FLAWED
VICTORY

FLAWED VICTORY

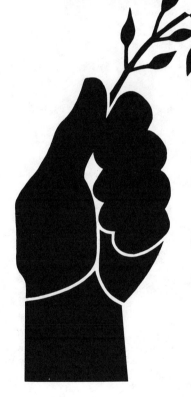

The Arab-Israeli Conflict and The 1982 War in Lebanon

Trevor N. Dupuy
Paul Martell

HERO BOOKS
FAIRFAX, VIRGINIA

FLAWED VICTORY
Copyright © 1986
by Trevor N. Dupuy

ISBN 0-915979-07-01

Printed in the U.S.A.

HERO Books
8316 Arlington Blvd.
Fairfax, Virginia 22031

Contents

PART II
The Fifth Arab-Israeli War, June 1982

PART III
The Lingering Crisis

List of Maps

Introduction

This book has truly been a work of collaboration between the co-authors. Sadly, however, this introduction is primarily the work of one of us. Before his untimely death a few months ago, Paul Martell reviewed the first draft and wrote almost two pages of comments which began:

"Your introduction is fine, BUT: . . . ."

Nothing could have been more typical of the understated style of that kind, diplomatic man, ever solicitous of the feelings of all of his colleagues, always self-effacing and diffident, yet also always ready to contribute unhesitatingly to joint endeavors of the products of a thoughtful, disciplined mind.

Thus, even though he did not have the opportunity to contribute fully to this introductory essay, I hope that it reflects most of his ideas, as well as my own. Therefore, I have retained his name at the conclusion of the introduction.

* * *

The authors had two purposes in writing this book. First, it is a sequel to an earlier book by one of the authors, *Elusive Victory: the Arab-Israeli Conflict, 1947-1974,** continuing that survey of the Arab-Israeli Wars for another decade. Regrettably that conflict continues, but we hope there will not be a need for a further sequel.

* By T.N. Dupuy; Harper & Row, New York, 1978; republished, HERO Books, Fairfax, VA, 1984.

The second, but not necessarily secondary, purpose is to provide to general readers, as well as those interested in military and politico-military affairs, an account of one of the great international tragedies of the 20th Century: Lebanon as a pawn in the Arab-Israeli Conflict, before and after, and partricularly during, 1982.

A starting point for a book with these two purposes is easy to establish. Not only did the previous book end in 1974 with the separation of forces agreements following the 1973 October War, but the shift in geographical focus of the Arab-Israeli conflict, to Lebanon, began almost simultaneously. Some background is provided in the first two chapters of Part One of this book. We believed it important for the reader to understand that the "fraternal hostilities" (Paul Martell suggested that it is "fraternal genocide") in that unhappy country is no recent or modern development. Only through such a historical review will the reader understand the context or background of the continuing hostilities in Lebanon.

The remainder of Part One is concerned with the gradual process whereby Lebanon became not only a battleground, but in fact the stage was being set for that tragically troubled land to become *the* battleground of the Arab-Israeli conflict.

Part Two of the book is concerned with the escalation of the conflict from a low-intensity, sporadic guerilla war to a brief, intense conflict, the fourth (or fifth, if the so-called War of Attrition is counted) Arab-Israeli War. This is the centerpiece of the book, literally, figuratively, and conceptually.

Part Three is virtually open-ended. It is a survey of the aftermath of that conflict of June of 1982. But that aftermath was still unfolding as this book was being written, and will continue to unfold, at least for months, and probably for years, to come. Furthermore, without the benefit of an unclouded crystal ball, there is no telling when that aftermath may (sadly) become the prologue to another conflagration. Since the authors are not soothsayers, and since our crystal ball is very clouded, we are not sure at what point our historical narrative becomes a mere recapitulation of current events. Quite arbitrarily we have ended the book with the departure of the so-called Multinational Force from Beirut, early in 1984. By coincidence, this is the conclusion of the decade following the October War.

One danger of writing and publishing a book about recent events in a volatile context is that new and unexpected happenings could so change the situation that earlier conclusions and assessments would become irrelevant, or even erroneous. After carefully considering the possible consequences, we are willing to take that risk. There have already been more such unexpected events—almost without exception tragic, dramatic and literally explosively newsworthy—than we had thought possible. Yet none of these has required the change of a single word in our efforts to combine hope with pessimism in the Epilogue.

One other point needs to be made.

We have been struck by the wisdom and perceptiveness of practically all who have, after the fact, commented about the inevitable consequences of the hostilities triggered by the Israeli offensive into Lebanon in June, 1982. Almost unanimously such commentators—particularly Israelis—point out that they recognized from the outset that this was a terrible mistake, which could have only tragic consequences for Israel. Probably most Israeli citizens are convinced that they are among the substantial proportion of their countrymen who opposed the war from the beginning.

In a very few instances the assertions of prescience can be substantiated from the public record. However, Appendix B would suggest that for the most part such wisdom has been retrospective.

We have many people to thank for assistance we have received in the preparation of this book. We know that Syrian, Lebanese, Jordanian, Palestinian, Egyptian, and Israeli friends who have helped us will almost inevitably disagree with some aspects of the book, and will be disappointed that we have not been as sympathetic to their ideas and perceptions as they would have wished. Some might even disagree with us so strongly that they will feel hurt or insulted if we give them credit for help. On balance, therefore, we have decided not to mention the names of any of them, and to convey to them, personally and privately, our thanks and appreciation.

We are under no such inhibitions in thanking those who helped us in the actual production of this book: our Publisher, Guy Clifton; our editor, Grace Hayes, and the ladies who typed various portions of our manuscript, particularly Virginia Rufner and Margaret Marsh.

It is, of course, the accepted thing for authors to say that whatever merits the book has are in large part due to all of the people who helped us, but that all of the shortcomings are our responsibility. In this case such a statement is more important than usual, and we mean it most sincerely.

T.N. Dupuy
Paul Martell

Fairfax, Va.
September, 1985

PART ONE
Lebanon
and the
Arab-Israeli
Conflict

Chapter 1
Tragedy and Hope:
The Origins of Turmoil
in
Lebanon

Early History

There was a time—in the years before 1975—when Lebanon was perceived by many westerners as a Switzerland of the Middle East, a western-type liberal and democratic state, an island of stability and social progress in a chaotic region. That perception was not accurate. In fact, modern Lebanon has been a feudal country, torn by religious, communal, and ethnic conflicts, riddled with violence and bigotry. Nevertheless, against all the odds, for some years in the middle of the 20th century the country did experience constitutional democracy. There was a multiparty system stretching from far left to far right, and there were freedom of speech, freedom of the press, and free enterprise. Although this situation was short-lived, it was an impressive accomplishment when one considers Lebanon's location in a region generally devoid of such liberties.

Lebanon occupies a strategic position along the eastern shores of the Mediterranean, bordering the Syrian Arab Republic on the north and east and Israel on the south. Its territory is about 4,000 square miles in area, and its population approximately 3,000,000, of whom some 450,000 are Palestinians who settled in the country after the State of Israel came into being in 1948.

Lebanon's history is usually traced back to the ancient Phoenicians who settled the coastal plain around 3500 B.C. and founded a number of independent city-states, including Tyre, Sidon, Beirut, and Tripoli. In the second and first millenia before Christ, the cities lost their independence and were ruled successively by foreign invaders—Egyptians, Babylonians, Persians, Macedonians, Greeks, and then the Romans.

During the Roman era, Christianity spread throughout the region, reaching deep into the Arabian desert. In Lebanon, European missionaries left Christian communities in the coastal cities and moved into the mountains to convert pagans living there, establishing numerous Christian settlements.

In the 6th century A.D. a small Maronite Christian community living on the banks of the Orontes River in northeastern Syria was caught in a violent religious conflict among Christian sects (Monophysites, Jacobites, and Nestorians), and was forced to flee west into the inhospitable mountains of central Lebanon. During the following century, more Maronites— fearing persecution by their fellow Christians—began seeking refuge in the rugged mountains. Soon the newcomers absorbed the indigenous population, erected monasteries, churches, and castles, and started to shape a new political entity.

Arrival of Islam

Early in the 7th century Islam appeared in the Arabian Peninsula, united the warring Arab tribes, and emerged from the desert seeking to bring the new religion to other lands. In 636, Arab Muslim forces defeated a Byzantine army in a battle at the Yarmuk River not far from Jerusalem. As a result, the Byzantines were driven into Asia Minor, leaving Palestine, Syria, Egypt, and Mesopotamia in the hands of the Muslims. In Lebanon, the victorious Islamic armies quickly subdued the coastal cities, but were unable to conquer the rugged mountains, homeland of the Christian Maronites.

Beginning in the 8th century, the Abbasid Caliphs decided to Arabize Lebanon. They moved entire tribes of Arab Muslims into the area. This changed the demographic and religious status of the country. The new arrivals nibbled away at the Christian territory in the mountains, and soon colonized the areas south and southeast of Beirut. Lebanon became an integral region of the Muslim Caliphate. Except in the most rugged mountain regions, Islam largely replaced Christianity, and the chief language became Arabic.

In the 10th century came a great schism in Islam. The followers of Mohammed became divided into the more orthodox Sunni and dissident Shiite sects. At the same time a few smaller sects, such as the Druze and the Alawites, emerged. Being minorities in a sea of Sunni Muslims, and fearful of persecution, the Shiites, the Druze, and later the Alawites began to drift into Lebanon, where the mountains provided an environment of reasonable security.

Crusaders and Mamelukes

When the Crusaders conquered the region in the 11th and 12th centuries, Lebanon became part of the Christian enclave on the littoral of the eastern Mediterranean. Northern Lebanon became part of the County of Tripoli; the south was made part of the Kingdom of Jerusalem. The Crusaders began a systematic campaign to evangelize the country's population. As a result, the Maronite Church gave up its Monothelite doctrine— the belief that Christ had only one will, rather than both a human will and a divine will. The Maronites also accepted papal supremacy, while keeping their own patriarch and liturgy.

After nearly one hundred years of domination, late in the 12th century the Crusaders were defeated near Tiberius by Salah al Din, Mameluke Sultan of Egypt and Syria, and the decline of the Crusader states began. A century later, in 1291, the last Frankish mainland strongholds of Tyre, Beirut, and Sidon surrendered to the forces of Sultan al-Ashraf Khalil. The remnants of the Crusader armies fled to Cyprus and Europe, leaving behind them in Lebanon a majority of Christians concentrated mainly in the Maronite bastion in the northern Bechare (Bsharri) region. To the south, in the Kisrawan area, the population was a mixture of Christians, Sunnis, Shiites, and Alawites. In the Shouf mountains and in the southern Gharb area the population was predominantly Druze, with a small Christian minority.

The victorious Mamelukes soon overran and pacified the mountain regions of Lebanon. The Christian entity, while preserving its social and religious institutions, lost its political autonomy. It was able, however, to retain cultural ties with Christian Europe.

Ottoman Rule

The Mameluke domination of Syria, Palestine and Lebanon was ended by the Ottoman Turks early in the 16th century. The Ottoman Empire retained sovereignty over the region until the end of World War 1. In general the Ottomans kept direct control over the coastal areas, while permitting the people of the Lebanon Mountains to manage their own affairs. Slowly a new social and demographic system developed. An appreciable migration of population occurred. The Shiites were driven from the northern provinces by the Sunnis and Christians, and moved en masse to the south and into the Bekaa Valley where they became a majority. In turn, a majority of the Druze moved from the south to the Shouf and central mountains. At the same time numerous Maronite peasants resettled not only in the cities, but also in the southern areas which had previously been inhabited by the Druze.

In the Lebanon Mountains, a Druze-Christian alliance was formed between Druze communities firmly established in the south, and Maronites who remained settled in the north. The Turks tolerated a limited autonomy in this mountainous region under the leadership of local emirs. The most distinguished among these was the Druze prince Fakhr al-Din of the Ma'ani family, who ruled from 1591 to 1633. Having consolidated his power base in the central Lebanon range—now often known as Mount Lebanon—he extended his authority over the mountainous areas to the south and east. He soon controlled the Bekaa Valley in the east, and the narrow coastal plain in the west. Thus, for the first time in centuries, most of what is now Lebanon was under one local ruler, who owed only nominal allegiance to Istanbul (Constantinople).

The Maronites, who were instrumental in bringing Fakhr al-Din to power, supported him loyally and provided him with experienced and well educated civil servants, and with links to European courts. This enabled Fakhr to carry out his own diplomatic initiatives and to make trade arrangements with foreign states. In return, Fakhr al-Din helped the Maronites to resist Sunni and Shiite pressure from the Bekaa Valley and coastal towns, and permitted Christian settlements in the Gharb and Shouf districts, hitherto a Druze domain. There is some evidence that Fakhr al-Din was secretly baptized a Christian.

The Ottomans, who at first accepted Fakhr al-Din's autonomous Lebanon, soon became suspicious of his ambitions. They were particularly distrustful of his highly organized and centralized Maronite power base. In 1633, Fakhr was defeated by a Turkish military expedition. He surrendered, and was taken to Istanbul, where he was executed two years later.

Endemic Anarchy and Chaos

Following the defeat and death of Fakhr al-Din, Lebanon suffered through a period of internal strife and political instability. The Shiites in the Bekaa Valley revolted and cut their ties with Mount Lebanon. The Sunnis, from their power base in the coastal areas and in the cities, challenged the authority of the princes. Thousands of Christians fled from Sunni and Shiite persecution in the lowlands, back into the mountains, where they found security in the Maronite and Druze communities.

Anarchy and chaos pervaded the region until 1697 when Bashir Shihabi, a Sunni Muslim, but a distant relative of Fakhr al-Din, rose to power in the mountains with the help of both the Druze and Maronite communities. Elected prince, as Bashir I, he subdued the feudal landlords and restored order. Domination of Lebanon by the Shihabi family lasted until 1842 and was marked by economic growth, prosperity, and only sporadic political crises. Under the Shihabis, some of whom secretly became Christians, the Maronite communities expanded over all of Mount Lebanon from Bsharri in the north to Jezzine in the south and again became dominant in the central mountain area.

In 1831 Egyptian troops of Mohammed Ali Pasha, in revolt against Ottoman rule, advanced on Lebanon through Palestine. Led by Ibrahim Pasha, son of Mohammed Ali, and a gifted general, the Egyptians drove the Turks out of Lebanon. The majority of the population welcomed the Egyptians as liberators. Prince Bashir II Shihabi (1788-1840) allied himself with the invaders, and the Egyptians allowed him to continue to rule. Bashir took advantage of the support of Mohammed Ali to increase his own power at the expense of the nobility. This, combined with an economic depression, led in 1840 to a popular revolt against the Shihabis. This uprising was supported by Anglo-Turkish intervention. Ibrahim Pasha and his troops were driven out of the country, back to Egypt, and Bashir fled into exile. This virtually ended the autonomous principality of Lebanon.

The collapse of local central authority led to renewal of sectarian clashes throughout the country. The Ottomans, always eager to "divide and rule," were happy to encourage inter-community tension and violence, anticipating that it would help them to reestablish their authority. Muslim communities, which had resented privileges which the Shihabis had accorded to the Christians, were determined to regain their lost rights. Similarly, Druze landlords wanted to recover lands which had been confiscated from them and given to Maronite peasants. Both Muslims and Druze resented the growing influence of western ideas which the Christians introduced.

In the autumn of 1841, Druze bands attacked Christian villages in the Shouf Mountains and massacred many Maronites. Druze leaders appealed to the Turks to restore direct Ottoman rule, in order to check the spread of European influence. The Turks were pleased to agree, and sent troops into the mountains to take charge. In January 1842 they announced the termination of Lebanese autonomy. At this point, Britain, France and Russia intervened, and forced the Turks to divide Lebanon into two provinces, separated by the Beirut-Damascus Road. The northern province was to be ruled by the Christians. The southern one was to be placed under Druze control.

It soon became evident, however, that this arrangement would not work, and two decades of turmoil ensued. In the Druze and Muslim territories, the Christian minorities were persecuted, while in areas under Maronite control there was similar discrimination, persecution and genocidal murder of Druze and Muslims. The turmoil was aggravated after 1848 when Christian peasants in the north—emboldened by the revolutions then sweeping Europe—rebelled against the nobility and the landlords. By 1859 this popular rebellion spread south to the Druze province, where Maronite peasants again led the uprising. Their efforts to incite their Druze neighbors failed, however; the Druze peasants sided with their aristocracy against the Maronites.

By this time the whole country was immersed in a confused civil war, part social, part sectarian. The Druze, backed by the Sunnis and Shiites, massacred tens of thousands of Christians not only in the mountains but also in the coastal towns and in the Bekaa Valley, while to the north, in areas under their control, the Christians took revenge on the Muslims, slaughtering them indiscriminately.

Uneasy Peace

The carnage again led to European intervention and to pressure on the Turks to restore peace and order. In 1861 the Turks accepted European demands to grant autonomy to the Mount Lebanon region, which was to be governed by a Christian governor, appointed by the Ottoman Sultan, and assisted by an administrative council and local authorities. Direct Ottoman rule continued over Beirut, the Bekaa Valley in the east, the Akkar Plains in the north, and the coastal plains in the south. Gradually an uneasy peace was established throughout the region.

This arrangement worked for over fifty years, until World War I. Muslims, Christians, and Druze coexisted, sometimes in tension, but in general without bloodshed. The country began to prosper economically and to mature politically. Close commercial ties with Europe were established, and the people became exposed to western ideas of freedom and democracy.

World War I and Aftermath

When, however, the Ottoman Empire entered World War I on the side of the Central Powers, the Turks ended Lebanon's autonomy and imposed martial law. Determined to crush all traces of nationalism and western influence, the Turkish Army occupied the entire country. Incessant military requisition of food between 1915 and 1917 resulted in widespread famine. Over 100,000 people starved to death in Lebanon, and many more became destitute.

As the Ottoman armies collapsed at the end of World War I, Lebanon was occupied by British forces. Accompanying the British in their advance into Syria and Lebanon was an Arab army commanded by

Hashemite Prince Faisal of Mecca, and advised by the legendary Lawrence of Arabia. Soon afterward, however, in accordance with the Sykes-Picot Agreement of 1918, which divided the former Turkish dominions between Britain and France, the British withdrew, and the French moved in. This was a devastating blow to Arab Muslim nationalists who had been encouraged by the British to believe that Syria and Lebanon would become part of a new Arab state, under the rule of Prince Faisal and his Hashemite family of Mecca and Medina.

In January 1919, at the Versailles peace conference, France was given a mandate over both Syria and Lebanon. The Lebanese Christians, and many of the Druze and Muslim inhabitants, accepted the Versailles decision. To most of them French authority was preferable to the rule of Hashemite Prince Faisal and his Arab-Syrian nationalist supporters.

However, on March 7, 1920, Prince Faisal defied the Sykes-Picot Agreement and the Treaty of Versailles, and declared himself King of Syria, including Lebanon and Palestine. He demanded that France cede to his new Arab kingdom all the territories under the mandate. The French government for nearly two years had been trying to reach an agreement with Faisal. They offered local autonomy, in partial acceptance of Arab demands for independence, in return for recognition of the French mandate. When it was obvious that a compromise was impossible, French troops occupied Damascus in July 1920, and expelled Faisal. Lebanon became an integral part of the French mandate of Syria.

Chapter II
The New States:
Lebanon and Israel

Lebanon Under French Mandate

Contemporary Lebanon came into being on September 1, 1920, when General Henri Joseph Gouraud, French High Commissioner in Lebanon and Syria, proclaimed Lebanon an independent republic under a French mandate nominally supervised by the League of Nations. This new nation included not only the predominantly Maronite Catholic region of Mount Lebanon, but also neighboring territories inhabited mostly by Muslims and Druze. These areas included: Beirut, which was almost equally divided between Sunni Muslims and Christians; the chiefly Sunni coastal plains and the cities of Sidon, Tyre, and Tripoli; the Bekaa Valley and the Jabal Amel region where the population was mainly Shiite Muslim; and the Shouf mountains with its predominantly Druze communities.

Some French officials—aware of the troubled history of the region—recognized that the inclusion of these diverse and inimical groups in one political entity would result in inherent instability. But their efforts to revise the borders established by Gouraud were opposed bitterly by the Maronites, who feared that if Lebanon were divided into Christian and Muslim regions, the Muslim portion would gravitate to Syria, resulting in such a powerful Syrian state that it would dominate a tiny, Christian Lebanon. In 1923 the present Lebanese frontiers were internationally recognized, and three years later, in 1926, a constitution was promulgated, in which the political predominance of the narrow Christian majority was recognized. Given the heterogeneous nature of the peoples of Greater Lebanon, the constitution was essentially fair in protecting the rights of the various communities.

However, most of the Muslims were dissatisfied with their status in the new Lebanese state. The concept of Lebanese nationalism, based on political pluralism and democratic institutions, was essentially alien to

Muslim attitudes and traditions. They considered this to be a colonialist arrangement imposed on them by a hostile French-Christian alliance under the mandate. Most of the Muslims had become imbued with the spirit of pan-Arabism that had swept through the region at the end of World War I. They considered union with Muslim Syria to be a prime objective.

Thus, from its origins, the new republic was split internally along sectarian and political lines. In essence, only the Maronites accepted the concept of a Greater Lebanon, and it was they who primarily felt a sense of loyalty to the state and were devoted to its future independence and sovereignty.

The far-reaching demographic consequences of this state of affairs were virtually ignored by the Maronites. The dangers of internal instability of the state, which resulted from the inclusion of a large Muslim minority, seemed to them far less perilous than any other possible political solution. The Maronites of Mount Lebanon had a long tradition of close links to Christian Europe, especially France, and under the Ottoman Empire had enjoyed a substantial degree of autonomy guaranteed by European powers. The establishment of Greater Lebanon was a fulfillment of their centuries-old dreams of a sovereign state of their own, free from fear of being dominated and persecuted by their Muslim neighbors. Access to the sea-coast and the Mediterranean Sea relieved them from their old claustrophobia. They felt close to the outside, non-Arab world, and finally free from the ever-present threat of political and cultural assimilation in the sea of Arab-Muslim society.

Independent Lebanon

In 1943, the French mandate was terminated and Lebanon attained full independence. To ease the strained relationships among the different religious and ethnic groups the National Covenant of 1943 was promulgated, structuring a sectarian distribution of power and state offices which reflected the multi-communal character of the society. Based on the 1926 constitution and the incomplete and inaccurate population census of 1932, the agreed formula for power distribution was 6:5 in favor of Christians. The distribution of the population, according to that census, was: Maronites, 29%, other Christians, 22%; Sunnis, 23%, Shiites, 20%; Druze, 6%. The Maronites were to hold the most powerful office—that of the presidency—and to control the army and the security forces. The prime minister was to be selected from among the Sunnis, the largest Muslim group, and the speaker of the parliament was to be a Shiite. The Druze were not included in the power-sharing formula.

Although all this seemed to be a reasonable solution to the woes of

Lebanon, except for the exclusion of the Druze, in practice it merely deepened the age-old distrusts and hatreds, and even sharpened the existing differences.

Nor were these internal differences helped by the tensions which existed between Lebanon and its newly-independent neighbor to the east, Syria, which had simultaneously achieved its independence. Most Syrians, in fact, refused to accept the existence of a separate, independent Lebanese entity which—like most Muslims—they regarded as a product of western imperialism. They believed that Lebanon was truly a part of Syria. Despite their general hatred of the French, the Syrians felt justified in this position by the fact that the French mandate combined Syria and Lebanon under one central administration. They saw the union of the two territories, furthermore, as important to the Syrian desire to achieve hegemony in the Fertile Crescent, which would enable Syria to compete successfully with Egypt and Iraq in the pan-Arab arena. Thus, Syria refused to establish diplomatic relations with Lebanon, for fear that this would be considered *de jure* recognition of Lebanese sovereignty.

The future of independent Lebanon was precarious, indeed.

Zionism and the Origins of Israel

The land where the modern state of Israel now exists became the homeland of the Jewish people some 35 centuries ago. The Jews came originally from Mesopotamia, and later from Egypt. After subduing local tribes, in the 12th century BC the Jews established their own state, with its capital in Jerusalem. (It must be noted that modern Palestinians consider themselves to be descended from the local tribes that held the land when the Jews arrived.) In a relatively short period of time the Jews developed cultural and religious values which were not only of national and regional, but also of universal, significance.

After a few centuries of independence, the Jews were conquered by the Assyrians about 750 BC. Subsequently, except for about one century from 168 to 63 BC, there was no independent Jewish state until modern Israel was established in 1948, although before 71 AD the Jews often had considerable autonomy under foreign conquerors.

After the great Jewish revolt against the Romans, in 70-71 AD, most of the survivors were dispersed throughout the Roman Empire, establishing Jewish communities in many lands. This began the period known to history as the Jewish Diaspora. This displacement from their homeland, however, did not eliminate from the transplanted Jews their strong feeling of identification with the ancient lands of Israel and Judea, often called Palestine. Impelled by historic and traditional attachment, Jews—no matter where they lived—continued to think of Jerusalem as their Holy City, and in their hearts every successive generation of Jews hoped to return to their homeland. Not only their aspirations, but also their prayers, focused on the "Promised Land" which God had decreed—according to the Bible—should belong to "Abraham and his seed". It was this divine promise, combined with the persecution meted out around the world to the scattered but close-knit Jews (who refused to be absorbed into the religions and cultures of their new homes) that was a major stimulus to the Zionist Movement, which began in the latter part of the 19th century.

In 1897, the first World Zionist Congress convened in Basel, Switzerland, at the summons of the spiritual father of the Jewish State, the founder of modern political Zionism, Theodor Herzl. The Congress declared as its objective the establishment of a Jewish National Home in Palestine secured by public law, and set up an organization to pursue this objective.

At that time Palestine—like neighboring Lebanon—was under Turkish control and inhabited by about 550,000 people, of whom only about 50,000 were Jews, with the remainder Arabs. Approximately one-quarter of the Arabs were Christians, and the rest Muslims. Although the Ottoman sultans, the sovereign masters of Palestine, did not endorse the Zionist aims of the Basel Congress, they did not prevent the entry into Palestine of several thousands of Jews—mostly from Eastern Europe—and their establishment of new Jewish communities.

Despite occasional friction with Arab neighbors, these Jewish immigrants were able to acquire land and homes peacefully. They could look forward to the possibility that—when the universally hated Turks were driven out—they might be able to share political control of Palestine with the Arabs.

The Balfour Declaration

World War I transformed the prospects for the Zionists. Once Turkey joined the Central Powers against Britain, France and Russia, the Zionists could hope that the ultimate Ottoman defeat would end Turkish sovereignty in Palestine and other Middle East countries. Thanks to the efforts of one of the Zionist leaders, Chaim Weizmann, the British Foreign Secretary Arthur Balfour gave further hope to the Jews that Palestine would again become their "National Home". On November 2, 1917, the British government issued the so-called "Balfour Declaration" in which it was stated that *"His Majesty's Government view with favour the establishment in Palestine of a National Home for the Jewish people, and will use their best endeavours to facilitate the achievement of this object . . . ."* The Declaration included also a provision that *"nothing should be done which may prejudice the civil and religious rights of existing, non-Jewish communities in Palestine."*

The Balfour Declaration, which was re-affirmed in the British mandate over Palestine awarded by the League of Nations, gave obvious international sanction to the historic connection between the Jewish people and the land of Israel as well as the right of the Jews to rebuild their National Home. This, combined with subsequent authorization by the British government of substantial Jewish immigration to Palestine, aroused alarm among the Palestinian Arabs. They noted with particular concern the fact that the terms of the British mandate referred to the political, civil, and religious rights of the Jews, but only to the civil and religious rights of the non-Jewish communities.

The Arabs believed that their historical rights to Palestine were at least as good as those of the Jews. They were particularly disturbed by Zionist reference to the "Promised Land". Since Arabs consider that their ancestors had been in Palestine before the Jews, and since they also considered themselves descendants of Abraham, they believed that their presence in Palestine was already a fulfillment of God's promise.

The Arabs were not mollified when the British amplified and explained the Balfour Declaration, and made explicit the policy that the establishment of a Jewish National Home was not intended to displace any Arabs from their land. Nor were they satisfied when in 1922 Britain divided the mandated territory which until then extended over both sides of the Jordan River. East of the river London established an Arab emirate under the name Transjordan, bringing in Beduin Prince Abdullah of the Hashemite family to rule the population of Palestine Arabs and Beduins. Jews were forbidden to purchase land or settle in the new Emirate.*

This exclusion of Transjordan from the promised Jewish National Home was worrisome to the Jewish Agency, which had been set up as the official political governing body of the Zionist Movement. This, like restrictions placed upon Jewish immigration even to Palestine west of the Jordan, suggested a possible weakening in British determination to carry out the promise of the Balfour Declaration. The Jewish Agency therefore redoubled its pressure on the British government not to forsake the interests of the Jewish population in Palestine.

---

* By making Abdullah, younger brother of Prince Faisal, Emir of Transjordan, the British were able to ease their embarrassment about what many people considered to be shabby treatment of their Arab allies of World War I. Not only had they allowed the French to eject Faisal from Syria, but they had given no support to their Hashemite allies when— at about this same time— Ibn Saud was driving the Hashemites from western Arabia, as he created his new Kingdom of Saudi Arabia. In addition to making Abdullah Emir of Transjordan, Great Britain elevated Faisal to the throne of the Kingdom of Iraq, in their mandate of Mesopotamia.

There was, indeed, considerable ambivalence in British policy with respect to Palestine in the 1920s and 1930s. Many people in the British government were worried about it. It was not clear to them how, physically or morally, Britain could carry out the provisions of the Balfour Declaration against the wishes of the Arab majority in Palestine, and the Arabs had made very clear their strong opposition to the establishment of the Jewish National Home. Thus, while Jewish immigration into Palestine was allowed, it was at times severely restricted and Jewish purchase of land was obstructed as Whitehall struggled with the problem.

In Palestine itself, Jewish policy fluctuated during these years. At times, the growing Jewish community and the Jewish Agency leadership cooperated with the governing British autorities. At other time, objections to British pro-Arab policies were manifested by organized protests or terrorist violence designed to increase British frustrations to the point where they would simply abandon Palestine and let the Jews and the Arabs settle their own problems.

But the crucial development affecting the future of Palestine took place not in Palestine but in Europe in the 1930s with the rise of Hitler to power in Germany, and in World War II when entire Jewish communities in areas under Nazi occupation were massacred. In this Holocaust nearly six million Jews—men, women, and children—perished at the hands of Nazi executioners.

The genocide of the Jews had two important effects on the peoples of the Free World, particularly in North America and Western Europe. First was the feeling of sympathy for the Jewish survivors of the massacre and an understanding of the natural desire of many of them to get to a new land, "the Promised Land", where the future, despite Arab opposition, seemed to be brighter for them than in Europe with its memories of rabid anti-Semitism, hatred, and persecution. Second, and reinforcing the sympathetic support for the Jews, was the realization in these countries that anti-Semitism had flourished in their own pre-war societies, just as in Germany, and the prevalent feeling that, at least indirectly, all such societies shared to some extent the guilt of the Nazi murderers. On top of this the Jews of Palestine had loyally supported the British in the war, and had contributed fighting units. This earned support of the World War II Allies.

Only after World War II did the British government recognize that it could not reconcile the two fundamentally opposed elements of its policy in the government of Palestine. London felt obliged to carry out the provisions of the Balfour Declaration in some form or other. At the same time, the British not only felt a humanitarian responsibility to protect the interest of the Arabs who were under their governmental authority, they also recognized their responsibility under the terms of the Mandate to prepare the region for self-government, which of course meant to the Arab majority that they would dominate the future government of Palestine.

Even if a theoretical solution had been possible, neither Jews nor Arabs would permit reconciliation of the issues. So, with Jewish—Arab disorders growing in Palestine, and with British military and civilian personnel being killed and maimed by Jewish and Arab terrorists (mostly Jewish at that time), the British made the decision for which the Jewish Agency had hoped. They shifted the burden of settling the Palestine problems to the United Nations. When that multi-national body dawdled in considering the thorny issues, the British government put a practical deadline on the discussions by setting a target date for withdrawal in May 1948.

The United Nations and Israeli Independence

The United Nations created a UN Special Committee on Palestine (UNSCOP), composed of representatives from 11 member states. They grappled with the issues during most of 1947, then recommended the partition of Palestine into two independent states, one Arab and one Jewish, with an international enclave around Jerusalem. By this time there were 1,269,000 Arabs (about three-fourths Muslims and one-fourth Christians) and 687,000 Jews in Palestine. The Jews, however, owned only about ten percent of the land area.

The boundaries of the two would-be states were based primarily on ethnographic considerations. The Jews were to get most of the western coastal areas, from Haifa in the north to Ashkelon in the south, the rich farmland region they had long been developing in eastern Galilee and northern Samaria near Lake Tiberias, and the largely unsettled region of the Negev Desert. The Arabs received most of central Samaria and Judea, western Galilee, the southern coastal region from Ashkelon to Rafah, and the northwestern Negev Desert. The Jerusalem area—where the old, primarily Arab, city was abutted by a modern Jewish city of 100,000 people—was to be under international control. Bethlehem was also to be part of this international enclave. This would assure that the places so holy to the three major religions—Christian, Jewish, and Muslim—would be preserved for all without dominance by any.

The Jews were not happy with the plan since it kept Jerusalem and much of the traditional land of the ancient Jewish states from their control. However, they felt that they could live with it. The Arabs, on the other hand, insisted that for political, economic, and historical reasons, the small region of Palestine could not and should not be partitioned. It should be one political entity with constitutional guarantees to the Jewish minority.

A United Nations Resolution based on the UNSCOP draft proposal was adopted by the UN General Assembly on November 29, 1947, by a vote of 33 for, 13 against, with 10 abstentions. Both the United States and the Soviet Union supported the Resolution. The Jewish Agency accepted it. It was rejected by Arab governments and by Palestinian Arab leaders.

The six months between the adoption of the UN Resolution in November 1947 and the end of the British mandate at midnight May 14, 1948, were marked by increased Arab violence against the Jewish community. The hit and run Arab attacks were aimed at the interruption of communications between Jewish towns and villages, isolating and capturing some of them, and above all conquering Jerusalem. Jewish fighters responded in kind against Arab communities.

On May 14 representatives of the Zionist Movement and of the Jewish community in Palestine assembled in Tel Aviv and declared the establishment of a Jewish state in part of Palestine, to be known as the State of Israel.

As soon as the Jews proclaimed the establishment of their state, armies of the neighboring Arab countries crossed the Palestine borders in an attempt to "liberate" Palestine and to nullify the partition resolution by force. The Jewish-Palestinian internal conflict thus became a war between the Arab states and Israel over Palestine. In this struggle, despite a population disparity against the Jews of more than 50-to-1, Israel was able to defeat the invading Arab troops. The victory was achieved by the much greater efficiency of the Jewish forces and by their skillful use of interior lines of communication. On most of the battlefields the theoretically outnumbered Jews were able to achieve numerical superiority and firepower preponderance.*

Lebanon's Part in the 1948-1949 Arab-Israeli War

On May 14, Prince Abdullah of Transjordan assumed the position of Commander in Chief of the United Arab Armies and, during the night of May 14/15, attacked the newly proclaimed Jewish state. The nations providing contingents were Transjordan, Egypt, Syria, Iraq, and Lebanon; there was also an international contingent called the Arab Liberation Army. According to a mutually agreed (but not very well-prepared) plan, the Lebanese contingent was to advance along the coast from Naqoura to Nahariya. The Syrians, crossing the Jordan above the Sea of Galilee, would strike for Zemach. The Iraqi contingent would move from its concentration area west of Irbid in Transjordan to establish a bridgehead across the Jordan south of the Sea of Galilee, and then advance to Netanya on the coast. The Transjordanians, whose British-trained 10,000-man Arab Legion

* See T.N. Dupuy, *Elusive Victory, The Arab-Israeli Wars, 1947-1974*, Fairfax, VA, 1984.

was the cream of the Arab forces, had two objectives: one brigade would seize Nablus in central Samaria; the second brigade would advance to Ramle at the outskirts of Tel Aviv. A third brigade was to remain in reserve to deliver the final blow to the Israelis at the place and time that would assure victory to the Arabs. The Egyptians based at El Arish on the northern Sinai coast also had two objectives: the main force would advance along the Coastal Road to seize Gaza and to be ready to advance further north toward Tel Aviv. A secondary force was to strike northeastward across the upper Sinai through Auja and Beersheba to seize and secure Hebron.

The combined total Arab forces committed to the war were about 40,000 men. To defend the country, the Provisional Government of Israel under Prime Minister David ben Gurion initially marshalled 30,00 badly armed effectives, and some 10,000 men ready for immediate mobilization in local defense.

The Lebanese Army, approximately 3,500 men strong, was least ready for war of all of the generally unprepared Arab armies. To cross into Palestine, Beirut committed four infantry battalions, two artillery batteries, and small armored and cavalry contingents. The Lebanese General Staff recognized the possibility of isolation from other Arab armies in the advance initially planned along the coastal road toward Nahariya. Instead, it decided to make the initial move into Palestine by an advance against the western face of the finger of Galilee that extends northward up the Jordan River and Huleh Valley to Dan. This placed the Israelis in northern Galilee under pressure simultaneously from two fronts, since the Syrians were crossing the Jordan into the eastern side of that finger a few miles to the east and southeast.

The Lebanese invasion route lay through the Arab village of Mal-kiya, just west of the powerful Arab-held police fort at Nebi Yusha, on the ridge dominating the Huleh Valley. Having observed the concentration of the Lebanese contingent, and anticipating its advance, a Palmach (Jewish Defense Forces) battalion of the Yiftah Brigade during the night of May 14/15 cut across the mountains on foot toward the Lebanese border, skirted the Nebi Yusha fort, attacked Malkiya and Kadesh, and had occupied both by morning. However, shortly after dawn, the Lebanese launched a counter-attack eastward across the border on Malkiya and forced the Israelis back with heavy casualties. Advancing in strength across the border, the Lebanese occupied the village and began to maneuver to threaten nearby Kadesh. Recognizing the vulnerability of that position, the Palmach evacuated Kadesh the next day, and the village was immediately taken by the Lebanese. Well satisfied with two successes, the Lebanese Army halted its advance and consolidated its position a few miles inside Palestine.

Not yet aware that the Lebanese advance had stopped, on the night of May 17/18 the Israelis attacked and captured the police post at Nebi Yusha, and began to organize the territory to block the road from Kadesh into the Huleh Valley.

After the Lebanese had remained motionless in the Malkiya area for a week, Colonel Shmuel Cohen, commander of the Yiftah Brigade, decided to take the offensive. His plan was to feign an attack on the villages of Nebi Yusha and Kadesh from the south while attacking Malkiya from the rear through Leabnon. On the night of May 28/29 he sent a force of armored cars and infantry in trucks, moving without lights, across the frontier from Manara to reach a road running parallel to the border west of Malkiya. The Lebanese in Malkiya were taken by surprise. The village fell after a short battle. Kadesh also was abandoned by the Lebanese, who withdrew completely behind their frontier.

On June 6, a combined force of Lebanese, Syrians, and elements of the Arab Liberation Army (ALA) attacked Malkiya. This time the Israelis were caught by surprise. The attacking units, about the equivalent of two brigades in strength, were seriously delayed by minefields that the defending troops had laid around Malkiya. The ALA and the Syrian contingents were too discouraged by the obstacles to continue the attack, but the Lebanese persisted, and by evening they had captured the village for the second time. Encouraged by this success they pushed ahead and the next day captured Ramat Naftali and Kadesh and opened the way to the Huleh Valley to the south. However, again the Lebanese did not make any major effort to continue to advance. Instead, they organized their newly won positions. Until October the situation on the Lebanese-Israeli front remained quiet, interrupted only by occasional fire exchanges and raids.

On October 29, the Israelis launched Operation "Hiram" (named after Hiram, King of Tyre), aimed at freeing Upper Galilee from foreign troops. As a part of this operation the Israeli 7th Brigade recaptured the territory the Lebanese had occupied in June. They followed the retreating Lebanese troops across the border, penetrated as far as the Litani River, and occupied ten Lebanese villages. These Israeli forces remained in Lebanon until the Armistice Agreement between the two countries was signed on March 22, 1949. Then they returned the villages and the occupied strip of land to Beirut authorities, and moved back to Israel proper.

1958 Crisis: Incipient Civil War in Lebanon

The first major crisis in Lebanon's modern, post-1943, history came in the summer of 1958. This was a result of the strong wave of Islamic-Arab nationalism—inspired by President Nasser of Egypt—which spread throughout the Arab World in the 1950s. In Cairo on February 1, 1958, Egyptian President Gamal Abdel Nasser and Syrian President Shukri al-Kuwalty proclaimed the union of Egypt and Syria in a United Arab Republic (UAR). They termed the union the first step toward an eventual federation embracing all Arab countries. The proclamation asserted that this united republic, which was the fruit of Arab nationalism, would remain open to any Arab state desirous of joining.

A large segment of the Muslim population of Lebanon was inspired by this movement to seek alteration of the existing power structure in Lebanon, so as to integrate the country into the recently-established United Arab Republic of Syria and Egypt. An opportunity seemed to offer itself with an approaching national election for president. Unrest and political agitation flared into violence; the country was moving toward civil war.

Then on July 14, 1958, King Faisal II of Iraq was deposed and killed and the regime headed by many-times Prime Minister General Nuri as Sa'ad was overthrown by General Abdul Karim el-Kassem, head of the "Free Officers" group. The new government proclaimed Iraq a republic, and on July 15 withdrew from the previous loose confederation which had existed between the Hashemite kingdoms of Jordan and Iraq. King Hussein, fearful of similar revolt in Jordan, blamed communists and Nasserites for the bloody coup in Iraq, and requested that Britain expand its small military contingent in Jordan. London acquiesced, and soon increased its garrison in Jordan to 4,000 men.

Already faced with an imminent threat to Lebanon's sovereignty and existence, and with tension rising because of the events in Bagdad, Lebanese President Camille Chamoun accused unspecified foreign governments of feeding the rebellion with propaganda, money, arms, and manpower. Obviously he was referring primarily to Nasser's United Arab Republic, and also to the Soviet Union. He officially requested United States military assistance under the provisions of the UN Charter. In his message to President Dwight D. Eisenhower, Chamoun stated that Lebanon would not be able to survive without prompt US action.

American Intervention

In response, on July 15, 1958, President Eisenhower ordered US forces into Lebanon. He justified this action as necessary to protect American lives and to assist the government of Lebanon in the preservation of the country's territorial integrity and independence, which were deemed vital to both US national interests and world peace. The President believed that the Soviet Union and the United Arab Republic were jointly responsible for the efforts to overthrow the legally constituted government of Lebanon, and that their objective was to incorporate Lebanon into the UAR. Eisenhower also stated that US forces would be withdrawn as soon as the United Nations had taken effective steps to safeguard Lebanese independence.

That same day two battalions of the US 2d Marine Regiment began landing, without incident, on beaches south of Beirut near Khalde. This was the advance element of a Marine task force of 5,000 men commanded by Brigadier General Stanley S. Wade, USMC. On July 15 and 16 the Marines took control of the Beirut International Airport and began to guard key areas in several districts of Beirut. All formal arrangements for the Marines' deployment, and their cooperation with the Lebanese Army, were closely coordinated between Major General Fuad Chehab, Lebanese Army Commander, and General Wade. Despite threats from Muslim insurgents, and appeals by former Prime Minister Saeb Salam (the leader of the Beirut-based rebels) to oppose the occupation forces, there were no attacks on the Marines, and their appearance had a calming effect on the situation.

Both the Atlantic and Pacific fleets of the US Navy were placed on an alert status, and additional US forces were sent to Lebanon from Germany. By July 22 the task force had grown in strength to over 10,000 men, including 7,200 Marines, 1,800 paratroopers from the 24th Division in West Germany, and 1,400 other Army personnel. There was a corresponding buildup of US Navy and Air Force units in the eastern Mediterranean region.

On July 21 Admiral James L. Holloway, Deputy Chief of Naval Operations, announced that all US combat forces in and near Lebanon, including ground, sea, and air elements engaged in the operation, had nuclear capabilities. However, he said he foresaw no circumstances requiring the use of such weapons.

The buildup of US forces in Lebanon reached its peak early in August with the landing of 2,800 men. This force included an Army armored battalion with 75 tanks, and increased the total US strength to 15,000 men. American troops assumed expanded guard and patrol duties in the Beirut area, but encountered no opposition.

Uneasy Peace in Lebanon

The incipient civil war simply faded away, ending inconclusively. While the prospective insurgents failed to achieve their pro-Nasserist, pan-Arab objectives, they were able to block Chamoun's plans to run for a second term as president. General Fuad Chehab, a Maronite, was elected president on July 31. He adopted a policy of reconciliation toward the Muslims and agreed to meet their demands for increased political, social, and economic equality. Prominent Muslim and Druze leaders, such as Rashid Karameh, Saeb Salam, and Kamal Jumblatt gained key roles in the government, and insisted on the withdrawal of US troops. Since the political situation—at least on the surface—seemed to be returning to normal, the departure of American forces began on August 12 and ended on October 25. Only a small US administrative unit was left to settle claims of Lebanese citizens arising from the presence of the task force in Lebanon.

While the civil unrest had subsided, and foreign troops had left the country, the fundamental problems which had been plaguing the Lebanese Republic since its independence in 1943 remained unchanged. Although the violence that preceded the American intervention could hardly be called a civil war, it had demonstrated the willingness of the major segments of the society to use force for the attainment of political goals. This was hardly a new development in the history of Lebanon, but it was a disturbing reminder of the past under the new circumstances of a 20th century democracy. Not only had the Muslims been prepared to resort to arms to assert their political demands, but the Christians had demonstrated their equal readiness to fight to preserve the status quo. The Lebanese state had made no perceptible progress in the difficult historical transformation of its diverse and antagonistic religious, cultural, and ethnic groups into an integrated and unified political order. The complex governmental infrastructure designed to create the unified society envisioned by the Constitution and the National Covenant had failed to accomplish its purpose.

The society remained segmented and internally divided on the basis of deeply rooted irrational religious and political fanaticism and hatred. There were 17 separate and mutually suspicious religious communities in Lebanon, each with its own identity and aspirations, each seeking to preserve its own traditions and to protect its own narrow interests. All they had in common were fear, prejudice and centuries-old hostility. The Lebanese Christians, and especially the Maronites, considered Lebanon to be traditionally an essentially western-oriented Christian state; they considered the Muslims to be treasonous pan-Arabists collaborating with various other Arab states with the aim of destroying independent Lebanon. Yet, there was little religious or political unity among the Greek Orthodox, Greek Catholic, and other Christian denominations, who feared and mistrusted the Maronite Church, and in many ways felt much closer to the Arab world than to the Maronites. On the other hand, neither were the Muslims a really unified community. No love was lost among Sunnis and Shiites who had little mutual religious or political rapport or understanding. They did close ranks, however, on basic issues of Christian-Islamic conflict, and refused to accept the legitimacy of a non-Arab, non-Islamic Lebanese state. For them the traditional orientation of Lebanon was as part of a vaguely perceived Arab "nation". The Druze, no inconsequential component of the population, felt particularly insecure; they had been ignored in the National Covenant; they fiercely mistrusted both the Maronites and the two major Muslim groups.

This was the environment into which Arab refugees from Palestine began to arrive in the late 1940s and early 1950s. These were people, mostly Muslims, who had fled from, or been driven from, their homes by the emergence of the new state of Israel during and following the successful Israeli War of Independence in 1948-1949. While most of the refugees had fled to Jordan, a number reached Lebanon seeking temporary asylum until—as they expected—the Jews were ejected from Palestine, and they could return to their former homes. They played little or no role in the 1958 violence.

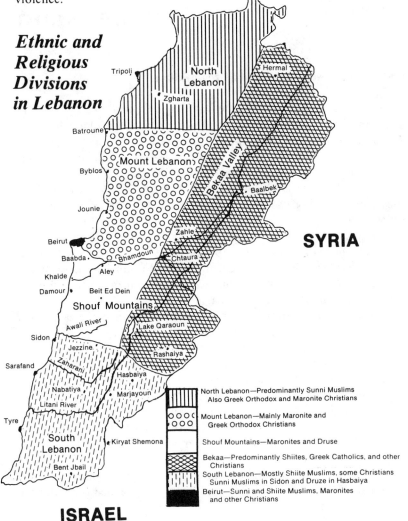

Ethnic and Religious Divisions in Lebanon

North Lebanon—Predominantly Sunni Muslims
Also Greek Orthodox and Maronite Christians

Mount Lebanon—Mainly Maronite and
Greek Orthodox Christians

Shouf Mountains—Maronites and Druse

Bekaa—Predominantly Shiites, Greek Catholics, and other Christians

South Lebanon—Mostly Shiite Muslims, some Christians
Sunni Muslims in Sidon and Druze in Hasbaiya

Beirut—Sunni and Shiite Muslims, Maronites and other Christians

Chapter III
The Palestinians
and the PLO
in Lebanon

Origins of the Palestine Liberation Organization

At the close of the 1947-1948 War—which the Israelis call their War of Independence—Transjordanian and Iraqi forces occupied much of central Palestine. The region under their control extended westward from the Jordan River, including much of the central mountain spine of Palestine, from Jenin in the north to Hebron in the south, with the ceasefire line running through embattled Jerusalem. On December 1, 1948, with the war obviously approaching its conclusion, Prince Abdullah of Transjordan proclaimed himself king of Arab Palestine. On December 13, the Parliament of Transjordan approved a union of Transjordan with the territory occupied by the Arab forces west of the Jordan River, the combined territory to be called the Hashemite Kingdom of Jordan. This new state of Jordan was virtually recognized by the ceasefire agreement between Jordan and Israel, negotiated on Rhodes in early 1949.

Until his assassination in 1951, Abdullah was clearly the recognized spokesman for Arab aspirations and interests in Palestine, including those portions of the region which were now the State of Israel. Abdullah was succeeded by his son, Talal, as King of Jordan. However, that mentally-disturbed monarch was deposed by the Jordanian Parliament on August 11, 1952, and his 17-year-old son, Hussein, became King of Jordan. The period of turmoil that followed provided an opportunity for the many Palestinians who did not wish their interests to be represented by the shaky Hashemite dynasty to establish their own centers of opposition to the Jewish control of most of their homeland.

In 1964 these various Palestinian groups were amalgamated into a loose confederation of anti-Israeli Palestinian Arabs, called the Palestine

Liberation Organization (PLO). This new organization soon became the institutional focus for the expression of Palestinian nationalism, independent of the nationalism represented by the Kingdom of Jordan. For several years the relationship between the PLO and King Hussein of Jordan was ambiguous. However, the 1967 Israeli conquest of the "West Bank" region of Jordan—the area which Abdullah had annexed in 1948—soon led to a polarization of the rival interests and adherents of the PLO and Hussein.

As an aftermath of the Six Day War of 1967, more Palestinian refugees poured into Jordan from the West Bank. The Palestine Liberation Organization, under the emerging leadership of Yasser Arafat, established a virtual state within the state of the Hashemite Kingdom of Jordan. Armed elements of the PLO mounted guerrilla raids into Israeli-occupied territory from bases in Jordan. The Israelis retaliated, and many Jordanians and some Palestinians suffered from the punitive raids conducted by the Israelis east of the Jordan River. To spare Jordan further Israeli punishment, Hussein demanded that the PLO cease using his kingdom as a base of operations against Israel. The PLO refused. Rather, well-armed and well-organized, the PLO ignored Jordanian authority and clearly posed a threat to the very survival of the monarchy. In September 1970, after the failure of several compromise efforts, Hussein reasserted his authority by a military operation in which, after a brief but bloody fight, that the PLO called "Black September", the Jordanian Army destroyed the PLO in Jordan. Arafat and close to 200,000 Palestinians fled to Lebanon, bringing the total Palestinian population in that country to almost half a million.

Components of the PLO

A new, cohesive, well-armed, and powerful ingredient had been added to the already simmering stew in Lebanon. While some of these Palestinian refugees were Christians they were unified as Palestinians under an essentially Muslim-Arab leadership. The PLO was not, however, a monolithic Palestinian entity. It was composed of a number of autonomous groups under a loose and collegial PLO central leadership. Each of the major component elements of the PLO is discussed briefly below:

• The Palestinian National Liberation Movement (Fatah), is the most active and the largest of the guerrilla organizations, and the dominant member of the PLO. Established in 1959, it began guerrilla or terrorist operations against Israel in 1965. By early 1982 it numbered some 6,500 armed men, organized in regular units.

• The Vanguard of the Liberation War (SAIQA) was established in Damascus in 1968 by the Syrian Ba'ath Party, to provide the Syrian government with means for influencing the Palestinian Liberation Movement. SAIQA's activities were and are directed by the Syrians, and the organization follows all orders received from the Syrian regime. Its political orientation remains (not surprisingly) close to that of the Syrian wing of the Ba'ath Party. SAIQA's military strength on the eve of the 1982 war was nearly 2,000 armed men.

• The Popular Front for the Liberation of Palestine (PFLP) was established in 1967. It is led by George Habash, a Christian. Ideologically close to Marxism-Leninism, it established friendly relations with the Soviet Union and Communist countries in Eastern Europe. In 1982 it was composed of some 1,500 members, most of them hard-core guerrilla-terrorists, engaged in terrorist activities in various countries. It has become the spokesman for the "Rejectionist Front" (those groups opposing any negotiations with Israel).

• The Democratic Front for the Liberation of Palestine (DFLP) was established in 1969 as a result of a split within the PFLP. The organization, led by Nayef Hawatmeh, also has a Marxist-Leninist ideology and has cordial relations with the USSR. Prior to June 1982 it numbered about 1,600 active members.

• The Popular Front for the Liberation of Palestine-General Command (PFLP-GC) was established in 1968 and is led by Ahmed Jibril. It also was the product of a split within the PFLP. The guiding principle of the organization is to carry out violent armed struggle against Israel. The PFLP-GC maintains close ties with Syria and Libya. It numbered over 1,100 members in 1982.

• The Palestine Liberation Front (PLF) was established in 1977 by a splinter group which broke away from the PFLP-GC because of pro-Iraqi and anti-Syrian political sentiments. The PLF belongs to the "Rejectionist Front" and is supported by Iraq. Its strength was about 700 men in 1982.

• The Arab Liberation Front (ALF) was organized in 1969 by the Iraqi regime and the Iraqi branch of the Ba'ath Party. The ALF is completely subservient to the Iraqi Government and serves the interests of Iraq. The ALF was composed of a few hundred guerrillas.

• The Palestinian Popular Struggle Front (PPSF) was established in 1967, and in 1971 merged with the Fatah. However, some 150 members of the organization refused to integrate and, under the auspices of Iraq, remained independent. The PPSF has no clear ideological leaning. Led by Dr. Samir Aousma, the group is unswervingly dedicated to the destruction of Israel.

• The Palestine Liberation Army (PLA) was established in 1964 as the military arm of the PLO. In theory it is subordinated to the Executive Committee of the PLO. But in practice its units are controlled by the countries in which the PLA is deployed. PLA headquarters is located in Damascus, and it operates according to orders received from the Syrian

General Staff. Before the June 1982 war, its strength was nearly 4,000 men, organized in three brigades and two independent battalions. One of these brigades was in Jordan, and was controlled by the Jordanian Army.

• The Abu Nidal Faction is a terrorist group headed by Sabri el Bana (Abu Nidal). In 1974 it broke off from the Fatah and operated under Iraqi protection until 1981, when it also established an office in Damascus. Prior to 1980 the group's primary targets were moderate Arabs. Afterward, Abu Nidal concentrated mainly on attacking Israeli and Jewish targets outside Israel.

The internal divisions and inherent volatility of the PLO were not widely recognized by the outside world, not even by the Arab world, which really should have known better. Yasser Arafat, the leader of the Fatah, and thus of the PLO, was able by a combination of diplomatic and public relations skills, as well as considerable charisma, to present himself as the undisputed leader of all Palestinians. This leadership seems to have been pretty generally accepted by the Palestinian Arabs still residing in the West Bank under Israeli occupation and elsewhere in Israel.

By the mid-1970s the PLO had become a political and semi-sovereign entity recognized by most of the Arab states as the authority representing Palestinian interests, independently of any of the Arab governments. As a quasi-government, it was the center of Palestinian political, social, economic, and cultural activities. For instance, it assumed responsibility for providing health education and other social services to the Palestinian people outside the State of Israel, for industrial training, information offices, and the National Fund. Initially it was not a strictly military organization, although its structure included the Palestine Liberation Army (PLA) for guerrilla and military operations against Israel. In time, however, largely as the result of Israeli victory in the Six Day War in June 1967, the PLO became more militant, as its leaders decided that armed struggle with Israel was the only way to liberate Palestine and to establish an independent Palestinian state. In prosecuting this struggle, the main aim of the PLO was implicitly and explicitly the destruction of the State of Israel. The Palestinian National Covenant, the primary political document of the Armed Palestinian Resistance Movement, adopted in June 1968 by the Palestine National Council, made the PLO responsible for the realization of the goals of the covenant, and for carrying out the Palestinian "National Liberation War."

The PLO Moves to Lebanon

After its bloody 1970 "Black September" defeat in Jordan, the PLO transferred its headquarters to Beirut. Its activities soon demonstrated a deliberate PLO design to take advantage of internal divisions in Lebanon in order to create conditions under which the PLO could carry on its war against Israel. An indirect and intermediate objective was pan-Arab radicalization of the Lebanese populace, and thus the destruction of the Lebanese state and society. The alliance of the PLO with Muslim and leftist organizations in Lebanon triggered a major arms race among the Lebanese sects and the paramilitary reorganization of Christian and Muslim militias. The pervasive feeling of insecurity in all Lebanese elements increased.

The Muslim communities strongly supported the Palestinian guerrillas and encouraged them in their struggle against Israel. There was an increase in Palestinian guerrilla and terrorist attacks initiated from Lebanese territory against Israel proper and Israeli citizens and property in third countries.

There was violent Israeli reaction. Actually, Lebanon had experienced Israeli reprisals even before September 1970. One of the most spectacular of these came on December 28, 1968, when helicopter-borne Israeli commandos raided the Beirut International Airport, destroying 13 civilian aircraft belonging to Arab airline companies. The assault was carried out by eight Israeli helicopters, of which six landed at the airport while two patrolled overhead. The Arab aircraft were destroyed by explosive charges planted in the nose-wheel well and the undercarriage wells of each plane. The Israelis were careful to confine their attack to Arab-owned planes.

The raid was retaliation for an attack by two Arab assailants on an El Al passenger plane on December 26, 1968, during a refueling stop in Athens. The plane was on its way from Tel Aviv to New York. One passenger and a stewardess were killed. The two assailants, members of the Popular Front for the Liberation of Palestine, who had arrived in Athens from Beirut two days earlier, were arrested by the Greek police. Although the Lebanese government denied any complicity in the Athens airport shooting, the Israelis did not accept this, and warned that any Arab government that permitted terrorism to operate from its territory must bear responsibility for the terrorist acts.

Aware of the increasing strength of the Palestinian guerrillas, and fearful of further Israeli reprisal raids, the Lebanese government tried to impose stricter control on the Palestinians in Lebanon. Yasser Arafat, Chairman of the PLO—who was then based in Jordan—was told that Palestinian guerrillas would not be allowed to operate across Lebanon's frontiers without approval of the government in Beirut. The Lebanese explained that such actions endangered the country's sovereignty and could be a pretext for Israeli annexation of border areas. Nevertheless, Lebanon did agree to permit a limited PLO guerrilla presence on its territory at that time.

The PLO, however, rejected any attempt to restrict its activities, and continued to carry out raids against Israel from bases in Lebanon. When discussions between Lebanese authorities and the Palestinian leadership reached an impasse in April 1969, the Lebanese Army and police moved in to clear out guerrillas from certain border villages in an effort to forestall Israeli reprisals. Violent clashes between the Lebanese Army and guerrillas lasted for seven months until November of 1969.

Mounting internal and external pressure led to negotiations in Cairo between a Lebanese delegation led by General Emile Bustani and Arafat. However, the Lebanese delegation soon found that it was negotiating at a great disadvantage. It was under great pressure not only from the government of President Nasser of Egypt, but also from the representatives of other members of the Arab League, the organization encompassing all Arab countries, which had its headquarters in Cairo.

1969 Cairo Accord

The result was the so-called Cairo Accord of November 3, 1969. It legitimized the presence of the Palestinian guerrillas and terrorists in Lebanon, and armed operations against Israel from Lebanese soil. The agreement guaranteed non-interference of either party—the Government of Lebanon and the PLO—in the affairs of the other. Thus the PLO became an entity enjoying political and military independence inside Lebanon. Palestinians living in Lebanon were permitted to domicile and travel freely around the country. The PLO was given the authority to control all Palestinian refugee camps, and to look after the interests of the Palestinians living there. Palestinians residing in Lebanon were permitted to carry arms, and to participate in the Palestinian armed struggle against Israel. The guerrilla units received assurance of free passage through Lebanon to border areas.

This was the beginning of Palestinian involvement in Lebanese politics. The country became virtually divided into two sovereign entities sharing the same national territory. On one side stood the Lebanese nationalist parties, largely representing the Christian communities, who were against armed Palestinian presence in Lebanon. They considered it a danger to the state, and demanded that the Palestinians be disarmed. On the other side was a combination of political forces consisting of Arab Muslim nationalists, Syrian nationalists, Marxists, and other leftist parties, who drew their support from the Muslim communities. They advocated freedom of action for the Palestinian guerrillas, and were in favor of armed raids against the Israelis from Lebanese soil.

In 1970, after the PLO guerrillas were expelled from Jordan, Palestinian political activity in Lebanon intensified. The PLO now joined the Lebanese Muslims in their efforts to decrease the influence and power of the Christians and of the Lebanese state. By the mid-1970s, parts of Beirut and of the Bekaa Valley, the coastal plains, southern Mount Lebanon, and the major cities in the north were virtually under the control of Palestinian and Lebanese leftists. The authority of the central government crumbled.

To the Lebanese Christians who still saw the entire country as their homeland, this was an intolerable state of affairs, and conflict became inevitable. The Lebanese government could not fulfill its duties to defend the state, to assure law and order, and to curb Palestinian activities, even though those activities brought about massive Israeli retaliation. The Phalangist forces, and the Maronite and other Christian militia took upon themselves the mission of restoring the dominant position of Christians in Lebanon and the nation's integrity and sovereignty.

Chapter IV
Civil War
and Syrian Intervention
in Lebanon,
1975-1976

The PLO Precipitates Civil War

The internal unrest in Lebanon in 1958 had provided evidence that the traditional rivalries of the Christian and Muslim communities in Lebanon might be so strong and intractable that the precarious balance of factions established by the Constitution of the Republic could never succeed. On the other hand, there was an interesting historical relevance to the figurative reference to Lebanon as "the Switzerland of the Levant." The early days of the now-stable Swiss Republic were as violent and volatile as those of the Lebanese Republic of the mid-20th century. Medieval Switzerland was torn not only by different religions, but also by different languages and allegiances to powerful neighbors in much the same way as modern Lebanon. So there was an historical basis for hope that stability might some day arrive.

But the arrival of the Palestinians made fulfillment of this hope impossible, and civil war inevitable.

The Civil War of 1975-1976 was precipitated by Palestinian support of the Muslim elements of the Lebanese population. The war brought about the collapse of the existing political system, stimulated military intervention by the Syrians, who occupied almost half of the country, permitted the establishment of an autonomous Palestinian mini-state in South Lebanon, and finally led to two Israeli invasions of Lebanon, the first in 1978 and the second in 1982.

The Civil War was essentially one more phase of the long-standing Christian-Muslim struggle for control of Lebanon. Nevertheless, the presence in Lebanon of about 500,000 Palestinian refugees, and especially of the well organized PLO guerrillas, numbering nearly 20,000 men, was a major catalyst in provoking the incidents which led to open warfare.

The fighting erupted in mid-April 1975. It was sparked by the so-called Rammanah incident of April 13, 1975. In retaliation for the assassination of a Phalangist commander in Beirut, the Christian militia ambushed a busload of Palestinian guerrillas returning from a rally in nearby Aley, killing 27 and wounding 19 of the Palestinians.

The ensuing violent struggle was essentially between Christians and Muslims. However, this was not just another sectarian civil war similar to those Lebanon had endured in the past. While the Christians were all Lebanese, the Muslims were a coalition of Lebanese, Palestinians and volunteers from other Arab countries. Because of the direct or indirect involvement of many Arab states, exerting their influence either through one of the several Palestinian organizations or through the various Lebanese Muslim groups, the conflict assumed a pan-Arab dimension. It resulted in the total collapse of the institutions of the Lebanese state, the utter breakdown of the judiciary system, and the disintegration of the army. Only a fraction of the troops remained in uniform; the majority, most of them Muslims, defected.

The precarious situation deepened the sense of danger among the people, who were impelled to seek security within the structure of their various clans and communities, each of which had its own militia or armed group. Direct affiliation of the majority of the Lebanese with para-military organizations constituted along sectarian lines led to a greater religious and ethnic division of the country.

After initial Christian successes in 1975, the situation of the vastly outnumbered Christians became desperate by early 1976. When it became clear that the Palestinian and leftist Muslim coalition was close to complete victory, the Maronite leadership, believing rightly that Syria would not want to see the emergence of a strong new Palestinian-controlled state in Lebanon, requested Damascus to intervene on its behalf.

Syrian Intervention

The consequent Syrian intervention changed the situation drastically. With its military superiority, the Syrian army quickly overwhelmed the Palestinians and the left-wing militias, enabling the Christians to survive. Soon after, however, Syria changed sides, seizing control of the Palestinian-Muslim coalition, and turning against the Christian establishment. It was a masterful demonstration by President Hafez Assad of Syria of the ancient precept of "divide and rule." The Syrian presence assumed the nature of a foreign military occupation.

Syria's readiness to move into Lebanon and impose its authority on that country was a manifestation of Syria's special historical and political interest in its neighbor, which most Syrians considered to be an integral part of Syria: "one country and one people." Syria also wanted to change Lebanon into a "confrontation" state in opposition to Israel. The Syrians were particularly disturbed by Lebanon's military weakness and lack of control over the southern part of the state, which had become virtually autonomous under PLO rule. They were concerned that, in the event of renewed hostilities with Israel, the area could be quickly overrun by the Israelis. Should this occur, Israeli forces could advance rapidly through the Bekaa Valley, envelop the western flank of the Golan Heights, and endanger Damascus from the west. Because of this concern, strong Syrian contingents were deployed south of the Beirut-Damascus highway. In this way Syria intended to neutralize such a threat by making it inexpedient for Israel to operate through Lebanon against Syria.

The Syrian involvement in Lebanon in 1975-1976 went through three main phases: the mediation phase, the limited military intervention phase, and the all-out invasion.

The mediation phase lasted from April until December 1975. During this period Syria attempted by political mediation to bring an end to both the civil war and Palestinian involvement in it. The Syrian objective was to preserve the pre-April status quo. Despite Syrian ties to, and support of, the revolutionary leftist rebels, pragmatic President Assad still favored the existing government, since it could serve as an efficient lever to maintain and increase Syrian influence in Lebanon. Assad realized that some of the leftist leaders—most prominent among them the Druze chieftain Kamal Jumblatt—were hostile to Syria, and were influenced by Arab opponents of the present Lebanese regime. If they were to gain absolute power in Beirut, this would not only weaken Syria's voice in Lebanon's internal affairs, but would strengthen the PLO, which might then be able to draw Syria into war with Israel at an unsuitable time.

The second phase, from January until May 1976, was characterized by Syria's increased political involvement and by limited Syrian military intervention. In January, the Syrians submitted their own peace proposal to the warring factions. It was a compromise plan, which—while leaving the governmental structure basically untouched—would make concessions responsive to some of the Muslim and Palestinian demands. This was rejected by the Lebanese left and the Palestinians, and the Syrians turned to a restricted military intervention.

In March 1976, Syrian commando units masquerading as elements of the Palestinian Liberation Army infiltrated into Lebanon. A few weeks later the Syrians deployed a tank brigade on the Lebanese frontier ready to cross the border at any time. This greatly increased tension in the area.

Differences between Syria and the Palestinians sharpened. The Palestinians identified themselves with the Lebanese left in its fight for the annihilation of the Christian establishment and the establishment of a revolutionary Arab Lebanon. They believed that a leftist victory would strengthen their hand in the struggle with Israel. "The road to Jerusalem," wrote Abu Iyad (a deputy to Arafat) in *Al-Safir* (May 24, 1976), "leads through Ein Turah and Jounie" (Christian communities). Commenting on this statement, President Assad warned that "the Palestinians fighting on the slopes of the Lebanese hills are not fighting for Palestine. Whoever wants to liberate Jounie and Tripoli, does not want to liberate Palestine, even though he may say so. . . . Remember, my brothers, what was said in 1970 in Jordan: 'Palestine will be liberated via Amman.' This statement is now being adapted to Lebanon." (*Tishrin*, Damascus, July 21, 1976)

The Syrian invasion of Lebanon and defeat of the leftist and Palestinian forces there in June and July 1976 initiated the third phase of Syrian involvement. The excuse for the entry of Syrian forces was the apparently approaching victory of the rebels, a victory which would assure Palestinian dominance and thus would undermine the Syrian status in Lebanon. As soon as the Syrian troops started to cross the border at Rakhle and via the Beirut-Damascus highway, the Christians adopted a resolution approving the Syrian intervention.

Syria's invading forces included its 3d Tank Division and a number of smaller units, which had already been deployed along the border and ready to cross at a short notice. The object of the invasion was to take Beirut, Sidon, Tripoli and surrounding areas, and impose a "Syrian" settlement on Lebanon. Intermittent fighting lasted all through the summer.

Since Syrian military intervention amounted to a *de facto* occupation of more than half of Lebanon, and since it was obviously not an act of self-defense or self-preservation, it was interpreted by those Arab countries sympathetic to the Muslim rebels and the Palestinians as interference in the internal affairs of an independent neighboring state.

On the other hand, although it disrupted the delicate balance that existed in Israel-Syria-Lebanon relations, the Syrian entry into Lebanon in 1976 had been tacitly accepted by Jerusalem, following US mediation. The terms of the consent were contained in a letter from then foreign minister Yigal Allon to the US Secretary of State, Henry Kissinger. Israel would not oppose the Syrian entry into Lebanon providing that the Syrian troops did not cross a line running from south of Sidon on the Mediterranean Sea to Mount Hermon in the east (this became known as the "Red Line"), that they did not use their air force against ground targets in Lebanon, and that they refrained from deploying ground-to-air missiles on Lebanese territory.

According to this understanding Israel retained freedom of action relative to areas in southern Lebanon where there were PLO military bases for operations against Israel. To locate and attack such bases, Israel insisted on the right to overfly parts of Lebanon.

There is no evidence that Syria officially accepted these terms. However, there was a clear, tacit understanding which the Syrians honored for nearly 5 years. Once, early in 1977, the Syrians sent an infantry company south of the Red Line to Aishiya, possibly to test Israeli reaction. Israel protested, through Washington. The Syrian troops were withdrawn within three weeks.

The Arab League Intervenes—and Leaves

Following the Syrian invasion, the foreign ministers of the Arab League countries convened in emergency sessions in Cairo. On June 9, 1976, they implicitly sanctioned the invasion as a peacekeeping effort, passing a resolution authorizing Syria to operate in Lebanon with part of its forces already there as a Token Arab Security Force. By fall, however, it had become obvious that Syria, acting alone as a Token Arab Security Force, could not end the internal conflict. Representatives of four Arab countries (Egypt, Saudi Arabia, Kuwait, and Syria) and the PLO then met in Riyadh, under the auspices of the Arab League, to consider the situation in Lebanon. On October 17, they agreed to the establishment of an Arab Deterrent Force (ADF) answerable to, and under the personal leadership of, the president of the Lebanese Republic. Arab states were asked to contribute troops. Sudan, the United Arab Emirates, Saudi Arabia, and North Yemen agreed to participate. Syria, which now had about 20,000 soldiers in Lebanon, insisted that those troops be incorporated into the ADF.

The mission of the ADF, as stated in the Riyadh agreement, was to implement a ceasefire, to halt combat activities, to separate the belligerent parties, to supervise the return of the combatants to the positions held before April 13, 1975, and to assist the Lebanese authorities in all governmental functions.

The ADF became operational in Lebanon in December 1976. However, it soon became clear that it could not fulfill its mission of bringing peace and security to Lebanon because it was dominated by Syria, whose national interests were not identical with the ADF goals. Instead of implementing the objectives put forward by the Cairo and Riyadh agreements of June and October 1976, Syrian forces, operating nominally in the name of the ADF, were using force and pressure to weaken the local centers of power and to establish a central Lebanese government subservient to Syrian dictates.

The stalemate in redressing the underlying issues of the Lebanese crisis remained unresolved. In April 1977, despite objections of other members of the ADF, Syrian artillery shelled East Beirut, the Christian part of the divided capital, killing and wounding many civilians. In July, after the June 13 murder of Toni Franjieh, son of the pro-Syrian Christian leader Suleiman Franjieh, the Christian-Syrian confrontations grew in scope. For several weeks the Syrians intentionally bombarded Christian civilian population centers, especially East Beirut, causing thousands of civilian casualties.

Early in the fall of 1977, realizing that public opinion was turning against them, and plagued by Israeli overflights as a show of strength, the Syrians decided to halt their activities against East Beirut, and instead to turn to Christian villages north of the capital. They began a systematic slaughter of anti-Syrian elements that resulted in the destruction of the Christian resistance. During this period other members of the ADF began dissociating themselves openly from the Syrian atrocities. Disappointed and frustrated by Damascus's intransigence, the governments of Sudan, Saudi Arabia, the United Arab Emirates, and North Yemen decided to withdraw their troops from the ADF. In February of 1978 the Sudan contingent left Lebanon, followed by Saudi Arabia in March and the United Arab Emirates and North Yemen in April, leaving Syria as the only member of the ADF whose troops remained in the country.

The Syrian presence in Lebanon, which was beginning to assume the nature of permanence, combined with Syria's improved relations with the Muslim left and the PLO, increased Christian suspicion and fear of the Syrians. There were growing demands from the Christian community that the Syrian forces leave Lebanon. The Christians were particularly concerned about the manner in which the PLO guerrillas were permitted freedom of action in most of Lebanon, and were increasing their control over southern Lebanon. The anti-Syrian Maronite Christians were successful in imposing their views on most of the other Christian sects, and the armed confrontation between the Christian militia and the Syrian army continued intermittently until the Israeli invasion in 1982.

Chapter V
From Jerusalem
To Camp David

Sadat Offers to Visit Jerusalem

Active operations in the 1973 October War were ended by the United Nations-sponsored ceasefire agreements of October 22 and 24, 1973. However, a state of hostility continued between Syria and Israel until those two countries—with the assistance of US Secretary of State Henry Kissinger's "shuttle diplomacy"—signed a disengagement agreement on May 31, 1974. While the three principal combatants—Egypt, Syria, and Israel—pondered and reacted to the many lessons all had learned in that war, the focus of attention in the Arab-Israeli conflict returned to the plight of the Palestinians and to the ongoing guerrilla warfare between the PLO and Israel. For all practical purposes, in light of the status of the PLO in Lebanon and the use of Lebanon as a base for the PLO's anti-Israeli activities, the PLO and Lebanon now occupied the center of the Middle East stage.

However, the focus of attention on Lebanon proved to be temporary. President Anwar Sadat moved back to the center of the stage in late 1977, and remained there for most of the next four years, although he was occasionally joined in that position—or jostled from it—by Prime Minister Begin of Israel, President Assad of Syria, and Chairman Arafat of the PLO.

Sadat shifted the focus of attention to himself by dramatically announcing on November 9, 1977 that he was prepared to go to Jerusalem to present his views on a peaceful settlement of the Arab-Israeli conflict personally to the Israeli Knesset. Two days later Prime Minister Menachem Begin of Israel responded by urging the Egyptian people to forsake war, and in turn expressed his willingness to travel to Cairo in the search for peace. Then on November 15 Begin—with the consent of the Knesset—issued a formal invitation to Sadat to visit Jerusalem to conduct talks about permanent peace between Israel and Egypt. Addressing the Knesset, Begin stated that he would also ask King Hussein of Jordan, President Hafez

Assad of Syria, and Lebanon's President Elias Sarkis to come to Israel for peace discussions.

The formal Israeli invitation to Sadat was given in Tel Aviv to US Ambassador Samuel Lewis for transmission to the American Ambassador to Egypt, Hermann F. Eilts, who delivered the document to Egyptian authorities.

President Sadat accepted the invitation on November 17 and announced that he would arrive in Israel on November 19.

The Background

It would have been impossible for Sadat, or any other Arab leader, to contemplate such a gesture for peace before the 1973 War. Even though that war reaffirmed the military superiority of Israel over its Arab neighbors, the facts that Arab troops performed well, and that the war ended in a virtual stalemate, provided the Arabs in general, and Egyptians in particular, a basis for regaining the pride that had been so badly damaged by the miserable Arab performance in the 1967 War. On the other hand, it was clear to Sadat and other Egyptian leaders that there was no possibility of regaining Sinai from the Israelis by force of arms.

Thus, in the years immediately following the 1973 War, Sadat was seeking some way in which he could honorably enter into negotiations with Israel. He was prepared to barter recognition of Israel in return for recovery of Sinai. It is not clear to what extent Sadat's thinking along these lines had been communicated to Israel, or—if so—through what sources. What is known, however, is that in the late summer of 1977, in a visit to Rumania, Prime Minister Begin hinted to President Nicolae.Ceausescu of Rumania that Israel would welcome an Egyptian peace initiative, and would be pleased to invite Sadat to visit Jerusalem for peace talks.

Acting as a go-between, President Ceausescu informed Sadat that, if he provided Begin with the opportunity, the Israeli would invite the Egyptian President to visit Israel. This was all that Sadat needed to take the action that galvanized the world.

Reactions

While the United States government strongly endorsed the projected visit to Israel, the Soviet Union was critical, charging that a separate Egyptian-Israeli dialogue would not serve either the Arab cause or peace in the Middle East, and would only give the Israelis an opportunity to make greater inroads into the hitherto solid Arab front.

The Arab world, in general, reacted negatively to Sadat's decision to go to Jerusalem and denounced it. The visit was interpreted as a threat to Arab unity. There were fears and suspicions that Sadat might negotiate a separate peace with Israel, and abandon the Palestinians. President Assad called the visit dangerous and declared November 19, the day of Sadat's arrival in Israel, to be a day of mourning. Libya and Iraq vigorously condemned Sadat's initiative as a serious deviation from Arab nationalism, and urged Arab masses to prevent Cairo's defection. Libya called for Egypt's expulsion from the Arab League and broke diplomatic relations with Cairo. The PLO rejected the visit, describing it as surrender to the Zionist enemy, and urged Sadat to cancel his plans.

Whereas most Israelis were in a state of excitement over the impending visit, some expressed concern, mistrust, and doubts as to whether the move would serve the Israeli national interest. Some even saw it as a trick or deception. A somber note was struck by Lieutenant General Mordechai Gur, the Israeli Chief of Staff, in a newspaper interview. He said that Sadat should realize that if he was contemplating another deception like the Yom Kippur War (the Israeli name for the 1973 October War), when Israel was taken by surprise, his intentions would soon become quite clear to Israel. Gur added that he could not ignore the fact that in recent months the Egyptian army had been conducting intensive maneuvers along the east bank of the Suez Canal in possible preparation for a war with Israel.

In Egypt the majority of the population supported Sadat, believing that his trip might end the vicious cycle of wars between the two neighbors that had cost Egypt thousands of lives and considerable economic deprivation. Nevertheless, other Egyptians had reservations, preferring the *status quo* of "no peace, no war" with Israel to a dialogue in which they might be deceived by the "untrustworthy Jews." Among these were Foreign Minister Ismail Fahmy and his deputy Mohammed Riad, who considered Sadat's step an ill-advised political move. They stated that they could no longer shoulder the responsibility for Cairo's foreign policy, and both resigned, on November 17 and 18, respectively.

Sadat in Jerusalem

Upon landing at the Ben Gurion International Airport in Tel Aviv at 8:03 P.M., November 19, President Sadat was accorded full honors of a visiting head of state, including an honor guard, a 21-gun salute, and a red carpet, despite the fact that not only were there no diplomatic relations between the two countries, but technically Egypt and Israel were still in a state of war.

As he stepped from the plane Sadat was greeted by the Israeli

President Ephraim Katzir, Prime Minister Menachem Begin, the entire Israeli cabinet, former prime ministers Golda Meir and Itzhak Rabin, members of the Knesset, and thousands of Israeli well-wishers. After a brief welcoming ceremony, Sadat and Katzir were driven to Jerusalem, where a special suite had been prepared for the Egyptian president at the King David Hotel. Immediately after arrival, Sadat held preliminary talks with Begin, Deputy Prime Minister Yadin, and Foreign Minister Moshe Dayan.

The next day, before addressing the Knesset, Sadat spent several hours touring Muslim and Christian holy places in East Jerusalem. He also went to Yad Yashem in West Jerusalem, the memorial to the six million Jewish victims of Nazi genocide in World War II, and later, in a surprise gesture, he placed a wreath on the monument to the Israeli war dead.

The highlight of Sadat's visit was his address to the Israeli Knesset in which, while striking a noticeably mild tone, he firmly adhered to the traditional Arab positions on the basic Arab-Israeli issues. While he held out the promise of Arab recognition of the Israeli state, Sadat warned that there could be no peace without a settlement with the Palestinians, based on justice and not on occupation of the land of others.

In the final, but not joint, communique issued shortly before Sadat's departure, hope was expressed that further steps would be pursued through a dialogue between Egypt and Israel, thereby paving the way toward successful negotiations leading to the signature of peace treaties between Israel and all of the neighboring Arab states.

During the following months numerous meetings were held between senior officials of the Egyptian and Israeli governments, aimed at reaching an agreement on a peace plan. A summit meeting between Sadat and Begin took place in Ismailia on December 25-26, without achieving any substantial progress. In an effort to break down the barriers to progress, the two leaders created two standing committees, one military and one political, respectively headed by the Egyptian and Israeli defense and foreign ministers. Soon, however, the committees became inactive and were dissolved. The peace process was not easy.

Camp David

In due time, Cairo and Jerusalem submitted separate peace plans to each other. Each of these was rejected by the other side, and each nation blamed the other for failure. Despite mediation efforts by the United States, the attitudes of the negotiators hardened and became deadlocked. Then, on August 8, 1978, the White House announced that President Jimmy Carter had arranged for President Sadat and Prime Minister Begin to meet with him on September 5 to discuss methods for resolving the Egyptian-Israeli impasse, and to seek a framework for peace in the Middle East. The summit meeting would be held at the presidential retreat at Camp David, some 80 kilometers northwest of Washington. It was agreed in preliminary exploratory discussion that the United States would play a full role in a tripartite effort to seek a just and lasting peace, and that the American participants would be free to make suggestions when they saw obstacles impeding progress.

President Carter opened the summit talks with President Sadat and Prime Minister Begin at Camp David on September 6. In a joint statement the three leaders expressed hope for success despite the grave issues which they were facing. While there was no agreed agenda, the main points to be tackled were negotiations on the framework for peace between Egypt and Israel, and solution to the conflict between Egyptian demands that Israel withdraw from occupied Arab territories, and Israeli insistence on secure borders.

The summit negotiations at Camp David lasted for ten days. The talks were difficult and often faced collapse on a number of points. On September 6 and 7 Sadat and Begin engaged in bitter and acrimonious disputes. The two did not meet again after that. Carter discussed with each of them separately the details of a slowly evolving agreement.

The talks concluded on September 17 with Egypt and Israel agreeing to an outline for a peace treaty and for the settlement of the broader Arab-Israeli dispute over the West Bank and the Gaza Strip. The agreement was embodied in two documents, each of which was signed by Begin and Sadat. President Carter, who had been personally conducting the negotiations, signed as a witness.

Under the first accord, both nations agreed to sign a peace treaty within three months. Israel would withdraw from the entire Sinai Peninsula, which was to be returned to Egypt and would be demilitarized. The Israeli pull-out would be made in phases, the first starting three to nine months after signing the treaty, and the final within two to three years from that date. Diplomatic relations between Cairo and Jerusalem were to be established. In the second document the two parties agreed to begin negotiations designed to achieve autonomy for Palestinians in the West Bank and the Gaza Strip.

The Peace Treaty

By mid-November 1978, two months after the signing of the Camp David accords, it was officially announced that a peace treaty had been negotiated and was ready for signature. But no signing took place. The signature was delayed primarily because President Sadat refused to agree to

Article VI.(5) of the Treaty, which read:

"Subject to Article 103 of the United Nations Charter, in the event of a conflict between the obligations of the parties under the present treaty and any of their other obligations, the obligations under this Treaty will be binding and implemented."

Sadat insisted that Egypt's previous obligations to other Arab states remained valid, and should not be set aside by the treaty with Israel. To the Israelis, Sadat's attitude meant that in the future Egypt could feel free to join other Arab nations in a war with Israel, as had happened four times in the previous 30 years. Begin, therefore, declared that any amendment of the Article VI.(5) was unacceptable and that he would not sign a document which permitted and legalized a new Egyptian war with Israel. The controversy became so acute that the entire peace process seemed to have fallen apart.

Then in March 1979, at President Carter's insistence, an interpretive article was added in the "Agreed Minutes" of Article VI.(5). "It is agreed by the parties that there is no assertion that the Treaty prevails over other treaties or agreements, or that other treaties or agreements prevail over this Treaty. The foregoing is not to be construed as contravening the provisions of Article VI.(5) of the Treaty. . . ." satisfied both Sadat and Begin.

President Carter visited Cairo and Jerusalem between March 8 and 13, and proposed to both sides compromises designed to resolve a number of other unresolved issues. Both sides agreed to these suggestions, and the peace treaty formally ending the state of war between Egypt and Israel was signed in Washington on March 26, 1979. Its key points were:

- Israel was to withdraw its military forces and civilian settlements from Sinai in phases over a 3-year period.
- UnitedNationsforces would be deployed in some Israeli-Egyptian border areas to monitor the agreement.
- Israel and Egypt would establish normal and friendly relations and exchange ambassadors.
- Israel's ships and cargoes would have free right of passage through the Suez Canal.
- Egypt would end its economic boycott of Israel.
- Israel would be permitted to purchase oil from Sinai under normal commercial terms, after the fields were returned to Egypt.
- Israel and Egypt would start negotiations for Palestinian self-rule in the West Bank and the Gaza Strip within a month after the exchange of ratification documents.

The Legacy of Camp David

Both Egypt and Israel achieved from the Camp David accords, and from the subsequent peace treaty, their respective major objectives. For Egypt, this was the return of Sinai. For Israel it was recognition by, and peace with, a major Arab state. Both countries, however, had to pay some penalties for these accomplishments. For Egypt the major penalty was ostracism from the Arab League and the pan-Arab movement, at least for several years. For Israel it was international opprobrium for willful refusal to adhere to the spirit of the agreement to provide some form of autonomy for the Palestinians living in the Arab territories Israel had conquered in 1967 (the West Bank and the Gaza Strip); loss of Sinai as a buffer territory; and forfeiture of the Sinai oilfields, so important to the Israeli economy.

Israeli intransigence over the issue of Palestinian autonomy, of course, added fuel to the arguments of Egypt's Arab enemies who had critized Sadat for putting selfish Egyptian interests ahead of the Arab cause in support of the Palestinians. Since this was at least partly true, the Egyptians were embarrassed, but not so much that they would consider abrogating the treaty and forswearing the return of Sinai.

While—as was evident from the dispute over Article VI.(5) of the peace treaty—Israel could not count on Egypt's never again being drawn into an Arab coalition against Israel, the peace treaty nonetheless effectively removed Egypt from the Arab anti-Israeli alliance. Further, there was no doubt in the minds of most Israelis that the Egyptians sincerely wanted peace, and welcomed the fact that this was assured by the treaty, short of gross and overt Israeli aggression that Egypt could not ignore. Thus, for the foreseeable future there was no possibility of the creation of any Arab alliance that—without Egypt—could seriously threaten Israel militarily. This was equally evident to the Arab countries, adding to their resentment of Egypt and Sadat.

One of the authors remembers a conversation he had in Damascus with General Mustafa T'lass, Minister of Defense of Syria, shortly after the peace treaty was signed. When T'lass discovered that his American visitor had just come from Cairo he remarked, somewhat bitterly: "Colonel Dupuy, you are a military historian. Why do you visit Egypt when that country is no longer at war?" On that same visit to Damascus the same author suggested to a Syrian major general that he could find the answer to a military research problem by discussing it with his Egyptian counterpart. The general sadly shook his head. "It is easier for us to visit Washington than it is to go to Cairo," he said.

The bitterness against the Egyptian Government, and particularly against President Sadat, was to be found not only in other Arab capitals, but also among many Egyptians. There is no question that the average Egyptian considered his lot had been improved by the peace treaty with Israel, but many were, nonetheless, embittered by their isolation from the rest of the Arab world, and by their belief that Sadat had betrayed the Arab cause.

These Arabs—including dissident Egyptians—now saw the PLO, and its continuing guerrilla struggle against Israel from its base in Lebanon, as the embodiment of the Arab cause and pan-Arabism. Thus Lebanon and the PLO again began to crowd Sadat from the center of the Middle East stage.

Chapter VI

1978
The Litani River Operation:
The Second Israeli Incursion

PLO Autonomy in Lebanon

The 1948 war was the only one of the Arab-Israeli conflicts in which the Lebanese Army actively participated. After Lebanon and Israel signed the Armistice Agreement at Rhodes on March 22, 1949, the Israelis withdrew from southern Lebanon. For nearly two decades the border between the two countries was quiet, and the populations along the frontier lived side by side in peace, although with little or no contact with each other.

The situation changed drastically early in the 1970s when the PLO established itself in Lebanon. Given its *raison d'etre*—the destruction of the Jewish state—the PLO could be expected to do everything in its power to harass Israel across the only border now open to it. This harassment was carried out in two major ways: terrorist infiltration, and firing long-range missiles into northern Galilee from positions inside Lebanon. By the spring of 1978 the PLO was so firmly established in southern Lebanon and West Beirut that it had, as we have seen, virtually become an autonomous mini-state. The Palestinian territorial stronghold extended from the Israeli border to Beirut, and from the Mediterranean Sea to the Anti-Lebanon Mountains, an area about 90 kilometers from north to south and 30 to 45 kilometers from east to west. On the south and west the PLO region was confronted by the Israeli Army and Navy. To the north and east it was facing Phalangist and Syrian forces. The Lebanese government, while desirous of restricting PLO activities against Israel, lacked the military power to enforce its will or exercise its sovereignty in the area controlled by the PLO. Arab states which could have put pressure on the PLO to take a more moderate stance were not interested in doing so, preferring instead to keep the tension high. And while Syria presumably did not want the PLO to

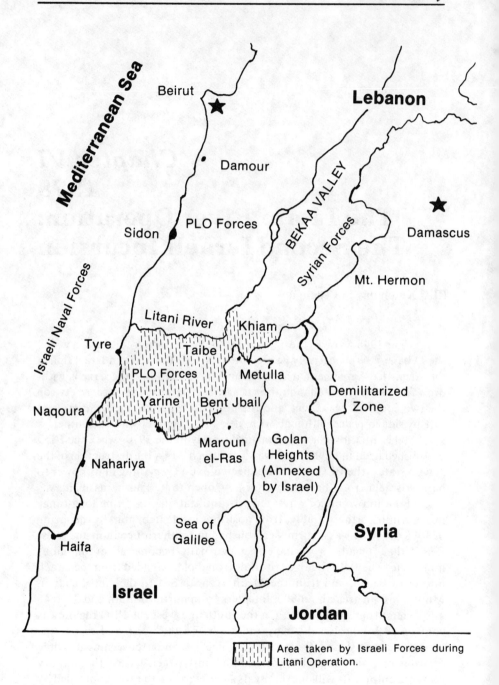

Litani River Operation 1978

precipitate a new war with Israel prematurely, it was prevented from exercising pressure because of the understanding with the Israelis not to move troops south of the "Red Line". Here was a paradox typical of Middle East relationships: the Palestinian guerrillas found a shelter in southern Lebanon under an Israeli umbrella which deterred the Syrians.

As the PLO established itself firmly in South Lebanon, it substituted its own administrative authority for the Lebanese political, economic, and administrative systems. Not only was the legitimate central governmental rule displaced, so too were local Lebanese government authorities. Replacing the standard political features of an established, civilized society were PLO guerrilla chieftains ruling by force and terror, and responsible only to the PLO administration of Yasser Arafat. These chieftains granted favors arbitrarily to their supporters while dealing harshly with opponents, in order to instill fear and obedience in the local population.

Increasing Intensity of PLO-Israeli Hostilities

The increased PLO guerrilla cross-border raids against Israel proper, as well as attacks against Israeli citizens and property outside Israel, resulted in hundreds of Israeli civilian casualties, including women and children. Since Israeli warnings to the Beirut Government and various international bodies did not restrain the PLO in Lebanon (as it had in Jordan and Syria), and since no sovereign government can fail to respond to attacks against its citizens and its frontiers, the Israeli Defense Forces (IDF) intermittently retaliated against known PLO installations in Lebanon with air raids and by surface forays made by special commando units.

This state of low-level, intermittent Israeli-PLO hostility reached a climax on March 11, 1978, when a group of 11 Palestinian guerrillas based in Lebanon landed on the coast of Israel about 20 miles south of Haifa, close to the settlement of Maagen Mikhael. The raiders, who had set out from Damour, apparently in fishing boats, came ashore in two rubber boats. Their first victim was a lone American woman strolling on the beach. They shot her after she told them where they were. Then the guerrillas walked several hundred yards east to the Tel Aviv-Haifa coastal highway. There they stopped a taxi, killing the driver and all of his passengers. Shortly afterward, they ambushed a bus bound from Tel Aviv for Haifa, and loaded with tourists. The gunmen seized the bus, killing or wounding several of the passengers. They then forced the bus driver to turn the bus around and proceed toward Tel Aviv. The gunmen fired at passing cars, inflicting more casualties. Another civilian bus was stopped north of Caesarea, and again a number of passengers were killed and wounded. The remaining passengers, including 30 children, were herded into the first bus, which—with the gunmen also aboard—then continued in the direction of Tel Aviv. Farther down the road a taxi was stopped and its six occupants taken hostage and loaded into the overcrowded bus.

By this time the Israeli security forces had been alerted. The police established several roadblocks in an attempt to halt the speeding bus, but were at first unsuccessful. Finally, near Herzliya, some eight kilometers north of Tel Aviv, a large barrier was erected near a road junction by specially trained units of police and soldiers, who had been helicoptered to the scene. As the bus approached the junction it was brought under heavy fire, and was halted. After a ten-minute exchange of fire, the vehicle blew up and burst into flames, killing many of the people inside. A total of 35 Israeli civilians were killed and over 74 wounded in this raid. Only two of the gunmen survived. The raid was the most costly to the Israelis since the establishment of their state in 1948.

The raiders belonged to Fatah, the official Fatah spokesman in Beirut acknowledged responsibility for the raid, and praised it as an inspiring success. He stated that PLO Chairman Yasser Arafat had personally approved the attack, in order to demonstrate that President Sadat's initiative to establish a peaceful relationship between Egypt and Israel would not bring peace to the area, since there could be no Middle East settlement without the Palestinians. The original plan had been to seize a hotel in Tel Aviv, to take hostages, and then to release them in exchange for Palestinian and foreign terrorists in Israeli prisons. Among the prisoners they hoped to free was the Japanese terrorist Kozo Okamoto, who had been sentenced to life imprisonment for the killing of 26 persons at Ben Gurion Airport in 1972. The guerrillas planned to demand that the British and Rumanian ambassadors and the UN representative in Israel surrender as hostages to guarantee the gunmen and the freed terrorists safe conduct to Damascus aboard a United Nations plane.

Israel was shocked by the carnage, which became known as the Coastal Road Massacre. The Israeli Government immediately denounced the wanton killings and—with strong popular support—warned of retribution. Israeli fury was further inflamed by official announcements from several Arab countries praising the raid as an heroic action. An Israeli counteraction was obviously imminent.

The Litani River Operation

During the night of March 14/15, while most of the world was reacting with horror to news of the massacre, IDF units, some 12,000 to 15,000 men strong, moved across the border into Lebanon and launched a limited attack against the guerrilla bases and other centers of the PLO. The objective of the operation was to clear the guerrillas from the area between the Israeli border and the Litani River in order to prevent any future Palestinian attacks on Israel.

During the next 36 hours the major PLO strongholds of Aalma-al Shaab, Naqoura, Yarine, Bent Jbail, Maroun er-Ras, al Tayybah, al Khiyam, and Ibias Saqi were captured by the Israeli Army. This made it possible to establish a so-called "security belt" seven to ten kilometers deep along Israel's 100 kilometer-long border with Lebanon. During the first two days of fighting, Israeli casualties were 11 killed and 57 wounded. The Palestinian losses were about 100 men killed and nearly 300 wounded.

Fighting continued as the Israelis consolidated their positions south of the river. By March 18 the Israelis had captured the PLO stronghold of Tebnine and 14 nearby villages in the central sector. In the eastern sector they halted their advance just south of the river to avoid confrontation with the Syrians and other elements of the Arab Deterrent Force.

When Israel declared a unilateral ceasefire on March 21, its forces were in complete control of the southern part of Lebanon up to the Litani River, with the exception of the port city of Tyre, and the Palestinian refugee camp at Rachidiye, which the Israeli Command decided not to take because of its large population. The Israeli Army also left open the bridge over the Litani River north of Tyre, in order to enable the Lebanese and Palestinian civilians to evacuate the area unimpeded.

The Israeli victory was quick, and was impressive in terms of captured territory. However, the rate of advance had been deliberate, due to the insistence of the Jerusalem Cabinet, to keep Israeli casualties to a minimum. This deliberate advance, combined with the three days' delay in reaction to the Coastal Road Massacre while the Israeli Government issued repeated warnings concerning the forthcoming retaliation, gave the Palestinian forces south of the Litani River plenty of opportunity to withdraw with relatively minor losses. The PLO forces slowed down the Israeli advance in some instances, particularly at the defensive strongholds of Bent Jbail, At Tayybah, and al Khiyam. Then they retreated northward in good order to establish a new line of defense running from As Sarafand in the west, close to the Mediterranean coast, to Nabatiye in the east. Casualty reports published for the first week of fighting up to March 21 were conflicting. While the Israelis reported that they had 20 killed and had inflicted 400 casualties on the Palestinians, the Palestinians admitted that 144 of their men were killed but asserted that 450 Israelis had been killed or wounded.

Although the Israeli ground forces did not advance beyond the Litani River during the course of the operation, Israeli planes and gunboats bombed and shelled Palestinian concentrations farther north. Among the targets struck were areas close to Sidon, Damour, Nabatiye, and strongholds in Palestinian refugee camps. No Israeli aircraft were lost in these operations.

The United Nations Interim Force in Lebanon

At the request of both Israel and Lebanon, the United Nations Security Council convened on March 17 to deal with the situation in South Lebanon. After two days of heated discussion, in which Israel and several Arab countries exchanged charges and countercharges, the Security Council approved US-sponsored Resolution 425. This called for strict respect for the territorial integrity, sovereignty, and political independence of Lebanon within its territorially recognized boundaries, withdrawal of Israeli troops from South Lebanon, and—to enforce the ceasefire—establishment of a 4,000-man United Nations Interim Force in Lebanon (UNIFIL).

On March 22, the first 100 UNIFIL troops arrived in Lebanon, via the northern Israeli town of Metulla. These were advance elements of contingents from Iran, Denmark, Ireland, Finland, and the Netherlands. They took up positions near the village of Ghandouriyeh, close to the Litani River. Units from Canada, France, Nepal, Norway, and Sweden followed in the next few days. Major General Emmanuel Erskine of Ghana was named the UNIFIL commander.

Israel informed the UN that it would not withdraw completely until the UNIFIL troops were deployed effectively and capable of preventing the return of Palestinian guerrillas to the border area. The UN provided appropriate assurances, stating that the UNIFIL would use military means to prevent the guerrillas from returning to their former positions. However, Yasser Arafat had already advised Mr. Kurt Waldheim, Secretary General of the United Nations, that the PLO had not accepted and would not accept Security Council Resolution 425. Nor would the PLO abide by the truce because, according to Arafat, "there is no ceasefire in the vocabulary of the Palestinian revolution."

Nevertheless, under international pressure, Israel started to withdraw its forces on April 11. The Israeli troops pulled back from their forward positions and turned them over to the UNIFIL troops. This left the Israelis in control only of a buffer zone about ten kilometers deep, a strip of territory they considered essential to the safety of the border region. The Israelis shared control of this zone with a small force of Lebanese soldiers and local militia commanded by Major Sa'ad Haddad of the Lebanese Army. Meanwhile, near Metulla, the Israelis had opened the border fence to permit Lebanese people to cross into Israel for work, to purchase supplies, and to receive medical assistance. This arrangement, which they called "the Good Fence", was highly publicized by the Israelis.

The Christian communities in the areas which had been occupied by the Israelis were distressed by the Israeli pullout. They did not trust the UNIFIL and insisted that the Israeli Army remain to protect them from the Palestinians. To calm them, the UNIFIL commander assured the Christians that it would safeguard them, would not interfere in their affairs within the enclaves, and would keep open the Good Fence.

The Israeli troops completed their withdrawal from southern Lebanon on June 13. Their relinquishment of the buffer zone, however, led to an immediate controversy. Instead of turning the area over to the UNIFIL, they left it under the control of Major Haddad and his militia. Israel's decision left Haddad as virtual governor of a strip of territory 10 kilometers deep, extending some 80 kilometers from Shouba in the east to Ras al-Biyada on the Mediterranean coast.

Israel contended that, since it had not occupied this largely Christian region during the March invasion, it could not hand it over to the UNIFIL. Jerusalem argued that Haddad represented legitimate Lebanese authority, since he had been sent to South Lebanon by the Beirut Government to organize an effective resistance to Palestinian encroachment.

Chapter VII
The Case of
Major Sa'ad Haddad

The Origins of "Free Lebanon"

Actually, Haddad had arrived in South Lebanon less than two years before the Litani operation. In October 1976 the President of Lebanon, Suleiman Franjieh, directed the Army Commander to find a suitable officer to command troops and militia in southern Lebanon. After the screening of numerous candidates, the choice fell on Major Sa'ad Haddad, a Christian line officer with a brilliant service record, whose original home was in Marjayoun in southern Lebanon. The Army Chief of Staff, General Hanna Said, ordered Haddad to establish his headquarters in Marjayoun, close to the Israeli border, and to restore order and Lebanese government rule in the region. This area was part of what had become known as "Fatahland," where Palestinian guerrillas were building bases and intimidating the local Muslim and Christian population.

The authors of this book, while visiting Lebanon in March 1983, had an opportunity to meet and interview Major Haddad, who told them about his difficult and unique task. Son of a Lebanese farmer, Haddad was born in 1937. After graduating from high school, he decided to break with the family tradition of farming, entered the military academy, and became an officer. Later he studied at the French Infantry School at St. Cyr, and at the US Army Field Artillery School at Fort Sill, Oklahoma.

Haddad was a Lebanese nationalist dedicated to an independent Lebanon in which Christians and Muslims could live together in peace. A Greek Catholic, he had been outspoken in efforts to persuade his Lebanese compatriots to overlook their confessional differences and join forces to work for the benefit of the country.

Haddad arrived in South Lebanon late in 1976 through Israel. "How else could I have come?" he said, shrugging his shoulders. "Southern Lebanon was completely cut off from Beirut by Palestinian guerrillas." So he came by ship from the small Lebanese port of Jounie, north of Beirut, to Haifa, and then across the border to Marjayoun. At that time a small area consisting of Marjayoun and its neighboring villages was held by a meager force of fewer than 500 Lebanese soldiers and militiamen under Lieutenant Adnan Housmi. Weary and fatigued, Housmi had repeatedly asked his superiors in Beirut to be replaced. He returned to Beirut on the same ship that had brought Haddad to Haifa.

Haddad kept in touch with the Lebanese Army Headquarters by radio, or by messengers sent through Haifa. He received his pay and that for his men from the Lebanese Ministry of Defense by bank drafts sent through Israel. The unused parts of salaries were deposited in Beirut banks in individual accounts. As he built up his forces, Haddad got most of his weapons and supplies from the Israelis, with the knowledge and approval of his superiors. Some of his equipment—like AMX tanks and spare parts— were sent to Marjayoun from Beirut by sea via Haifa, since the Israelis did not have the necessary parts for these items of Lebanese materiel.

Haddad considered his cooperation with Israel as being of service to his own country. He was full of contempt for the political hypocrisy of Arab states who refused to recognize Israel. He believed that admitting Israel into the Middle East family of nations would benefit the entire region.

Between his arrival late in 1976 and the Israeli Litani operation in March 1978, Haddad built up his strength to nearly 1,000 men. He accepted both Muslim and Christian volunteers into his force, and turned his original ramshackle army into a more disciplined and better fighting unit than any other in Lebanon. Under the banner of Free Lebanon, and the slogan "Lebanon for the Lebanese", his troops were engaged in a never-ending struggle with nearby PLO guerrillas and their local Muslim leftist allies.

Renegade or Patriot?

Subsequently, on April 18, 1979, Haddad proclaimed the area under his control the Independent Republic of Free Lebanon and called all freedom-loving Lebanese without regard for religion and sectarian origin to join him in liberating the country from foreign occupation. This was a bold and courageous step by a noble and brave man, who asked his fellow Lebanese to bury fears and animosities against their fellow countrymen, and give their loyalty to their state and not to the family clan. However, Haddad was condemned by many Lebanese Muslims, and by most of the other Arab countries. He became the target of a vicious propaganda campaign, despite the fact that he was carrying out a mission assigned to him by the highest authority of the Lebanese Army, and was paid regularly by the Lebanese government.

Many observers believed that, given time, Haddad's approach might have borne fruit. But the vicious and malicious propaganda conducted by the Arab and western press was effective. Denounced as a traitor, turncoat, deserter from the Lebanese Army, an Israeli puppet, Haddad was described in the world press as a renegade and warlord. But those who knew him, including his superiors and friends in the Lebanese Army and in the government, were aware of the truth.

Haddad was neither a traitor nor a renegade. He was a loyal Lebanese Army officer, cooperating with the Israelis in accordance with his officially assigned mission. Unfortunately, his premature death from cancer prevented him from playing the major role his ability and performance warranted in the continuing struggles of his unfortunate country. In retrospect, in light of the fact that the Israelis had liberated half of Lebanon from what was unquestionably a harsh and ruthless occupation by the PLO, Haddad must be respected as a man of wisdom, intelligence, foresight, and integrity.

Intrigued by the controversy surrounding Haddad, early in 1983, while talking with a senior Lebanese Army officer in his comfortable office in the imposing Ministry of Defense building at Yarzeh in the Beirut suburbs, we asked his opinion of Haddad. "Major Haddad—I know him well. A fine soldier and a patriot. He has been doing his duty in accordance with his instructions for the past several years."

Remembering that Haddad was a Christian, we asked another Lebanese general, who is a Sunni Muslim, what he thought about charges made against Haddad. "Haddad is a fine man and soldier; a great patriot," was his answer. "He was given a mission and he carried it out. It was possibly an illegal mission, but he did not question his orders. Another officer rejected a similar mission, which was his right. But Sa'ad did what he was told to do, and did it well. I expect him back in Beirut and in the regular army soon."

Next day, we again raised the question of Major Haddad with one of the top generals of the Lebanese Army, like Haddad, a Christian. "Haddad is a splendid officer," he stated. "For years we have served together. During his time in the south, he has been following official instructions. He and his men are paid through banks in Beirut. In recent months I have seen him from time to time. I enjoy his company, and respect his judgment. He will be welcomed back to the Army when it is time for him to return."

Still another Lebanese officer, a young, outspoken and dynamic lieutenant colonel of the General Staff, said "Haddad is a great patriot." He pronounced the word patriot with pride and repeated it several times. "A very fine man. He was a member of my class in officers' school. I have his name on the reunion list, which we shall have three weeks from now. How I envied him," the colonel continued, "during the years when the only place the Lebanese flag was flying freely was in his command."

Could all these generals and senior officers of the Lebanese Army, Muslims and Christians alike, be speaking of the man so often described by the media as a renegade, a deserter from the Lebanese Army? Although during the period when Syria was dominating the Lebanese government, Haddad had been formally discharged from the Lebanese Army and later court martialled, this was done under foreign pressure, dictated by the occupants of the country, without any regard to true facts, fairness, and law. Significantly, even after the court martial, Haddad and his men continued to receive their pay and supplies from the Lebanese Army, through Israel.

On January 5, 1984, just ten days before his death from cancer, the Lebanese State Court in Beirut reversed the old ruling by which Haddad had been nominally deprived of his rights in the Lebanese Army. The judges, two Muslims and one Christian, ruled unanimously that Haddad should be immediately reinstated in the Army and should regain all his rights and privileges.

Chapter VIII
The Resurgence
of the PLO
in South Lebanon

Increasing Strength and Activity of the PLO

The deployment of the UNIFIL across southern Lebanon in the spring of 1978 had been intended to establish a physical obstacle preventing further PLO incursion into northern Israel. However, despite this, and despite the presence of Major Haddad's Free Lebanon forces in the border strip along the Israeli frontier, the PLO continued to use significant areas in southern Lebanon as bases for operations against Israel.

Since the PLO guerrillas were generally unable to penetrate Israeli land frontiers, they resorted to artillery and mortar barrages, primarily on civilian targets in northern Galilee. Between April 1978 and April 1981 the PLO carried out over 50 shellings of Israeli territory, killing 10 Israelis and wounding 57. However, the number and intensity of shellings were considerably less than before the Litani operation. During that period, the PLO made two efforts to carry out raids using hang gliders, but both attempts failed. However, on April 22, 1980, a four-man Fatah raiding team came ashore near the Israeli coastal town of Nahariya. They broke into an apartment building, where they murdered a 4-year-old girl and her father. In an ensuing gun battle with the police, one policeman was killed and four civilians wounded. Two of the gunmen were killed and two taken prisoner.

In claiming the responsibility for the Nahariya raid, the PLO spokesman in Beirut asserted that its aim was to emphasize "Arab rejection of the Egyptian-Israeli peace treaty".

To carry out operations against Israel from South Lebanon, the PLO had set up two headquarters. One of these, known as the Forward Command Headquarters, was in Tyre, and was commanded by Azami Zarayer, a Fatah battalion commander. The other one, designated as the

Main Command Headquarters, was in Sidon under Haj Ismail, the Castel Brigade commander.

Despite protests from the local population, and in contravention of internationally recognized rules of war, PLO commanders deployed most of their heavy weapons—such as artillery, mortars, multiple rocket launchers, anti-tank and anti-aircraft guns—inside or close to towns and villages. They did this because they believed that the Israelis would be reluctant to retaliate by shelling and bombing the deployment areas because this would endanger civilians. For the same reason they placed their ammunition depots, headquarters, and troop billets in refugee camps, churches, mosques, hospitals, and office buildings which they confiscated for this purpose.

Israeli Reaction

Increased activities of the PLO guerrillas inside and outside Israel caused the Israelis to carry out extensive retaliatory air and ground strikes. During the same three-year period between April of 1978 and April of 1981, the Israeli Army mounted 32 ground operations against PLO installations in South Lebanon. Israeli planes repeatedly bombed the PLO base camps in the Damour, Sidon, and Tyre areas. PLO targets within range were heavily shelled by gunboats and by artillery. Palestinian casualties from Israeli ground, air, and naval assault were estimated at over 1,200. A considerable amount of equipment was destroyed as well.

The hard-hitting retaliatory response of the IDF had a marked impact on the PLO establishment. Realizing that the war of attrition was not going in its favor because of damage from the Israeli retaliation, the PLO began to change its tactics and carried out a reorganization to fit the changing military and political situations. Intense efforts were devoted to building fortified defense areas and constructing bunkers and shelters to protect headquarters and troops. With Soviet assistance the PLO had acquired large numbers of heavy weapons, including T-34 tanks; guns and howitzers of 100mm, 122mm, 130mm and 152mm calibers; 30 and 40 tube varieties of BM-21 Katyusha multiple rocket launchers; BRDM-2 reconnaissance cars; BTR-152 armed troop carriers; SA-7 and SA-9 surface-to-air missile launchers; and the deadly ZSU-23-4 radar-guided mobile antiaircraft guns.

From late April to late May 1981 there was a lull in Israeli operations against the PLO, due mainly to the concentration of Israeli attention upon an increasingly serious confrontation with Syria. This confrontation, precipitated by Syrian deployment of air defense missiles into eastern Lebanon (see chapter IX), led American President Ronald Reagan to appoint

Ambassador Philip Habib (former Undersecretary of State for Political Affairs) as his special envoy to the Middle East to attempt to defuse the crisis.

The Mission of Philip Habib

Both the PLO leadership and the Syrian Government were hostile toward Habib's mission. Through its spokesman, the PLO repeatedly asserted that the United States could be neither an arbiter nor a mediator in the Arab-Israeli conflict since its long-standing support of Israel made it one of the foremost parties involved in the crisis. Syrian government-controlled media were no less negative, strongly criticizing the Habib mission. Assad himself called the effort futile, and insisted that Syria did not fear any threat and would neither retreat nor compromise.

Israel, on the contrary—with national elections only a few weeks away, on June 30, and the raid on Osirak (see chapter IX) boosting its morale and feeling of military superiority—agreed to give Habib ample time to carry out his mission. Begin nevertheless kept his military options open by stating that the talks could not go on indefinitely, and that if diplomacy did not achieve positive results, Israel would deal with the missile problem unilaterally.

The Strife Intensifies

While Habib persevered in his attempts at mediation, trying to end the Syrian-Israeli missile crisis, Israel—after a month's lull—resumed its attacks on PLO concentrations in South Lebanon. On May 28 Israeli commandos, landing from the sea, raided a PLO guerrilla base near Damour, approximately 15 kilometers south of Beirut. In the same area, the Israeli Air Force attacked and destroyed four Libyan-operated SA-9 missile batteries deployed in and around the guerrilla camp of Ahmed Jabril's Popular Front for the Liberation of Palestine—General Command. In the attack on the camp, about 80 guerrillas and several Libyans were killed or wounded. Libya, which had kept a contingent of troops in Lebanon since 1972, had deployed these missiles early in April, a few weeks before they were hit. The Israelis also bombed PLO positions in the Arkub area—a stronghold in the heart of Fatahland on the slopes of Mount Hermon in southeastern Lebanon.

A few days later, on June 2, six Israeli planes bombed and destroyed a Fatah base and regional headquarters at Abu Swad, just north of Tyre. Six guerrillas were killed and about 45 wounded. After that incident, a tense pause in fighting lasted until almost mid-July.

On July 10, an Israeli air strike against PLO positions in southern Lebanon started around midday and lasted for nearly one hour. The attack was directed against a multiple rocket launcher base, some ten kilometers south of Sidon, and against an artillery deployment and ammunition depot at Habbush, four kilometers north of Nabatiye. Three guerrillas were killed and about 25 wounded. Israeli planes encountered antiaircraft fire, but all returned safely.

In retaliation, only a few hours after the bombardment of the guerrilla targets, a dozen Katyusha rockets were fired from the Rumman Arnoun area at the northern Israeli resort town of Kiryat Shemona, wounding 14 residents and destroying a synagogue and several other buildings.

The PLO retaliatory strike brought the Israeli planes back over southern Lebanon. On July 12 Israeli aircraft hit weapon storehouses, ammunition depots, and guerrilla deployment areas all along the Lebanese coast, from Tyre in the south to Damour in the north. Almost 25 people were killed or wounded. Two days later the IAF attacked PLO training bases and weapon and ammunition depots in the Damour and Nabatiye areas. Eight guerrillas and local residents were killed and 38 wounded. Several Syrian MiG-23s intercepted one group of Israeli planes. In the ensuing dogfight one Syrian MiG was shot down without any losses to the Israelis.

On July 15 Palestinian guerrillas responded to the air attacks by shelling several northern Israeli towns. Katyusha rockets and artillery hit the cities of Nahariya and Kiryat Shemona, killing three and wounding 35 civilians. This was the most intensive shelling of the area in several years. Israeli public opinion was outraged and demanded that the government take appropriate steps to prevent such occurrences. The official Israeli response was more air strikes, and the vicious circle of attacks and counterattacks seemed to have become irreversible.

On July 16, in the most severe air attack to date, Israeli planes ranged widely over southern Lebanon. They bombed PLO forward positions in South Lebanon for two hours. They also attacked and destroyed five bridges across the Zahrani and Litani rivers on key supply routes linking Palestinian gun and Katyusha positions with their rear base areas. The headquarters of the Popular Front for the Liberation of Palestine and of the Arab Liberation Front were hit. Serious damage was inflicted on the guerrilla training camps and firing positions.

On July 17 Israel further escalated hostilities by a 20-minute raid on Beirut, the first since the air strike on that city in 1974. The target was the PLO headquarters located in the heavily populated Fakehrani District of Muslim West Beirut. The office of the Fatah, the main PLO guerrilla army, and of the Democratic Front for the Liberation of Palestine, were severely damaged. Some 300 people were killed or wounded, most of them Palestinian and Lebanese civilians. This Israeli attack was strongly deplored by many people, both outside and inside Israel. Many Israelis believed that by killing civilians Israel had lost its moral advantage in the struggle against the PLO and badly hurt its image in the West. Prime Minister Begin was accused of disrupting the peace mission of Ambassador Habib and of setting back the whole course of securing a solution of the missile crisis. The United States condemned the bombing of West Beirut and the escalation of violence along the Lebanon-Israeli border, and suspended delivery of several F-16 aircraft, which were to have arrived in Israel in July and August.

The Israeli government defended its action, stating that its air force never intentionally directed its attacks against the civilian population. However, if the PLO continued to attack Israel, while at the same time intentionally placing its headquarters and other military bases near or within civilian communities, the IAF had no choice but to attack them as legitimate military targets. The Israelis said they would not be intimidated and would strike again. They said that the blame for eventual civilian casualties should be placed on the PLO, which was totally disregarding international agreements on the law and customs of war, which prohibit deployment of military installations in populated areas.

Between July 17 and 22 Israeli Air Force planes hammered daily at various PLO headquarters, ammunition dumps, weapon depots, camps, and artillery and rocket sites near Tyre, Rachidiye, Nabatiye, Sidon, and Damour. They destroyed five more bridges across the Zahrani and Litani rivers, making a total of ten bridges out of service. The Israeli command believed that this would seriously hamper the PLO's ability to supply the forward units shelling Israeli territory. Particularly hard hit was Beaufort Castle, a 12th century crusader stronghold, used by the PLO as an observation post to direct artillery fire at targets in Israel. On July 20, an Israeli naval commando unit landed beside the Zahrani estuary south of Sidon; after a short encounter with PLO guards, the commandos destroyed nearby ammunition, oil, and weapon depots.

The PLO responded to these Israeli attacks by shelling northern Israeli towns and villages, including Nahariya, Kiryat Shemona, Metulla, and a number of kibbutzim in Galilee. In Nahariya a maternity hospital was struck, wounding four women. A rocket attack on Kiryat Shemona on July 19 killed a teenage boy and his mother, and wounded 23 civilians. No military targets were hit.

The escalation of long-range violence clearly presaged the possibility of full-scale hostilities. President Reagan instructed Ambassador Habib to devote all of his effort to ending the violence between Israel and the PLO and to mediating an understanding between the two.

Habib Obtains a Ceasefire

Habib immediately went to work. Seeking cessation of hostilities, he met with Israeli and Lebanese leaders, with whom he discussed ways of finding acceptable solutions to the conflict. Being restricted by the US commitment to Israel not to negotiate directly with the PLO, Habib established indirect contact with the PLO through Saudi Arabia.

On July 24, 1981, after a week of arduous negotiations, the Israeli government and the PLO endorsed separate ceasefire agreements, ending the fighting along the Israeli-Lebanese border. Although the ceasefire was accepted by PLO Chairman Yasser Arafat, the Popular Front for the Liberation of Palestine—General Command, led by Captain Ahmed Jabril, refused to participate in the agreement and continued to shell Major Haddad's Free Lebanon enclave. However, Jabril too agreed to the ceasefire on July 29.

The storm in Lebanon seemed to have blown over. In fact, however, issues raised by the ceasefire were to precipitate a new war in less than a year.

Chapter IX
From Bekaa to Osirak to Cairo; Missiles, Airpower, and Assassination

The Israeli Air Force had carried the principal burden on the Israeli side during the 40 months of low-level hostilities between Israel and the PLO following the Litani River operation and up to the ceasefire of late July 1981. Most of the Israeli operations were air raids against PLO installations inside Lebanon. The bulk of the intelligence behind the planning of the several commando raids was gathered by Israeli reconnaissance aircraft. These operations were often airborne assaults, and almost invariably were carried out with substantial air support. During the late spring and summer of 1981 two incidents highlighted the special significance of airpower to the defense and security of Israel, and were of major significance in the events leading up to, and following, the July ceasefire.

Syrian Air-To-Air Missiles in the Bekaa Valley

During the spring of 1981 the Syrians had become concerned about the effectiveness of Phalangist and Israeli cooperation against the PLO. Unexpectedly the Syrians—while avoiding a direct confrontation with Israel—entered into this situation by besieging the Christian city of Zahle, near the Beirut-Damascus highway, in the north-central Bekaa Valley. As the plight of the Phalangist defenders of Zahle became desperate, the Israelis began to fear that a major defeat there could seriously threaten the viability and survivability of their principal Christian allies in Lebanon. On April 28 Israeli planes intervened for the first time in the struggle for Zahle, shooting down two Syrian helicopters which were attacking the Christian militia. The Israelis justified this action by stressing Israel's commitment to the survival of the desperately threatened Christians. An Israeli spokesman revealed that in August 1978 Israel had made a secret promise to the Lebanese Christians that it would provide air support to defend them against air attacks by Syria.

On April 29, in response to the Israeli destruction of its helicopters, Syria began to deploy Soviet-built surface-to-air missiles in Lebanon's Bekaa Valley. By early May, the Syrians had moved three SA-6 batteries, with a total of 36 missiles, into Lebanon. In addition, they deployed two SA-3 batteries, one SA-2 battery, and one tank brigade on the Lebanese-Syrian border.

Israel considered that the emplacement of air defense missiles on Lebanese soil was a breach of the tacit Israeli-Syrian understanding that Syria would not install such weapons inside Lebanon. Although Syria insisted that the missiles were merely defensive weapons, Israel regarded the presence of SA-6s in the Bekaa Valley as a threat to the air reconnaissance which it considered vital to its security. Prime Minister Menachem Begin warned that Israel would use force to remove the missiles unless Damascus withdrew them voluntarily. While President Hafez Assad realized that the superior Israeli Air Force could destroy the SAMs at any time, he rejected the Israeli demands, insisting that Syria had full right to defend its troops by deploying the missiles in Lebanon, and that this was not a violation of the prior understanding.

Syrian-Israeli Tension Mounts

By his unequivocal threat to destroy the missiles, Prime Minister Begin had maneuvered himself into an unenviable position. He now had only two options: either to launch a military strike against the Syrian missiles in Lebanon—with the danger that this could precipitate war—or to seek a diplomatic solution to the crisis in a way that would allow Jerusalem to maintain its credibility.

At this point, Moscow decided to act. Only a few days before Philip Habib, the US Special Envoy to the Middle East, arrived in Damascus to negotiate a settlement between Israel and Syria, the Soviets sent First Deputy Foreign Minister Georgiy Korniyenko to Damascus to discuss the situation with President Assad. After several days of consultations with Assad and senior Syrian officials, Korniyenko concluded his visit, urging Syria to stand firm and not to retreat or compromise.

Syrian control of Lebanon was consistent with the Soviet grand design for the Middle East. The Kremlin was seeking to extend its influence in the region for several reasons, among them to secure ready access to the Persian Gulf oilfields, to obtain a possible route to the Indian Ocean, and as a means of weakening NATO's southern flank. For the Kremlin, Syria had become a power base in the area. Moscow saw Syrian control of Lebanon as an enhancement of that base, which could be a springboard for Soviet subversion in the region, as well as a possible thrust toward the oil-rich regions. The Soviets also encouraged Syria to consider their operations in Lebanon as useful ground, naval, and air training for the Syrian forces.

President Assad, who had been plagued by increased internal turmoil created by the Muslim Brotherhood, was pleased to accept the Soviet advice. If his stand on the missiles should precipitate another round of fighting with Israel, he might lose on the battlefield, but he stood to gain much politically. An Israeli attack would give him a good reason to control the Brotherhood's activities, by uniting all Syrians against the common Israeli enemy. It would affirm Assad's claim to be the leader of the Arab world in the struggle against Zionism, and would mean the end of the accepted status quo in Lebanon which had limited his freedom of action in that country. It would also place Egypt, which had recently signed a peace treaty with Israel, in an awkward position. Would Cairo abide by the treaty and remain neutral, or would popular and pan-Arab pressure force Egypt to join a fraternal Arab country in its fight against Israeli aggression?

Another factor important to President Assad was that for some time the Syrians had treated the eastern part of the Bekaa Valley as Syrian territory. Syrian money was legal tender in the region. Syrian traffic signs had replaced the old Lebanese signs. In the towns and villages, Assad's photographs were displayed much as they were in Syria, with no photographs of Lebanese leaders. The Bekaa Valley offered a possible avenue of advance by Israeli forces to threaten Damascus, and the Syrians were very sensitive to this threat. Thus, Assad welcomed the fact that the Israelis had given him an excuse for moving the missiles into the Valley, hence strengthening Syrian defenses along the route of a potential Israeli advance.

For years it had been Israel's policy to preserve its freedom of operation in the skies over Lebanon. However, military action against the Syrian missiles in the Bekaa Valley could not be taken lightly. Since 1976, Israel had tacitly accepted the Syrian military presence in Lebanon north of the Red Line, while Syria had reconciled itself to Israel's pre-eminent role in the south. Each side scrupulously avoided military encounters, other than occasional dogfights in the sky near the Lebanese-Syrian border. The Syrians did not take military action in response to Israeli retaliation strikes against the Palestinian guerrillas, and—prior to the Zahle incident—Israel had not directly intervened in Syrian operations against Christian areas in the north. However, it was plain to both sides that neither could tolerate the total destruction of its allies—for Syria, the Palestinians; and for Israel, the Christians.

The consequence of a strike against the missiles could be serious for Israel. Not only would the military benefits be dubious, but the potential price could be high. Furthermore, it would provide Assad with an excuse for strengthening his control in Lebanon. The Israeli government also had to consider internal public opinion. The people generally agreed with the leadership that the Syrian missiles must be removed from Lebanon, but were against action that would drag the country into another costly war. Therefore, the Israeli press called for patience and negotiations.

Habib Defuses the Crisis

These considerations were very much in the minds of Israel's decision-makers when they decided to curb the rhetoric of their most militant leaders and continue diplomatic efforts to solve the crisis. The US special envoy, Philip Habib, who had been shuttling between Jerusalem, Damascus, Beirut, and Riyadh, was given more time to negotiate a settlement. In fact, Habib's presence in the region made it all but impossible for Israel to execute military action against the Syrian missiles. Use of force under these circumstances would have severely strained American-Israeli relations.

On the other side, the Israeli military establishment could not agree to limit the freedom to maneuver that Israel had enjoyed in Lebanon since 1976 in dealing with the Palestinian guerrillas, in conducting aerial reconnaissance missions over the Lebanese heartland, and in advancing Israeli-Christian cooperation in southern and northern Lebanon. Particularly frustrating to them was the fact that with each passing day the Syrians were probably improving the capability of their SAMs to withstand an attack.

In strictly tactical terms, the deployment of SA-6 missiles did not affect Israel's ability to attack guerrilla bases in southern Lebanon, or to fly over the coastal area. Improved SA-2 missiles, which had already been deployed on the Syrian side of the border, covered as much of Lebanon as the newly deployed SA-6s in the Bekaa Valley. Nevertheless, the Israelis were afraid that once the principle of no Syrian missiles in Lebanon was violated, and the violation accepted by Israel, the Syrians would advance their missiles deeper into Lebanon, and directly threaten Israel's ability to fly over any part of that country.

The Nuclear Threat From Iraq

While the attention of most of the world was focused on Ambassador Habib's efforts to defuse the threatened war in Lebanon, in fact the attention of Israel's leadership was really focused on what it considered to be an even more serious threat to the security of the state.

Since 1975 the Israelis had been closely observing an apparent effort by Iraq to acquire a nuclear weapons capability. In that year Iraq made an agreement with France for the construction of a nuclear reactor at Osirak, about 18 kilometers southeast of Baghdad. France had also agreed to help Iraq establish a nuclear research and training center. In an effort to diversify their sources of nuclear material, the Iraqis followed up the agreement with Paris with yet another with Rome, whereby Italy would sell Iraq four research facilities to be used for reprocessing irradiated fuel elements and extracting plutonium. France and Italy justified sales of sensitive nuclear material and equipment to Iraq by citing Baghdad's signature of the Nuclear Non-proliferation Treaty prohibiting the manufacture of nuclear arms. Israel and other critics of the agreements considered this a fragile assurance in light of Iraq's belligerence and internal instability. These critics—including internationally known scientists, political analysts, and diplomats acquainted with the area—argued that Iraq's nuclear reactor was meant not for peaceful use, but for the production of nuclear weapons to be deployed against Israel, Iran, and other countries inimical to the Baghdad regime. It was even suggested that once Iraq had acquired a nuclear capability, Baghdad might use its new weapons to blackmail friendly Arab countries to submit to its will. Experts agreed that by 1985 the amount of high-grade uranium supplied by France and other countries would enable Iraq to produce three to six 20-kiloton Hiroshima-type atom bombs, each capable of wiping out as many as 150,000 to 200,000 people.

On the other hand, the International Atomic Energy Commission (IAEC) was monitoring the project and insisted that its inspection had shown that the Osirak reactor would not have any military capability. When, however, Iraq kept IAEC inspectors from visiting the reactor site for six months in 1980-81, the IAEC began to review the situation again. As a result of this review it accepted the probability that the Iraqi installation could manufacture atom bombs.

The development of the Iraqi reactor was troubled from the start by a number of violent incidents. On April 5, 1979, saboteurs—assumed, but never proven to be, Israeli agents—destroyed the core of the 70 megawatt reactor lying in storage at Seyne-Sur-Mer near Toulon, awaiting shipment to Baghdad. Next, in June 1980, a key man in the Iraqi nuclear program, an Egyptian-born scientist, was killed in a Paris hotel, probably by Iranian assassins. Three months later in Rome, a bomb destroyed the offices of the Italian SNIA Techint Company, which was supplying nuclear technology and equipment to Iraq. That same day an abortive bomb attempt was made on the life of Jean Jacques Graf, a French scientist involved with the Iraqi nuclear program. Responsibility for the last two attacks was claimed by the "Committee for Safeguarding the Islamic Revolution," an Iranian terrorist organization.

Israeli concern about the developing Iraqi nuclear capabilities increased when it became known that, in addition to constructing the French reactor, the Iraqis were investing huge sums in procuring missile technology and were negotiating with the Soviet Union as well as with western countries for the manufacture of a surface-to-surface missile system with a 3,000 kilometer range. This could only be intended to deliver a nuclear warhead.

By February or March 1981, on the basis of both western and Israeli intelligence reports, it became obvious to the Israeli authorities that by September Iraq could have its 70 megawatt reactor in operation. Thus Israel would soon have to give serious attention to an Iraqi nuclear weapon capability. This prodded the Israeli Government to make a final decision on a matter long under consideration.

The Israeli Plan to Attack Osirak

The idea of attacking and destroying the Iraqi reactor had been under study by the Israeli Armed Forces for many months. Israeli pilots had been training for the operation on a large model of the reactor site built in the Negev desert. Different types of planes were tried out in rehearsal raids, in order to select the one most suitable for the strike. Meanwhile, intelligence agencies continued to gather information necessary for the success of the attack. The raid could have been carried out in late 1980, but it was postponed indefinitely after the Iranians bombed the reactor on September 30, 1980. Following this, the 180 to 200 French and Italian specialists assigned to the project left the country. However, they returned in February 1981, and Israeli intelligence learned that after they resumed their work rapid progress had been made. Thus, despite the interruption, it now seemed that the project would still be completed as originally planned, toward the end of September.

The Israelis considered destruction of the reactor vital to Israel's security, and an act of self defense. They knew, however, that the raid would cause a very negative international reaction and might harm Israel's relationships with many friendly countries. They expected an American condemnation coupled with increased military assistance to Saudi Arabia. They also anticipated strained relations with France and Italy, whose scientists were deeply involved in the project.

Taking all of the pros and cons into consideration the Israeli cabinet decided that, in the long run, nothing could be more important to Israeli survival than inflicting a major setback to the Iraqi nuclear aspirations. Jerusalem wanted to postpone the strike as long as possible in case some kind of satisfactory solution could be found by peaceful means. However, to strike as late as September, when the reactor would be already loaded and operational, would greatly increase the danger of radiation casualties among the civilian population of Baghdad and would arouse greater international outrage against Israel.

Another factor which the Israeli government had to consider was the possible impact of the planned attack on the next Israeli national election, scheduled for June 30. It would leave Prime Minister Begin and his ruling coalition open to the charge that the raid was undertaken to gain an electoral advantage. But responsible politicians in the cabinet realized that the raid did not necessarily imply electoral gains. While votes might be gained by a successful bombing, they would be more than offset in the event of failure, major loss of life, or serious international repercussions.

Security considerations prevailed, and the raid was scheduled for May 10. However, this was soon changed when it was realized that the French presidential elections were to be held on the same day. This postponement gave Israel a chance to try to persuade the newly elected president, Francois Mitterand, and other suppliers to stop the flow of uranium to Iraq.

When Mitterand's new socialist government reaffirmed French commitment to the Iraqi agreements, Prime Minister Begin and his cabinet decided to act. They believed that the chances of Arab unity and a common front in the event of an Israeli attack on Iraq were slim. Jordan and Egypt had already declared that they would not join Syria in case of war with Israel, and there was little reason to assume that they would change this attitude if Iraq were attacked.

As for the possible Iraqi reaction, the Israelis were not greatly concerned. Iraq had already been weakened by its war with Iran. Considering the poor performance of his armed forces in that war, Iraqi President Saddam Hussein could do nothing to respond to a slap from Israel. Iraq had no common boundary with Israel. It might consider using its SCUD missiles, but their range was limited, and to hit Israeli targets they would have to be deployed closer to Israeli territory, in either Jordan or Syria. In the very doubtful event that Jordan would agree, the deployment would take time. It would be readily detected by Israeli intelligence, and pre-emption would be quick and easy. Even less likely was the possibility of moving Iraqi SCUDs to Syria. For years, relations between those two countries had been strained, and in Iraq's war with Iran, Damascus had sided with and supported Iran.

Nevertheless, practical and technical problems facing the Israeli Air Force in carrying out the raid on the nuclear reactor were complex and difficult. To achieve surprise, Israeli aircraft had to baffle Jordanian, Saudi Arabian, and Iraqi radar and air defenses along the route. They would also have to circumvent American-operated AWACS, the world's most sophisticated airborne early-warning system, which was deployed in Saudi Arabia. Israeli planes would then have to deal with Iraqi ground-to-air missiles on the site, and be ready for the possibility that the Iraqi Air Force might scramble in counterattack. All this had to be done at a time of high Iraqi vigilance, since Iraq was at war with Iran, and the Saudis and other Gulf countries were also on alert because of the danger of Iranian air strikes. Furthermore, after accomplishing the mission, the return of the planes had to be protected. By this time, of course, their presence would be known, and they would have to fly some 1,000 kilometers over hostile Arab territory before reaching Israel.

The Osirak Raid

Fourteen aircraft participated in the raid on Osirak. Six F-15s served as fighter escorts. There were eight F-16s. Of these, four were to carry out the actual bombing; the remaining four were flying in reserve, ready for action if needed. The operation took place on Sunday, under the assumption that the foreign experts working at the installation would not be there on a Christian holiday. In fact, of some 150 French, Italian and other western experts working on the project, only one was killed.

The strike force took off from an Israeli base late in the afternoon of June 7. All had clearly visible Israeli markings. They flew at high altitude over Jordan, using Jordanian radio signals and formations so as to be taken for a Jordanian training flight. Then they cut across the northern tip of Saudi Arabia, where they identified themselves as Jordanians. The air defense systems of Arab countries are not integrated and there was no exchange between Jordanian and Saudi Arabian air defense systems about the flights. The Israeli planes were also undetected by US AWACS planes based in Saudi Arabia; they were patrolling along the eastern Saudi frontier, more than 1,500 kilometers from the route of the Israeli planes, and had their surveillance equipment directed toward the Persian Gulf and Iran.

On entering Iraqi air space, the Israeli planes dropped close to the ground to avoid Iraqi radar. Only as they approached Osirak did they start climbing. At exactly 6:30 P.M. Baghdad time four F-16s appeared over the target and dropped eight 2,000-pound bombs with great precision. They destroyed the main reactor and reportedly damaged a smaller one. Surprise was total. The Israelis were neither engaged by Iraqi fighter planes, nor taken under fire from surface-to-air missiles. At first the Iraqi leaders did not know exactly who had attacked them, and they waited more than 24 hours before confirming the attack. Initially they assumed that the attackers were Iranians. In fact, had the Israelis not officially announced, a day later, that it was they who struck at Osirak, Israeli involvement might not have been suspected, with the Iranians being blamed—or credited, depending on the point of view—for the attack.

Aftermath of the Raid

The raid was almost unanimously condemned throughout the world. The Arab League denounced Israel and called the attack a dangerous precedent that threatened world peace and security. But it did not ask its member states to undertake military reprisal, nor did it suggest an oil embargo against Israel and its allies, as it had after the 1973 October War. In Cairo, President Anwar Sadat—who just three days before the raid had met in Ophira with Prime Minister Menachem Begin—felt greatly embarrassed and vehemently condemned the Israeli action as unlawful and provocative. His Foreign Minister, Kamel Hassan Ali, called the bombing irresponsible, shameful, and illegal.

In Washington, the administration denied any advance knowledge of the raid, disassociated itself from it, denounced it, and suspended the delivery of four F-16 aircraft scheduled to be transferred to Israel in the next few days. The French government, which perceived the raid as a violation of international law, decided nevertheless not to change France's basic attitude toward Israel. British Prime Minister Margaret Thatcher, speaking in the House of Commons, totally and utterly condemned the raid and branded it a grave breach of international law. The Indians, who had developed their own nuclear capacity, and were concerned with Pakistani countermeasures, called the attack an unprovoked act of aggression that made a mockery of accepted norms of international conduct and behavior.

The Soviet Union and other Communist countries uniformly denounced the raid as the acme of international terrorism. The Soviet press agency Tass called it an act of gangsterism and a link in the long chain of Tel Aviv's crimes which the US tolerated and supported.

On June 19, after several days of heated discussions, the UN Security Council unanimously passed Resolution 487, strongly condemning Israel for its June 7 air attack on the Osirak nuclear reactor, and called upon Israel to refrain from such attacks or threats in the future. Israel was urged to submit its own nuclear facilities to international inspection. The resolution stated that Iraq was entitled to appropriate redress for the damage it had suffered, and which had been acknowledged by Israel. The United States joined the other 14 members of the council in condemnation of the act, which it called shocking and undermining the stability of the area.

The Israeli government unqualifiedly rejected the UN resolution, calling it immoral and a striking example of the double standards of morality that prevailed at the United Nations. In Jerusalem's view, Iraq's dictatorship had built a reactor in order, in cunning secrecy, to construct atomic bombs to be dropped on Israeli cities. Thus, claimed Israel, the condemnation should be directed at the producer of the deadly atomic weapon, and not its potential victim. Iraq had the means to deliver an atomic bomb. It could use Soviet-made Tu-22 bombers and Su-20 and MiG-23 fighter bombers. An Iraqi atomic bomb on Tel Aviv could have caused about 100,000 casualties.

Whereas officially most governments reacted in a fashion highly critical of the Israeli raid, many leading politicians and diplomats, and numerous articles in the press were moderate and defended the Israeli action as an act of legitimate self defense. Even some Arab leaders, especially from Israel's neighboring states, while officially expressing their outrage, in private conversations with the authors—who at the time of the attack were travelling in the Middle East—indicated relief that, at least for some time, Iraq would not have a nuclear potential with which it could effectively blackmail them and force them to submit to Baghdad's hegemony.

Those few people who publicly defended the Israeli raid argued that—in light of the given circumstances, and under recognized principles of international law—Israel had a legal right to bomb Iraq's nuclear installation. Given the generally accepted concepts of what action constitutes self defense between belligerents, these defenders asserted that this was an act of legitimate self defense. Unfortunately, law plays little part in attitudes toward the Arab-Israeli conflict. It is invoked by enemies and friends alike when it suits them, and is ignored otherwise.

Iraq and Israel were certainly belligerents. Iraq considered itself to be in a state of war with Israel, and despite relevant resolutions of the United Nations had refused to renounce belligerency against Israel. It had never agreed even to negotiate a ceasefire or armistice, as all of Israel's other Arab enemies had done in 1949. During the 1948, 1967, and 1973 Arab-Israeli wars, Iraq had sent troops and planes to fight the Israelis. However, when Israeli aircraft attacked an Iraqi objective regarded by the Israelis as endangering their country, the Iraqis, with most of the rest of the world, condemned it, considering it unlawful, and an act of aggression. Whatever one may think of the rights and wrongs of the Arab-Israeli struggle, and of Israel's attitude toward Resolution 242 and toward the provisions for West Bank autonomy under the Camp David accords, the bombing of the Iraqi reactor was not illegal under international law.

The destruction of the Iraqi nuclear plant was an eloquent act in a complacent world that watched silently when the Egyptians used chemical weapons in Yemen, India exploded a nuclear device, and Iraq invaded Iran. With hindsight, taking into account Iraq's use of chemical weapons in its war with Iran, in direct violation of the Geneva Protocol prohibiting "use in war of asphyxiating, poisonous, and other gases," which Iraq ratified in 1931, one can easily perceive that Baghdad would probably not have hesitated to use nuclear weapons against Iran, given Iraq's desperate situation in that dragging war. Nor would Iraq be likely to hesitate to use the weapons against Israel.

Legal experts have noted that in attacking the reactor Israel did not even have to plead self defense. The raid was simply an act of war in the course of a continuing state of war, and not qualified by any agreement to suspend hostilities. Toward the end of World War II Americans twice blew up heavy water installations where the Germans worked on the atomic bomb, thus delaying or preventing production of that bomb. Just as Germany was in a state of war with the United States, and open to any military action on its facilities, Iraq has been in a state of war with Israel since 1948.

Obviously, the bombing of the reactor was an extreme step. However, under the circumstances a responsible government in Israel did not have many alternatives. The government might have tried to use more diplomatic efforts to discourage France and other countries from cooperating with Baghdad in nuclear matters, but the chances of success had already been shown to be slim.

Jerusalem might also have opted for a policy of mutual nuclear deterrence and a balance of terror, and learned to live with an Iraqi nuclear bomb in its backyard. But would this have worked in Israel, a small country with fewer than 4,000,000 people concentrated mostly on the coastal plains between Tel Aviv and Haifa? Nuclear deterrence implies logical decision making, national responsibility, and respect for human life. In a dictatorship such as Saddam Hussein's, already involved in an illogical, costly and nearly suicidal war with Iran, one may question the importance of considerations of this kind. Deterrence means the ability to launch a second strike against the attacker which will be so devastating as to make his use of nuclear weapons inconceivable. But when surviving even a first strike is impossible, deterrence becomes meaningless.

At present, in 1985, there is the possibility that Iraq may now have enough of the highly enriched uranium fuel originally supplied by France for Osirak to manufacture a nuclear weapon. Another danger has been introduced by the Soviet commitment to provide Iraq with a nuclear plant similar to those also promised to Syria and Libya. Presumably the Soviet installation will not provide direct access to material for nuclear weapons. However, Iraq might eventually be able to extract it from the reactor's spent fuel, using a "hot cell" previously supplied by Italy, a heavily shielded facility in which radioactive material can be safely handled.

The Osirak raid may only have been the first act of a longer and more deadly drama.

Immediate Implications of the Raid

The Israeli raid probably assured postponement of the war that had seemed so threatening in Lebanon with the introduction of surface-to-air missiles into the Bekaa Valley. The Israeli military, basking in the glow of a splendidly executed attack, had reason for confidence that at any time, if necessary, they could deal with the Syrian missiles which had been installed earlier, and were reluctant to make any hasty move that could lead to a full-scale war. The Syrians, on the other hand, watching the timid reaction of the Arab world to the Baghdad raid, came to realize that in case of war they would undoubtedly be left alone to face the formidable Israeli enemy. The search for a peaceful *modus operandi* thus continued with renewed vigor on both sides.

The Assassination of President Sadat

A dramatic and tragic event in Cairo, five months later, was also to contribute to the increase in tension throughout the Middle East, and to add fuel to embers soon to burst into flame.

On October 6, 1981, the armed forces of Egypt conducted their eighth annual parade celebrating the success of the Egyptian surprise crossing of the Suez Canal which initiated the October War of 1973. The parade began at about 12:30 P.M., with President Sadat, resplendent in his field marshal's uniform, in the place of honor in the first row of the reviewing stand, which was crowded with other Egyptian dignitaries, as well as the foreign diplomatic corps.

Shortly before 1:00 P.M., as troops in trucks were rolling past the reviewing stand, there came an impressive fly-over by Mirage jets of the Egyptian Air Force, swooping low over the parade column, and dipping their wings in salute to the President. While all eyes in the stands were watching the aerial display, a truck on the inside lane of the truck procession suddenly halted, and from it jumped four uniformed soldiers, each armed with the regular issue submachine gun, the AK-47. They immediately started to run across the 30 meter space between the parade column and the reviewing stand, at first unnoticed, since even the security guards had their eyes glued on the Mirages overhead.

Then the running men opened fire with their weapons at the front row of the reviewing stand where President Sadat was flanked by the Vice President, Hosni Mubarak, and the Defense Minister, Field Marshal Mohammed Abou Ghazala. Chaos broke out in the stand, as everyone dove for cover.

The four attackers continued to rush forward, firing their weapons.

As they reached the wall of the grandstand, they raised their weapons over their heads. They continued to fire, now over the wall and down at the mass of people and chairs on the floor of the stand, aiming particularly at the President. Bullets ricocheted through the stand, and many people were hit. But this continued for only a few seconds because, finally, the stunned and ineffective security guards had moved into action, overpowering the assassins, killing two of them in the process.

Sadat, mortally wounded, was rushed in a helicopter to a military hospital at the outskirts of Cairo, where he died from multiple wounds before 4:00 P.M. without ever regaining consciousness. (He may even have been dead upon arrival at the hospital.) Eight other persons on the reviewing stand also were killed, and dozens were wounded. Among these, neither seriously hurt, were Vice President Mubarak and Defense Minister Abou Ghazala.

The assassins were fanatics belonging to an outlawed Muslim fundamentalist group, *Takfir wa-Hijrah*, an even more violent offshoot of the extreme Muslim Brotherhood. The name can be translated as "Departure from heresy" (*takfir* means "infidel" or "heretic", *hijrah*—or *hegira*—refers particularly to Mohammed's flight from Mecca in 622). By this title the group proclaimed its disassociation from modern Egyptian society which it considered heretical, and which was represented for them by President Sadat, hated by the members as the arch-heretic. In general, the members of this group rejected all modernization as leading to impious deviations from traditional Muslim values, and condemned the institutionalized official version of Islam in Egypt as being hopelessly infected with modernism.

The ringleader of the assassins was Army Lieutenant Khaled Ahmed el-Istambouly. On the day of the parade Istambouly granted leave to three regular members of his unit and replaced them with members of his organization disguised as military reservists. Although these four alone carried out the attack, they were part of a larger conspiracy to kill Sadat. Nearly 20 people had been involved. All of these were arrested during the following weeks.

While in the West and in Israel Sadat's death was sincerely mourned, in most of the Arab world the assassination was met with joy and approval. In these lands, and in the world at large, the tragic event was misinterpreted. Almost everyone assumed that Sadat had paid with his life for his policy of peace with Israel. In fact, this was only a marginal consideration in the minds of the conspirators, for their primary motives were Sadat's opposition to fundamentalist Muslim fanaticism, and his efforts to modernize Egypt. Nevertheless, the false perception colored most reactions to the assassination.

Many Arabs, both radical and so-called "moderate", rejoiced when they learned of the crime, and they praised the assassins for having rid the

Arab world of the man who had collaborated with US imperialism and with Zionism.* Then they went on to warn that any other Arab leader who continued to follow Camp David policy would meet the same fate.

* The authors were in Amman, the capital of "moderate" Jordan, when this event occurred. We were shocked by the public display of elation, and by an official announcement from the Minister of Information praising the assassins. Privately, however, many thoughtful Jordanians told us of their shock, sorrow, and concern about what had happened.

PART TWO
The Fifth Arab-Israeli War, June 1982

Chapter X
A Ceasefire
Sets the Stage
For War

Hostilities Become Inevitable

Hardly had the ceasefire agreements of July 24 and July 29, 1981, gone into effect between Israel and the PLO along the Israel-Lebanon border when two new—and eventually critical—controversies emerged. In the first place, there was the question of Israel's right to carry out reconnaissance flights over Lebanese territory. As far as the Israelis were concerned, this was not an issue. They maintained that the flights were necessary to protect Israel's security, and as such had been recognized in the agreement. The PLO and Syria disagreed and called such flights a violation of the agreement.

The other controversy was over the PLO claim that the ceasefire covered only border hostilities, and that terrorist operations inside Israel and against Israeli targets in third countries were a separate issue, and should be recognized as legitimate resistance to Israeli occupation of Palestine. Not surprisingly, the Israeli government interpreted the cessation of hostilities as universal, and regarded any PLO terrorist attack, anywhere, against Israeli targets as a breach of the understanding that would justify retaliation.

It quickly became obvious, therefore, that the ceasefire had little chance to remain effective. For the PLO to refrain from any attacks on Israel by shelling, by raids, or by terrorist operations, would mean abandonment of its *raison d'etre*. And Israel would certainly not remain inactive in the face of attacks on its citizens at home and abroad. Furthermore, with its towns and villages still vulnerable to shelling from the PLO sanctuary in southern Lebanon, Israel was eager to seize any opportunity to destroy the PLO and remove the cause of constant tension on its borders. Both sides

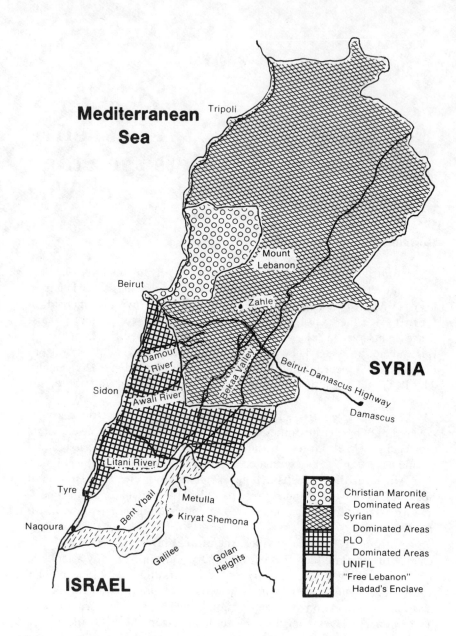

Mediterranean Sea

Tripoli

Mount Lebanon

Beirut

Zahle

Damour River

Bekaa Valley

Beirut-Damascus Highway

SYRIA

Sidon

Awali River

Damascus

Litani River

Tyre

Bent Ybail

Metulla

Kiryat Shemona

Naqoura

Galilee

Golan Heights

ISRAEL

Christian Maronite
   Dominated Areas
Syrian
   Dominated Areas
PLO
   Dominated Areas
UNIFIL
"Free Lebanon"
   Hadad's Enclave

The Division of Lebanon on the Eve of War

therefore expected a major confrontation to break out again; the only question was when. Israel increased its forces just south of the border, and conducted several large-scale maneuvers in the frontier area. The PLO reacted by bringing additional armor, long-range artillery, and multiple rocket launchers into southern Lebanon. Military training was also intensified and the PLO command structure was overhauled. The result, as the Israelis grimly noted, was that new PLO weapons and fresh forces with growing military capability were deployed within striking range of the upper Galilee panhandle.

Meanwhile, in the Bekaa Valley, the missile crisis had receded somewhat and there was no longer immediate danger of military action to resolve it. Nevertheless, continued restraint on the part of Syria and Israel remained essential if the danger of escalation were to be avoided, and any possibility for a peaceful solution were to be achieved.

Between August 1981 and June 1982 Israeli had four times massed forces near the Lebanese border in preparation for an attack, but each time called off the planned invasion as a result of internal and external pressures. However, it was clear that the Israelis needed only a provocation to launch a mortal blow against the PLO. This time the Israeli General Staff was not thinking of another Litani campaign, which had left the PLO almost intact. Instead, the concept was the annihilation of PLO military capability. The plan was to destroy the strongholds and infrastructure of some 6,000 Palestinian guerrillas deployed in South Lebanon. This would put all Israeli settlements in Galilee out of reach of PLO artillery and terminate the threat to the lives of their inhabitants.

The Israeli planners recognized, however, that it might not be possible to avoid hostilities with the Syrians while fighting the Palestinians. It is not clear whether the IDF really hoped to keep Syria out of the war, or whether plans merely provided for avoiding engagement with the Syrians until the PLO was defeated. Certainly plans were ready for hostilities with Syria, and seem to have envisaged the possibility of pushing the Syrians out of Lebanon. The operation against the PLO was planned as a rapid advance in depth, bypassing pockets of resistance (which were to be dealt with later), and cutting off the main combat elements of the PLO in southern Lebanon from their reserves and bases located in the Beirut and Damour areas. The action against the PLO was to be completed in 72 hours.

The PLO leadership apparently did not realize the seriousness of the Israeli intentions. PLO actions and various statements in early 1982 suggest that they did not anticipate an all-out Israeli drive, but assumed that the Israelis would again undertake a limited operation like that of 1978. The Palestinian leadership even looked forward with relish and defiance to an Israeli invasion. Although an Israeli attack could cause them some losses, they believed that it would result in a tremendous political victory for the

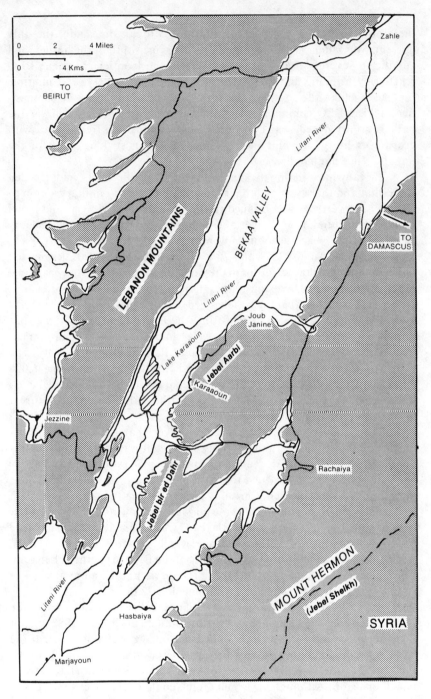

The Bekaa Valley

PLO. That is why they insisted that the ceasefire negotiated by Ambassador Habib was applicable only to military operations across the Israeli-Lebanese border. They continued acts of terror against Israeli civilian targets inside Israel, on the West Bank, and in foreign countries, realizing that in this way they were goading Israel, knowing well that Israeli patience would end sooner or later.

That, in fact, is what happened. The waiting period came to an end after a series of terrorist attacks, inside Israel and all around the world, culminated on June 3, 1982, in the shooting of Mr. Shlomo Argov, Israel's Ambassador in London. Three days later a massive Israeli thrust into Lebanon commenced, given the code name, "Peace for Galilee".

The Setting

In making their plans for the operation in Lebanon the Israelis had to give serious consideration to the terrain. Lebanon's geography makes offensive operations very difficult. This was as true in 1982 A.D. as it had been when Alexander the Great fought the Persians and the Phoenicians in the 4th century B.C. The rugged mountains of the Lebanon and Anti-Lebanon ranges provide excellent defensive positions. Even with limited forces, a defender can offer strong resistance and inflict heavy casualties on an attacker. In the coastal strip many towns and villages with narrow streets and stone houses slow down advancing forces and make urban combat precarious. Numerous orange, apple, and banana groves restrict movement and offer excellent staging areas for hit and run attacks.

Geographically Lebanon is divided into four narrow, parallel north-south zones. From west to east these zones are: the coastal plain; the Lebanon Mountain chain; the Bekaa Valley; and the Anti-Lebanon Ridge, the crest of which is the border between Lebanon and Syria.

The coastal plain lies between the Lebanon Mountains to the east and the Mediterranean Sea in the west. It is an intensively cultivated narrow strip of land from one to seven kilometers wide. The plain is the most heavily populated area in Lebanon and includes the major cities of Tyre, Sidon, Beirut, and Tripoli, as well as many Palestinian refugee camps. The coast has numerous natural bays and harbors.

A number of rivers and streams flow westward from the Lebanon Mountains to the Mediterranean Sea, creating natural obstacles for north-south troop movements. The major rivers in the area are, from the south: Litani, Zahrani, Awali, Damour and Beirut.

The road network is poor. The main communications axis is the Coastal Road, running parallel to the coast from the Israeli border to Beirut. From it a number of roads lead eastward into the mountains.

The Lebanon Mountain chain (or Mount Lebanon) lies between the El Ostouane River in the north, the Litani River in the south, the coastal plain in the west, and the Bekaa Valley to the east. It is very difficult mountainous terrain, with peaks as high as 3,000 meters, very steep eastern slopes, and more moderate western slopes descending in some places to the sea.

Roads in the mountains are narrow and winding, most of them running from east to west; they would be difficult to drive on, even if adequately maintained, which they were not. There is only one main south-north road from Jarjoua, through Jbaa, Jezzine, Kfar al Shouf, and Dir el Kamar to Ain Zhalta, and it then links with the Beirut-Damascus highway. It is extremely difficult for tanks to operate off roads in these rugged mountains.

There are numerous villages in the region, inhabited primarily by Christians and Druze. Many springs—especially along the midwestern slopes of the mountains—support intensive cultivation of land.

The area can be easily sealed off by relatively small forces. The very abrupt eastern slopes create a solid barrier between the coastal plain and the Bekaa Valley, severely complicating coordination of military operations west and east of the mountains.

The Bekaa Valley, a northward continuation of the Huleh and Jordan River valleys, lies between the Lebanon and Anti-Lebanon mountains. Its length from south to north is about 120 kilometers, and it varies in width from 5 to 20 kilometers. Although the Bekaa is one of the few areas in Lebanon where armor can be used readily, nevertheless armored maneuver is hindered by numerous irrigation canals and cultivated fields, some of which can be quickly flooded. The Bekaa is dominated by the high mountains to the west and east. Fire can easily be brought to bear from these heights on forces operating in the valley. Approaches to the southern Bekaa from Israel are controlled from Beaufort Castle, surmounting the Beaufort Hills, which rise very steeply from the Litani River to a height of about 750 meters. These heights provide excellent observation of the entire area; the view from the castle on a clear day is breathtaking.

A small north-south range with two ridges, Jabal bir ed Dahr and Jabal Aarbi, blocks the southern part of the valley, like a cork in a bottle, and creates a transverse link between the Lebanon and Anti-Lebanon mountains. Any movement from the south into the Bekaa must negotiate the flanks of all of these mountain ranges.

There are three major longitudinal, north-south communication axes through the valley: the western road (Delfi Bridge, Mashghara, Kabb Elias); the central road (Kaoukaba, Yohmor, Karaoun, Joub Jannine, Bar Elias); and the eastern road (Hasbaiya, Kfar Meshki, Majdel Aanjar).

The Anti-Lebanon mountain range terminates in the south at towering Mt. Hermon, known to the Arabs as Jabal Sheikh. These steep, rugged mountains, which reach altitudes of over 2,800 meters, form a natural barrier between Lebanon and Syria, and severely constrain military operations; the only passages between the heights are narrow gorges. There is little vegetation, and the area is thinly populated. Winding through Fatahland along the western slopes of Mt Hermon are two roads; one runs from Hasbaiya to Rashaiya further east, and higher up on the slopes; the "Arafat Trail" runs from el Mari to Aaiha, thence to the northeast to the Syrian frontier.

On the whole, the geographical peculiarities of the country seriously complicate combat activities, and require meticulous planning and preparations for any kind of offensive operations. The narrowness of the country and its mountainous character make for most abrupt changes in climate. One can go from subtropical to Alpine environment in a distance of 15-20 kilometers. A force advancing along the coast or across the Bekaa can effectively outflank defenders only by resorting to mountain warfare. The coastal plain and the Bekaa Valley can both be easily blocked and covered by enfilade fire from positions along the mountain heights and slopes. Cities such as Tyre, Sidon, Damour, Beirut, Jounie, and Tripoli—and the smaller towns and villages which lie between the sea and the foothills—can be avoided only by traversing difficult mountain roads and trails. The cities, therefore, are also formidable obstacles.

Probably no geographical area in the world has been so long and so often traversed by military forces as has the eastern littoral of the Mediterranean Sea. More than 3000 years after this land had been fought over by the Hyksos kings of Asia Minor and the pharaohs of Egypt. It was once more about to become a battleground.

Chapter XI
Opposing Deployments, Forces, and Plans

PLO Strength and Deployment

At the beginning of June 1982, the PLO had about 15,000 regular fighters organized in battalions ready for battle in Lebanon. These were backed up by an additional 18,000 militiamen recruited from among Palestinian refugees. All of these forces were under the command of the PLO's Supreme Military Council, with headquarters in Beirut.

The PLO forces had vast quantities of weapons, armor, and ammunition, supplied primarily by the Soviet Union and other communist countries, paid for mainly by oil-rich Arab states, and shipped either directly to the PLO, or through Arab countries such as Syria, Iraq, Libya, Algeria, and South Yemen. The list of military hardware included approximately 300 tanks (T-34, T-54, T-55); 150 APCs (BTR-152 and BTR-60); 200 to 300 large antitank weapons (including high velocity recoilless guns and "Sagger" antitank missiles); over 350 artillery pieces, including multiple rocket launchers and a number of long-range 130mm guns; over 200 antiaircraft guns; great quantities of heavy and light machine guns, grenades, pistols, and rifles; and individual antitank rockets and the portable SA-7 air defense missiles.

Given the PLO's justification for existence—dedication to the expulsion of the Jewish population from Palestine (Israel) and the establishment of an independent Arab-Palestinian state—it had long been inevitable that the Palestinian armed presence in Lebanon would lead to a full-scale conflict with Israel. Nevertheless, despite intensive efforts, the PLO had never developed the military competence or strength to constitute a serious threat to the existence of the state of Israel. Hitherto, the PLO had been able—especially since the early 1970s—to use guerrilla and terrorist tactics to pose a mortal peril to individual Israelis in Israel and abroad, and particularly (though sporadically) to the civilian population in northern Galilee. However, by 1982, thanks to its growing arsenal of Soviet-supplied weapons, the PLO was developing a significant military capability.

The PLO forces in Lebanon came from eight main Palestinian political groups:

1. The Fatah had four infantry brigades, one tank group, and one artillery group—altogether over 6,500 men under the direct command of PLO Chairman Yasser Arafat;

2. SAIQA had about 2,000 men in three infantry battalions and smaller units;

3. The Popular Front for the Liberation of Palestine, under George Habash, had nearly 1,000 men in four battalions;

4. The Popular Front for the Liberation of Palestine—General Command, under Ahmed Jabril, had about 900 men;

5. Democratic Front for the Liberation of Palestine, under Nayef Hawatmeh, was organized in about 10 company-sized units with a total strength of about 1,000 men;

6. The Palestine Liberation Front, a small splinter group not represented on the PLO Executive Committee, had some 600 men;

7. The Popular Struggle Front, another small splinter group not represented on the PLO Executive Committee, had about 300 men;

8. That part of the Arab Liberation Front affiliated with the Iraqi Army had about 800 men; and another faction of the Arab Liberation Front, under the command of the Fatah, consisted of two infantry battalions and one tank group—about 1,500 men altogether.

There were also one brigade and smaller units of the Palestine Liberation Army, a trained military force under Syrian control, which the Damascus government had for the first time released to the PLO command.

All across southern Lebanon, just north of the UNIFIL area, stretching from the coastal plains to the slopes of Mt. Hermon, the PLO deployed the Castel Brigade, some 6,000 men commanded by Brigadier Haj Ismail. This area included the cities of Tyre, Sidon, Nabatiye, and Jbaa. The brigade concentrated approximately 2,000 men (belonging mostly to the Fatah) in the Tyre, Qana area. These were deployed in well-prepared positions running from Ras el Ain in the south to the Kasmiya Bridge in the north, with detachments in the densely populated refugee camps of Rachidiye, El Bass, and Borj ech Shimali, in the city of Tyre, and in the hilly triangle Qana-Jouaiye-Aames. In the 25-kilometer length of the coastal strip, between the Litani and Zahrani rivers, there were about 1,000 com-

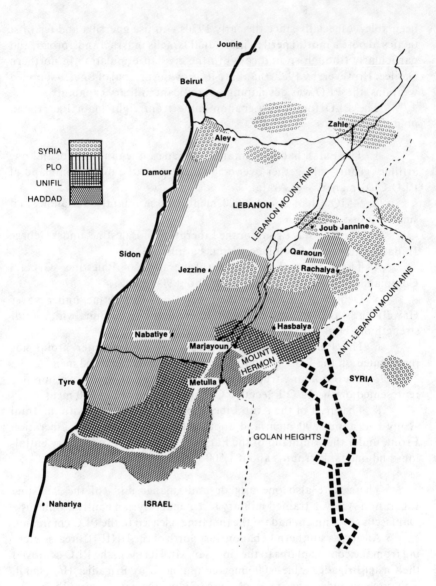

Deployments in Lebanon on the Eve of War

batants from Fatah, SAIQA, and the PLA, deployed in towns, villages, and training camps. The area was used as a logistic rear echelon where supply depots, repair facilities, and some intermediate headquarters were located.

The greater Sidon region, between the Zahrani and Awali rivers, was defended by a force of 1,500 men. The area contained many important rear installations and major headquarters groups. In the mountains to the east, and in a large refugee camp on the outskirts of the city, there were well-prepared defensive positions, including bunkers, trenches, gun emplacements and command posts.

The Nabatiye region, which included the strategically situated Arnoun Heights, provided excellent observation over much of northern Israel and commanded the main roads between the southern end of the Bekaa Valley and the coastal plains south of Sidon. This region was controlled by about 1,000 PLO combatants.

Two units were deployed to the north and east of the Castel Brigade: a battalion of the Yarmuk Brigade, some 600 men in the Aishiye-Rihane sector; and the Karame Brigade, which had 1,500 men in Fatahland, located mainly along the western ridges of Mt. Hermon. The Yarmuk battalion had two missions: first to interdict a possible Israeli attack toward the coastal lowlands from the north and northeast; and second, to hold the western flank of the Bekaa Valley in the Kaoukaba sector adjacent to the right wing of the Karame Brigade. That brigade was to defend the western ridges of Mt. Hermon and the southeastern Bekaa.

The region between the Awali and Damour rivers was controlled by the Ain Jalud Brigade of the PLA. This brigade of fewer than 1,000 men was undoubtedly better trained than those to the south, and was under the direct command of the PLO Headquarters in Beirut.

The central coastal strip between the Damour River and Beirut, including the cities of Damour and Beirut, housed the PLO General Headquarters, various command posts, training camps, logistical installations, and reserve units. Beirut was prepared for defense; construction of fortifications had begun in 1975. There were about 6,000 PLO military personnel in the area. Some of these were combat troops, the remainder were reserves and service units in logistical and weapon depots. As in the Tyre, Sidon, and Nabatiye districts, the PLO forces were concentrated in urban areas and scattered among the civilian population. Not only did these dispositions of forces permit the defenders to turn entire city blocks into fortified areas, but they made it difficult for an attacker to carry out an all-out attack because of the danger of civilian casualties.

Along the Lebanese coast, in Tripoli, Beirut, Sidon, Tyre, and in several tiny harbors, the PLO had small naval bases. They were used partly as staging areas for coastal raids against Israel, as well as being storage depots and ports of entry for military supplies.

Syrian Forces

On the eve of the war the Syrian contingent in Lebanon, under Major General Adib Ismail, consisted of the 1st Tank Division (including two tank and one mechanized infantry brigades), one independent mechanized infantry brigade, sixteen SA-2, SA-3, and SA-6 missile batteries, and a number of commando, artillery, antitank, air defense and engineer battalions. Also included in the Syrian contingent were two infantry brigades and one tank regiment of the PLA (one of these infantry brigades was, as noted earlier, attached to the PLO). The total Syrian-PLA strength in Lebanon was about 25,000 men, 300 tanks (T-55 and T-62), over 300 artillery pieces (122mm and 130mm guns, multiple rocket launchers, 120mm and 160mm mortars), nearly 100 missile launchers, about 100 antiaircraft guns, approximately 200 crew-served anti-tank weapons, and 300 APCs, including BMPs and BTR-152s. In addition there were individual small arms, several thousand machine guns, and several hundred individual antitank and antiaircraft missiles.

Northwest of Damascus, and close to the Lebanese border, Syrian General Headquarters had concentrated additional armor and infantry units—the equivalent of about one division—ready to move into Lebanon if the situation required.

Following the Syrians' entry into Lebanon in May 1976, they had started to fortify the areas under their occupation. By the spring of 1982 they had organized two principal defense zones. The forward defense zone included Damour, Jabal Aarbi, and the slopes of Mt. Hermon, and the second defense zone encompassed Beirut, Zahle, Rayak, Jdeidet Yabus, and Dir el Ashiyer. In addition there was apparently a "security belt" of observation posts just north of both the UNIFIL area and Major Haddad's Free Lebanon enclave.

The main concentrations of Syrian forces were as follows: in the Lebanon Mountains area—one mechanized infantry brigade supported by artillery, tanks, and commando units; in the Bekaa Valley—one tank brigade (T-62), artillery, antitank elements, and a commando group; in the Anti-Lebanon Mountains—one tank brigade (T-62), mechanized infantry, commando units, artillery and antitank elements; in the Beirut area, which was a part of the Syrian second defense zone—one mechanized infantry brigade, one PLA infantry brigade (in addition to that under PLO command), and one PLA tank regiment (about 50 T-54 and T-55 tanks). To the north of the Beirut-Damascus highway, there were additional mechanized infantry units. Also in the Bekaa Valley, south and east of Zahle, there were four SAM brigades.

Israeli Forces and Plans

The official Israeli objective of the planned thrust into South Lebanon was the destruction of the PLO military capability to carry out bombardment of Israeli territory. No less important was destruction of the PLO bases from which it had mounted terrorist attacks against Israeli civilians inside and outside the country. In fact, the Israelis intended to smash the entire PLO infrastructure in Lebanon and end its autonomous rule over large portions of the country. The operation was apparently planned so as to avoid—at least initially—clashes with the Syrian Army. However, it was obvious that Israeli moves against the PLO would, despite warnings, sooner or later force the Syrians into the battle. In such a case, and this was probably to the liking of Defense Minister Ariel Sharon and other hawks in the IDF General Staff and in the government, the IDF would be ready to strike and to deal firmly and quickly with Syria, forcing its forces to withdraw from Lebanon.

The Israelis intended to prevent the Palestinians from mobilizing and deploying all of their forces, and to capture their enormous supplies of weapons and ammunition, which were known to be stored in various depots and dumps. The Israeli General Staff decided to use enough troops to reach and take the principal terrain objectives quickly. Thus the guerrillas would be unable to regroup and force the IDF to fight step by step for every village, house, wadi or hill. This would also minimize Israeli casualties and make it more difficult for the Syrians to react effectively either in Lebanon or on the Golan Heights.

The Israeli General Staff ordered a partial mobilization to provide a force strong enough to shock the Palestinian establishment, to be able to advance deep into Lebanon, and, if necessary, to defeat the Syrian Army. Half of the combat force reserves—infantry, armor, and artillery—and less than 50 percent of the reserve logistical depots were activated.

The Israeli Chief of Staff, Lieutenant General Rafael Eitan, directed that the operation in Lebanon be carried out by forces of the IDF Northern Command under Major General Amir Drori. For the operation, the Northern Command was to commit seven mechanized and tank divisions, and several independent brigades and special units. Altogether the Northern Command fielded some 76,000 men, 1,250 tanks and 1,500 APCs. The advance was to be supported by the Israeli Air Force and the Israeli Navy. General Drori was given 48 hours to achieve the initial objective of reaching the mouth of the Awali River in the west and the southern tip of the Bekaa Valley in the east.

Upon receiving instructions from the General Staff, the Northern

Command staff prepared a final directive for the operation, which read, in part, "In order to prevent artillery fire and terrorists'* incursion across the border, the Northern Command will attack the terrorists, and destroy their infrastructure in South Lebanon. The Northern Command is prepared to destroy the Syrian Army in Lebanon, should the Syrians attack the IDF."

To fulfill the assigned misson, General Drori decided to advance along three main axes: a western axis, along the coastal area; a central axis, over the ridges of the Lebanon Mountain range on both sides of the central spine; and an eastern axis, through the Bekaa Valley and along the western slopes of Mt. Hermon and the Anti-Lebanon chain.

The success of the operation depended in great degree upon the implementation of two basic tactical concepts. In the first place momentum was to be obtained by a swift advance without stopping; pockets of resistance would be bypassed and dealt with by follow-up forces. Second, there would be amphibious landings from the sea in the PLO rear areas north of Sidon, to prevent an orderly northward retreat by the PLO fighters, and at the same time cause panic and disruption in rear areas and on lines of communication. These landing forces were to link up with IDF units advancing from the south and east and encircle the main PLO forces in southern Lebanon.

The 76,000 IDF troops which were assigned to the operation were organized in several *ugdah*, or division-sized task forces. Three of the task forces and additional units were combined into a corps-type command (about 35,000 men and 800 tanks) called the Bekaa Forces Group (BFG), under the command of Major General Avigdor "Yanush" Ben Gal, with the mission of destroying Syrian forces in the Bekaa Valley, should the Syrians intervene in support of the PLO. (General Ben Gal had commanded the 7th Armored Brigade in the critical actions that stopped the Syrian invasion of the Golan Heights in October 1973.)

The missions and deployments of the task forces were as follows:

• Task Force A consisted of the 91st Division (six reserve mechanized infantry brigades, and the 211th Armored Brigade from the 162d Division, temporarily assigned to Task Force A) under Brigadier Itzhak Mordechai. This force was to advance northward along the Coastal Road and across the hills to the east, up to the Awali River. Mordechai was to take Tyre, Sidon, and other urban areas in his sector, and to destroy PLO concentrations and installations. Task Force A was organized in mixed battalion-sized battle groups of infantry and armor.

---

* In Israel the PLO is invariably referred to as a "terrorist" organization and its members as "terrorists".

• Amphibious Task Force B, commanded by Brigadier General Amos Yaron, was made up of elements of the 96th Division, naval commandos, the 50th Paratroop Battalion of the 35th Paratroop Brigade, armor and engineer units, all transported by about 15 landing craft. This force was to land at the mouth of the Awali River (north of Sidon) and isolate the area of operations from the north, engage PLO forces in the area and block the roads parallel to the coast. After linking up with IDF units advancing from the south and southeast (Task Forces A and C), Task Force B—reinforced by additional armor units from those task forces—was to move northward to prevent PLO reserves from joining the battle in the south.

• Task Force C consisted of the 36th Division (less the 7th Armored Brigade) under Brigadier General Avigdor Kahalani. Organized in several mixed infantry and armor battle groups, it would advance on the central axis, destroying PLO concentrations in the Nabatiye and Arnoun Heights areas, capturing Beaufort Castle, crossing the Litani River at the Hardale Bridge under Beaufort Castle, and taking the Habush Bridge so as to open the road to Jezzine. Part of the Task Force would then turn westward along the Zahrani River to join with Task Force A near Sidon, and the remaining units, reinforced by Task Force D, the Northern Command reserve, would advance northward toward Besri in the Shouf Mountains east of Beirut and thence to the Beirut-Damascus highway.

The early capture of the Nabatiye-Arnoun Heights area was considered essential since it would be the base for future strikes along the Jezzine-Ain Dara axis, which were intended to split and fragment the PLO deployment. From this area the IDF could also threaten the right flank and rear of the southernmost Syrian positions in the Bekaa, and threaten Syrian control of the Beirut-Damascus highway, the Syrian lifeline in Lebanon.

• Task Force H was part of the Bekaa Forces Group (BFG), composed of several infantry and armor battle groups of the 252d Division (less the 460th Armored Brigade) under Brigadier General Immanuel Sakel. This force was to advance on the eastern axis, moving out from the Metulla area toward Kaoukaba and Hasbaiya and from Har Dov along the "Arafat Trail" toward Kfar Shouba and Hasbaiya. The task force was to destroy PLO concentrations in Fatahland and be ready to repel Syrian attacks, should these occur.

• Task Force V of the Bekaa Forces Group (the so-called Vardi force, named after its commander, Brigadier General Danni Vardi) was composed of one armored and one mechanized brigade, organized in infantry and armor battle groups. It was to become engaged only if the Syrians entered the battle. It would then be committed to the west of Task Force H and break through the first Syrian defense line in the Lake Karaoun area, destroy the Syrian forces there, and continue northward toward the Beirut-Damascus highway.

• Task Force Z of the Bekaa Forces Group was the 90th Division, under Major General Giora Lev. It was to follow behind Task Forces C and D along the central axis, capture the Jezzine area, and link up with other IDF forces operating in this sector to the east and west.

• Task Force D was the 162d Division (less the 211th Armored Brigade, which was attached to the 91st Division) under Brigadier General Menachem Einan. This was the Northern Command reserve. If the Syrians entered the battle it would be available to reinforce Task Force H in the eastern sector. Otherwise it would follow Task Force C to Nabatiye, and then advance north toward Jezzine, the Besri Bridge in the Shouf Mountains, Barouk, and Ain Zhalta close to the Beirut-Damascus highway.

Included in the Bekaa Forces Group was also a Special Maneuver Combined Force of approximately two mixed brigades under Brigadier General Yossi Peled. It was essentially an antitank force and its main mission was to prevent Syrian reinforcements from entering the Bekaa Valley. The 880th Division, commanded by Brigadier General Yom Tov Tamir, was the Bekaa Forces Group reserve.

• The Israeli Air Force was to maintain air supremacy over Lebanon, and protect Israel's air space. It was also to support ground operations on call, carry out interdiction, attack PLO targets (and Syrian targets if the Syrians entered the war), provide helicopter lift for infantry elements, and evacuate wounded by air.

• The Israeli Navy was to carry out interdiction as necessary on the high seas and coastal waters, to shell specific PLO targets along the seashore, to land Israeli amphibious forces at the mouth of the Awali River, to land small commando groups at other specially designated areas, to maintain naval supremacy, and to protect the Israeli coast line.

Pre-operation Activities June 4-5

According to an IDF count, in the period between May 9 and June 3, 1982, the PLO had launched 28 different attacks in Israel and abroad on Israeli targets. However, none of these was considered serious enough to focus world attention on the terrorist problem, and to justify Israeli retaliation. The attempt in London on the life of Israeli Ambassador Schlomo Argov was carried out late at night on Thursday, June 3. The Israeli Cabinet met the next morning, and approved a retaliatory air strike, to take place that afternoon. The Cabinet members did this, even though they recognized that this would almost certainly provoke a PLO bombardment of Galilee, which in turn would force them, ineluctably, to approve the long-planned, often-delayed invasion of southern Lebanon.

At 3:15 P.M. on June 4 the Israeli Air Force raided PLO targets just south of Beirut and in southern Lebanon. The first two targets hit were between Beirut and the Beirut International Airport to the south. One was Bourj el-Barajneh, the Fatah's training camp, containing eight buildings, numerous huts and tents, machine gun positions, and over ten antiaircraft gun emplacements. The second target was a nearby arms and ammunition depot situated under the grandstand of the soccer field near the Sabra refugee camp. The reinforced concrete stands provided protection for thousands of small arms rounds, and mortar and artillery shells belonging to the Fatah, the Palestinian Liberation Army, and the Lebanese leftist guerrillas, supporters of the PLO. Other targets in the same area included PLO headquarters, communication facilities, troop concentration areas, and bunkers.

At 5:00 P.M., immediately following these strikes, PLO artillery—mortars and multiple rocket launchers (MRL)—shelled Israeli settlements in the Galilee panhandle. This in turn provoked another Israeli response. IDF artillery units and naval guns opened fire on PLO concentrations in South Lebanon, including Beaufort Castle, Nabatiye Heights, Tyre, and the Zahrani estuary. The Air Force continued its strikes against PLO camps, headquarters, and artillery emplacements, and also interdicted traffic on main and secondary roads. Missile boats silenced Palestinian sources of fire near Sidon.

Heavy PLO shelling of Israeli territory continued on June 5. Some 23 towns and settlements came under intermittent artillery, mortar and MRL fire, resulting in several casualties and considerable damage. One person was killed and 15 wounded and hospitalized. The IAF maintained its attacks on PLO targets: weapons and ammunition depots, troop concentrations, tanks, and bunkers and other fortifications as far north as Damour. The Israeli aircraft also hit artillery positions (including several 130mm gun emplacements), caves where ammunition was stored, MRL positions, and bridges. Israeli long-range artillery and naval guns succeeded in silencing most of the PLO batteries in southern Lebanon.

Unconfirmed reports mention nearly 200 Palestinian fighters killed or wounded in the preliminary air strikes and artillery bombardments. Apparently fearing that Israel was about to launch its long expected ground offensive, the civilian population was swept by panic, and thousands of refugees jammed the roads leading north.

Israel's 40-Kilometer Territorial Objective

The issue that faced the Israeli Cabinet when, at the conclusion of the Sabbath, early on the evening of Saturday, June 5, it convened again was approval of the invasion. With some misgivings, the Cabinet gave its approval after discussion of the military objective of the operation. It announced its decision, however, only at 4:00 P.M. on June 6, five hours after the Israeli forces began crossing into Lebanon. From that discussion the Cabinet members (including the Prime Minister) almost certainly believed that they had received an assurance from Defense Minister Ariel Sharon, and from the Israeli Army Chief of Staff, General Eitan, that every effort would be made to avoid hostilities with Syria. They were also assured that the objective was to occupy southern Lebanon up to a distance of 40 kilometers from the Israeli border. This distance was selected because it would place all of northern Israel beyond the range of any known PLO weapons emplaced north of such a line. Apparently no member of the Cabinet asked Defense Minister Sharon how the Israelis would get to this line in the region east of the Lebanon Mountains without fighting the Syrians, who held positions that in some places were less than 20 kilometers from Metulla, in northern Israel. The objective of stopping at a line 40 kilometers north of the frontier was mentioned several times by Prime Minister Begin and other members of the Cabinet—including Sharon—in the early hours of the invasion.

On Sunday, June 6, Prime Minister Begin informed President Ronald Reagan that the Israeli forces invading Lebanon had been instructed to push back the PLO units 40 kilometers to the north so that all Israelis in Galilee would be relieved of the constant threat to their lives from PLO bombardment. Terminology describing the depth of the Israeli advance was vague, and probably this was deliberate. The Prime Minister did not specify from where the 40 kilometers would be measured.

In his message to Reagan, Begin also claimed that the Israeli offensive was an act of self defense, for the PLO guns had been shelling only civilian populations in northern Israel, even though there were many military targets in the area. He went on to say that Israel "does not covet one inch of the Lebanese territory" and wished to sign a peace treaty with a free, independent Lebanon, with its territorial integrity intact.

There seems little doubt that Prime Minister Begin was sincere in his repeated insistence that Israel intended to go no more than 40 kilometers north of the frontier. On the other hand, he does seem to have recognized the difficulty of keeping that pledge in case Syria, despite assurances that its forces would not be attacked by the IDF, should enter the war.

Thus, on June 7 Begin asked US Ambassador Philip Habib to go to Damascus, not only to assure President Assad that Israel would not attack Syrian troops, but also to ask Assad to pull back all Palestinian units at least 40 kilometers from the Israeli border, and withdraw the SAMs that the Syrians had moved into Lebanon in 1981. It seems incredible that Begin should think that Assad would entertain such a suggestion, and there seems to be at least some question of Begin's reluctance to attack Syria. On June 9, after Habib had delivered the Israeli warning to the Syrian government and while he was waiting to see President Assad, the Israeli Air Force attacked Syrian SAM batteries in the Bekaa Valley. This sudden attack made Begin's promise meaningless and Habib's mission invalid.

There must be serious question about the frankness of the assurances which Defense Minister Sharon and Chief of Staff Eitan gave to the Cabinet regarding the intention of not attacking the Syrians, and the territorial objective of 40 kilometers. The course of operations begun on June 8 suggests that neither of these intentions was an element of the military plan being carried out by the IDF.

The Israeli Time Table

The Israeli plan envisaged a timetable of three days for the destruction of the PLO Castel Brigade in southern Lebanon. H-Hour was set for 11:00 A.M. on June 6, when Task Forces A, C, and H were to cross the border and advance in their respective sectors. At 10:00 P.M. that night Amphibious Task Force B was to land in the rear of the Castel Brigade at the mouth of the Awali River. By 11:00 A.M. on June 8 all the PLO areas in South Lebanon up to the Awali River, including the city of Sidon, were to be overrun. Consolidation was to be completed in the next 24 hours.

General Drori's Northern Command was the operational headquarters responsible for the operation. The campaign was directed from Drori's command post in the Rosh Pinna area.

Chapter XII
Israeli Assault
on the PLO

The operations precipitated by the Israeli invasion of southern Lebanon can be divided into three major phases. First, beginning June 6, was a three-day battle in south and southwest Lebanon, in which the Israeli forces focused their attention on the military destruction of the PLO and its installations south of Beirut. The second phase of the operations began on June 8; this was the three and one-half day battle of the Bekaa Valley (which also encompassed the mountain chains to the east and west of the valley) between Israel's Bekaa Forces Group and elements of the Syrian forces deployed in Lebanon; major air battles were included. The third phase consisted of operations around Beirut against combined Syrian-PLO units, beginning on June 9.

Because of the speed and dazzling maneuvers of the Israeli forces, these operations were complicated and overlapping. It is difficult to draw a clearcut line between Israeli operations against the PLO and against the Syrians. To enable the reader to understand, and to follow, the combat actions, they are discussed day by day, and sector by sector. Since the Israelis had seized the initiative, the combat sectors automatically coincided with their activities. Even the most objective historians must therefore link operational descriptions to the movements of the several Israeli task forces and task groups.

The First Day (June 6, 11:00 A.M.—June 7, 5:00 A.M.)

Task Force A (Western Sector). Late on June 5, 1982, the commander of Task Force A, Brigadier General Itzhak Mordechai, received an order to commence the operation at 11:00 A.M. on June 6. Task Force A, deployed on the western axis, was to advance along the coastal plain and the hilly western slopes of the Lebanon Mountains, facing the Mediterranean

Sea. The ground attack was to be supported by a small amphibious daylight landing near the mouth of the Litani River.

Promptly on schedule, the Israelis quickly advanced through the Free Lebanon enclave and then across the belt controlled by the UNIFIL, meeting no resistance from the United Nations contingent. An armored unit, designated Battle Group A-4 (the 211th Armored Brigade under Colonel Eli Geva), attacked along the Zarit-Iskandarouna axis on the coastal road. At the same time the landing group—a small force of mixed armor and infantry—came ashore north of Tyre, then advanced rapidly southward toward Tyre. In the afternoon, under the cover of tank fire, Battle Group A-1, composed of mechanized infantry, enveloped Tyre from the east, advancing between the city and the large Palestinian refugee camps Rachidiye and Borj ech Shimali. The defensive positions of three Castel Brigade battalions, designated "Abu Youssef el Najar," "Middle Sector," and "Beit el Mukades", were isolated and heavily battered.

At first the PLO fighters offered spirited resistance, but they soon were overwhelmed by superior forces. Aware of the danger of encirclement, they started to retreat toward Tyre and the refugee camps which were their main strongholds. General Mordechai directed Battle Group A-4 to advance as rapidly as possible, regardless of opposition, to link up with Battle Group A-1, and to continue northward.

Battle Group A-1 was soon fighting near and around the refugee camps Borj ech Shimali and el Bass, and captured the Kasmiya Bridge over the Litani River. The bridge, which had been destroyed by the IAF a day earlier, was quickly replaced with a Bailey bridge, and Mordechai's troops readily crossed the river. At the same time the tanks of Battle Group A-4 were advancing swiftly north along the coastal highway, bypassing occasional roadblocks. By nightfall Tyre was encircled, but consideration for saving the lives of the civilian population prompted General Mordechai to postpone an assault on the city until daylight the following morning.

During the night of June 6/7 Battle Group A-4 sped northward past Tyre to link up with amphibious Task Force B. According to plan, that force had landed north of Sidon at the mouth of the Awali River shortly before midnight. Soon after midnight Geva's Battle Group A-4 reached and captured Aadloun, almost halfway between Tyre and Sidon. By this time PLO forces in the western sector had ceased to operate as organized units, except for a few centers of resistance, mostly in and near Tyre. Individual PLO soldiers were retreating in panic either to the mountains in the east, or to Tyre in the west, leaving most of their equipment behind.

Israeli aircraft supporting Task Force A encountered no resistance in the air. However, an Israeli Skyhawk was hit by a PLO missile and crashed in the area between Tyre and Nabatiye. This was the only Israeli fixed-wing aircraft shot down during the active combat period of the war.

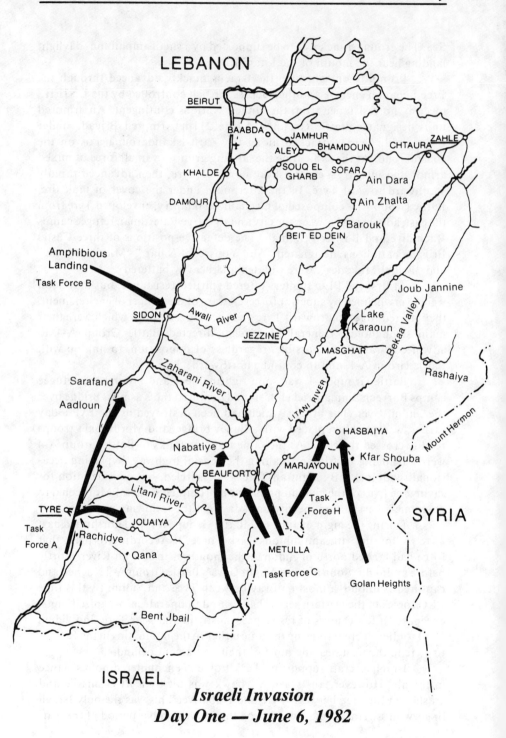

LEBANON

BEIRUT

BAABDA

JAMHUR

ALEY   BHAMDOUN   CHTAURA   ZAHLE

SOUQ EL   SOFAR
GHARB

KHALDE   Ain Dara

DAMOUR   Ain Zhalta

Barouk

BEIT ED DEIN

Joub Jannine

Amphibious
Landing
Task Force B

SIDON   Awali River

Lake
Karaoun

JEZZINE

MASGHAR   Rashaiya

Zaharani River

Sarafand

Aadloun   Mount Hermon

Nabatiye   o HASBAIYA

BEAUFORT o   MARJAYOUN   Kfar Shouba

Litani River   Task
Force H   SYRIA

TYRE   METULLA
Task   JOUAIYA
Force A   Rachidye

Qana   Task Force C

Golan Heights

Bent Jbail

ISRAEL

Israeli Invasion
Day One — June 6, 1982

The pilot was captured by the PLO. Also hit and destroyed were two Israeli helicopters.

Task Force B (Western Sector). On June 6, when the forward elements of the IDF were crossing the frontier into Lebanon, the Israeli amphibious armada was already at sea. The Naval Task Force—some 15 vessels, including missile boats, landing ships, and landing craft—had left Haifa and Ashdod the previous night. They sailed north with orders to land Task Force B on the beach a few hundred meters north of the mouth of the Awali River. This force was composed of elements of the 96th Division, naval commandos, paratroopers, engineers, tanks, APCs, and artillery. The amphibious operation was commanded by General Amos Yaron.

The landing had long been planned, and most of the troops had trained specially for the mission. The landing area was well known to the Israelis, who had carried out several raids there during previous years.

At 10:00 P.M. the first two groups of naval commandos landed on the beach without meeting any resistance. One group blocked the coastal highway, the other secured the beach for the landing of the main forces. Shortly after midnight, as soon as the beach was secured, the main amphibious force of several infantry battalions of the 96th Division, and units of the 50th Paratroop Battalion of the 35th Paratroop Brigade under Colonel Yair "Ya-Ya" Yarom started to land. As each group landed it moved immediately inland toward assigned objectives. The paratroopers captured Baksta Hill to the east of the coastal road and the Awali River bridge. PLO vehicles moving on the road were ambushed and destroyed. The PLO retreat toward Beirut was blocked.

The IDF landing caught the PLO defenders by surprise. After the beachhead had been secured by the commandos, and while the paratroopers were landing, Palestinian artillery, mortars, and multiple rocket launchers opened fire on the ships and troops on the beach. However, the fire was inaccurate and Israeli guns and missiles from the ships soon silenced the PLO guns. No ships were hit, and the Israelis suffered only minor casualties. Hurriedly organized counterattacks by elements of the Castel Brigade on Baksta Hill were unsuccessful, and the PLO fighters in the area began to withdraw toward the mountains.

By sunrise, units of the Castel Brigade deployed in the western sector found themselves cut off from their rear bases and from PLO headquarters in Beirut. The only escape route from the Sidon area was toward the mountains to the northeast, but this too was already threatened.

Task Force C (Central Sector). Following orders received on June 5, Brigadier General Avigdor Kahalani, the commander of Task Force C, sent his troops across the border into Lebanon at 11:00 A.M. on June 6. The success of the operation depended on a swift crossing of the Litani River canyon—which in some places was more than 120 meters deep—and taking the Nabatiye-Arnoun Heights, which were defended by the Jirmak Battalion of the Castel Brigade.

The approach to the Nabatiye-Arnoun Heights area from the southeast was possible only along two axes, both requiring fording of the Litani. One of the crossing points was in the Hardale Bridge area, covered by fire from Beaufort Castle and nearby hills. The other was across the Akiya Bridge, which traverses a deep Litani River gorge.

With heavy air and artillery support, reinforced reconnaissance and engineer companies of the Golani Infantry Brigade attacked north and west of Beaufort Castle, while armored Battle Group C-3 crossed the UNIFIL area to capture the Akiya Bridge. Battle Group C-2, composed of mechanized infantry, followed Battle Group C-3 across the Akiya Bridge. In a lightning stroke, the two Israeli battle groups advanced along narrow, easily blocked roads, scattering occasional pockets of PLO resistance. They cut through the center of the Castel Brigade's defensive positions and separated the Jirmak Battalion from its neighbor to the west, the Beit el Mukades Battalion. By afternoon, battle groups C-3 and C-2 reached the Habush Bridge and cut off the Jawad Abu el Shaar Battalion. The tanks of Battle Group C-3 now approached Nabatiye from the west.

While the advance of battle groups C-3 and C-2 isolated the Jirmak Battalion from the main forces of the Castel Brigade, the reconnaissance and engineer companies of the Golani Brigade advanced to the east and south of Nabatiye. This action cut off the headquarters of the PLO battalion and its supply depots from the troops in the field.

When Battle Group C-3 captured the Akiya Bridge, Battle Group C-1 advanced to take the Hardale Bridge, which was the only remaining bridge over the Litani River south of Lake Karaoun still under PLO control. This group then advanced to capture the northeastern Nabatiye ridge, bypassing defensive positions at Aishiye where, in addition to the PLO, a small Syrian detachment was deployed. Next the Israelis advanced against strong resistance along mountain roads up to Arab Salim. In the Aishiye area Israeli troops, for the first time, came under fire from Syrian artillery, which was deployed in forward positions southwest of Lake Karaoun.

At nightfall, the only strongpoint in Task Force C's sector still remaining in PLO hands was Beaufort Castle, strategically perched several hundred meters above the Litani gorges. The castle, crowning a rocky spur, had been built around 1140, during the Crusader era, by Count Fulke of Anjou. The PLO defenders of the castle pledged that they would resist the Israelis, just as their forebears in the 12th century had resisted the Crusaders.

To the Israelis and their Lebanese allies from the Haddad enclave, Beaufort Castle had become more than a symbol. Invulnerable to air and artillery strikes, with a commanding view of southern Lebanon and Israel's Galilee panhandle, the castle had served for ten years as a forward observation post for the PLO. From there the Palestinians directed artillery, mortar, and MRL fire against Israeli and southern Lebanese towns and villages.

An Israeli force of about 200 men from the reconnaissance and engineer units of the Golani Brigade arrived in APCs and other vehicles at the western foot of Beaufort Hill at dusk. Soon afterward they started their assault up the hill on foot. The defenders offered strong resistance, firing artillery, mortars, and hand weapons from strategically located positions, bunkers, trenches, and communication trenches. Israeli artillery, however, was now in position on the plateau and responded, hitting some of the PLO positions, and neutralizing most of the PLO fire. The advance was slow. As the forward Golani unit approached the top of the hill, the PLO fire died out and the defenders disappeared in the darkness, leaving behind about 35 men killed and wounded. Shortly after midnight the battle was over. Israeli losses were 6 killed and 18 wounded. The capture of Beaufort Castle, although not the most important, was the most dramatic event of the day. Unlike 300 years earlier, when the defenders had managed to withstand a siege for nearly two years, the PLO fighters gave up the castle after about two hours of combat.

During the night, as elements of Task Force C established themselves on the Arnoun Heights, and encircled Nabatiye, General Kahalani ordered his main forces to advance rapidly northwest to link up with Mordechai and Yaron (Task Forces A and B, respectively) in the Sidon area. Battle Groups C-3 and C-2 crossed the Habush Bridge and pushed westward toward Doueir and Kfour and the Coastal Road.

Task Force H (Bekaa Forces Group; Eastern Sector). General Ben Gal, commander of the Bekaa Forces Group, ordered General Sakel's Task Force H to cross the Israeli—Lebanese border at two points on June 6 at 11:00 A.M., and to occupy Fatahland. This area was defended by elements of the PLO Karame Brigade. Task Force H was also to secure the eastern flank of IDF forces operating against the Castel Brigade. Israeli commanders were to make every effort to avoid confrontation with Syrians, even if PLO units were in areas under Syrian control. To avoid provoking the Syrians into the battle, the task force was ordered to halt its advance along the line between Kfar Shouba, Hasbaiya, and Kaoukaba, to the south of the forward Syrian defense position. Syrian non-intervention in the opening stages of the war was considered by the Israeli General Staff to be crucial if the basic goals were to be achieved in three days. Having to deal with Syrians as well as the PLO would slow the advance and cause additional difficulties.

At 11:00 A.M. two columns of Task Force H jumped off in the

direction of Hasbaiya along two roads: Battle Group H-2 advanced from Metulla (in Israel) to Al Khiyam, and on to Hasbaiya; Battle Group H-1 followed the road from Har Dov (in Israel), to Kfar Shouba, and on to Hasbaiya.

Mechanized infantry and armor units of Battle Group H-2, moving into Lebanon from the Metulla area, crossed the nearby valley controlled by the Free Lebanese Forces of Major Haddad, and continued through territory under the UNIFIL's jurisdiction. Then, without meeting any serious resistance, they pushed into Fatahland, across the hilly terrain up to the Hasbaiya-Kaoukaba line. There they took up defensive positions.

Battle Group H-1—composed of mechanized infantry, armor, and engineer units—advancing along the eastern axis (Arafat Trail) toward Hasbaiya, ground to a halt shortly after crossing the border. About 500 meters north of Kfar Shouba the mountain road caved in after only five APCs had passed. The battle group commander ordered the five APCs to continue to Hasbaiya as planned, while the rest of his force waited until the road was repaired. The spearhead APCs, overcoming light resistance, reached Hasbaiya by nightfall. There they found Battle Group H-2, which had arrived earlier.

As soon as IDF troops entered the Hasbaiya area, Syrian artillery opened fire, and PLO antitank teams began to harass the leading Israeli elements. During the night units of the Karame Brigade deployed in the town withdrew without a fight to the mountains further east and north. They left behind large quantities of weapons and ammunition, and well-equipped training centers.

Chapter XIII
The PLO Collapse

The Second Day **(June 7, 5:00 A.M.—June 8, 5:00 A.M.)**

Task Force A (Western Sector). By sunrise on June 7 Battle Group A-1 had overrun large areas south of the Litani River, and Geva's armored Battle Group A-4 had left Aadloun and was advancing toward Sidon. General Mordechai now committed two new infantry battle groups, (A-3 and A-5) to combat on the coastal plain. A few hours later Battle Group A-6 crossed into Lebanon at Biranit, some 20 kilometers east of Rosh Hanikra, and by mid-morning Task Force A had six battle groups engaged in combat all across southwestern Lebanon.

As the new troops entered the combat area, they began mopping-up operations. Mixed infantry and armored elements of Battle Group A-3, advancing past Tyre, turned eastward along three roads, leading to Kana, Tair Debba, and Abassiye. Soon they linked up with Battle Group A-6, which was coming from the Biranit area. The two battle groups enveloped the remnants of the PLO Middle Sector Battalion, which was primarily deployed inside UNIFIL territory (in violation of the accord reached after the Litani operation in 1978). By nightfall, that battalion had been annihilated and most of the territory south of the Litani River was under Israeli control. The Israeli troops crossed the river and continued northward toward Sidon.

At the same time Battle Group A-7 (a mixed group of infantry and armor) joined other Israeli units already engaged with PLO defenders of the Rachidiye refugee camp just outside Tyre. By midday the camp was encircled. While scores of its inhabitants followed IDF warnings—announced by loudspeakers—and abandoned the camp to look for safety behind the Israeli lines, many hundreds of others remained inside, being held hostage by the PLO troops.

Shortly after midday the IAF dropped leaflets on Tyre, giving the population a two-hour warning to leave their homes and go to the beach to avoid being caught in the fighting for the city. The warnings were also repeated over loudspeakers. These announcements deprived the Israelis of surprise, which they sacrificed for the goodwill of the Lebanese populace. The Israelis were clearly determined to minimize civilian casualties, not only to avoid domestic and international condemnation, but also to avoid antagonizing the local Lebanese population. Some 12,000 inhabitants actually left the city after the warnings and concentrated on the beach, where a few thousand had already gathered.

Later the Israelis used this same method to get civilians out of danger in mopping-up activities in Sidon and Nabatiye. In both places a considerable number of the local population followed the Israeli advice.

Around 3:00 P.M., after the two hour deadline had passed, mopping-up operations began in and around Tyre. By nightfall the Israelis had occupied most of the city, with the exception of a few pockets of resistance. The area north of Tyre, up to the Kasmiya bridge on the Litani River, was also cleared. The PLO Abu Youssef el Najar Battalion had totally disintegrated. Its remnants, abandoned by their commanding officer, Azami Zarayer, made desperate attempts to defend a few fortified blocks in Tyre.

Meanwhile, supported by tank and direct artillery fire, infantry elements of Battle Group A-7 pushed slowly into the Rachidiye Camp to mop up continuing resistance. Soon, however, it became clear that the camp had become a huge fortress, well-stocked with weapons and ammunition. To avoid civilian casualties the Israelis used their superior firepower sparingly and selectively. The advance was slow. The PLO had dug many tunnels under the camp, linking the numerous strongholds, enabling easy movement of reserves from one point to another. Late in the evening about half of the camp area was in Israeli hands, and hundreds of prisoners had been taken.

During the morning, while mopping-up operations south of the Litani River were still in progress, Battle Group A-4 continued to speed northward along the coastal plain toward Sidon. Units of the Castel Brigade tried to halt the rapidly moving Israeli tanks, but were unsuccessful. Geva's troops bypassed several PLO strongholds, and in the evening linked up at the mouth of the Zahrani River with forward elements of Task Force C, striking from the east. A major petroleum refinery with a huge oil depot and excellent port facilities fell into Israeli hands. Soon after, both forces moved north toward Sidon and joined with elements of Task Force B arriving from the beachhead north of the city, completing the encirclement of Sidon. Geva, however, continued his northward advance, bypassing Sidon, trying to catch up with other elements of Task Force B, which were already approaching Damour.

Task Force B (Western Sector). In the morning the Israeli Navy brought additional units of the 96th Division from the Nahariya area to the

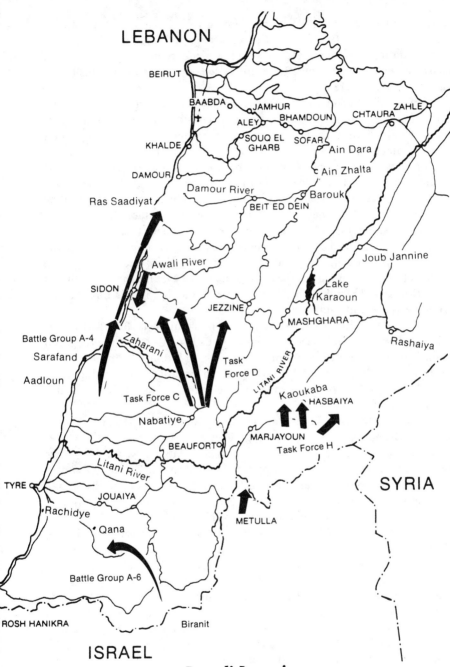

Israeli Invasion
Day Two — June 7, 1982

beachhead near the Awali River, reinforcing Task Force B with additional infantry, tanks, artillery, and APCs to a strength of about four battalions. As the landing ships and craft carrying the reinforcements approached the coast, they were shelled by PLO artillery located in the mountains to the east, but no hits were registered.

General Yaron then organized Task Force B into three battle groups. One group pushed north along the coastal road. By evening, after meeting only slight resistance, this group reached Ras Saadiyat, only about seven kilometers south of Damour and barely 20 kilometers from Beirut. The move was supported by air force bombing raids up the coast as far as Naame, some 15 kilometers south of the Lebanese capital.

A second, smaller, battle group enlarged the beachhead area to the east, forcing the PLO defenders to retreat into the mountains. The third group went south, blocking Sidon from the north and northeast. As at Tyre, the Israelis gave the 200,000 residents a two-hour warning to evacuate the city. After the deadline expired the Israelis moved in, and fighting took place in the northern part of the town. Late in the evening the group linked up with forward elements of Task Forces A and C approaching the city from the south and southeast.

Task Force C (Central Sector). By morning, with Beaufort Castle taken and Nabatiye encircled, Battle groups C-3 and C-2 (less units engaged in the Nabatiye area) advanced northwest toward Sidon. They moved along both banks of the Zahrani River, using several parallel roads leading to the west. In the evening they linked up with elements of task forces A and B south and east of Sidon.

Meanwhile tanks and infantry units of Battle Group C-1 crossed the Hardale Bridge early in the morning. They were soon reinforced by elements of Battle Group C-2. The group then occupied Nabatiye—where resistance was negligible—and mopped up the Arnoun-Nabatiye Plateau. By evening the PLO Jirmak Battalion, which had defended the area, had ceased to operate as an organized force. Individual fighters or groups either surrendered or fled into the mountains to the north.

Two other PLO battalions—Jawad Abu el Shaar and Abu Hassan Salemeh—melted away as Task Force C passed through their areas. Some of the men ran into the mountains; others escaped to Beirut.

The linking up of elements of Task Forces A, B, and C in the Sidon area closed the ring around that city and meant the end of the Castel Brigade as a viable combat formation, even though pockets of resistance were still fighting in several strongholds, including Sidon, and a few refugee camps. Within 40 hours the PLO had lost most of South Lebanon, many installations, and great quantities of equipment and supplies.

Task Force D (Central Sector). General Einan's Task Force D, composed of elite regular units, had not been involved in combat in the opening phase of the operation, but followed behind Task Force C. At 9:00 A.M. the forward detachment of Task Force D, Battle Group D-1, passed through combat deployments of Task Force C near Arab Salim and pushed northward. The mission of this battle group, composed of armored units and reinforced by Nahal infantry,* was to cut off the coastal plain theater of operations from the Bekaa Valley, by striking through the southern part of the Lebanon Mountains and capturing the Besri Bridge north of Jezzine. The mountain roads on which Battle Group D-1 proceeded were treacherous and narrow (the maximum width being no more than 5 meters), with sheer cliffs often dropping 200 meters. The battle group advanced along the axis Akiya Bridge-Habush Bridge-Jarjoua-Jbaa-Beit Adin-Besri River.

During the day the tanks and infantry of Battle Group D-1 advanced nearly 30 kilometers, encountering only light resistance from Syrian commando units which organized ineffective ambushes along the road. In the Jezzine area the Israelis were shelled by Syrian artillery and mortars. To prevent escalation against the Syrians, Einan avoided direct action, only returning fire to silence their artillery. By evening, forward detachments of the task force were only a few kilometers south of the Besri River.

Task Force H (Eastern Sector). There was little action in the area. Task Force H consolidated its positions along the Hasbaiya-Kaoukaba line and exchanged desultory fire with PLO and Syrian elements. Forward detachments took Ain Keniya, some 3 kilometers to the east of Hasbaiya.

Air Activities. During the day the IAF provided support to the ground forces on call. It also continued its attacks against PLO rear areas, hitting troop concentrations, supply depots, and known command posts. Much of the air activity was focused on the principal concentration of PLO rear area elements in the southern fringes of West Beirut. During one of the air attacks on West Beirut, a Syrian MiG-23 was shot down in a dogfight with Israeli planes. This was the first sign of Syrian air involvement since the initiation of the Israeli offensive against the PLO the previous day.

The Third Day (June 8, 5:00 A.M.—June 9, 5:00 A.M.)

Task Force A (Western Sector). Task Force A continued to mop up Tyre, the Rachidiye refugee camp, and a few other areas where remnants of the Castel Brigade still offered resistance. Progress was slow, because the PLO units were deployed among civilians, and the Israelis continued to abstain from using their full firepower capability, in order to avoid noncombatant casualties.

---

* Nahal troops are conscripts who choose to serve part time in the Army and work part time in a kibbutz. They are regarded as highly motivated fighters.

At noon General Mordechai was ordered to end further offensive operations and to start mopping up the western sector south of the Awali River. Several of his units were detached and assigned to Task Forces B, C, and D. Mordechai was to flush out all the remaining PLO fighters in the region under his command, and to take Sidon and the nearby el Hilwe refugee camp, both of which were already encircled. Because of caution to avoid civilian casualties, these mop up operations took almost one week to complete.

During the first phase of the operation, Task Force A had completed all of its missions. In 48 hours it had advanced some 60 kilometers in difficult, partly mountainous, terrain, had crossed two major water obstacles (the Litani and Zahrani rivers) and had taken numerous towns and villages.

The achievements of Task Force A were attributable to several factors: the simultaneously successful operations of Task Forces B and C; coordination of all arms; imaginative use of available resources by commanders at all levels; up-to-date intelligence; combined ground and sea operations to envelop PLO forces; and effective support by the Israeli Air Force and the Israeli Navy.

Task Force B (Western Sector). During the day spearheads of Task Force B crossed the Damour River southeast of Damour and took up positions southeast of the city. At night a paratroop unit carried out an envelopment maneuver from southwest to northeast. Then, from positions east of Damour, it advanced eastward into the hills along the road leading to Kfar Matta.

Task Force C (Western Sector). The previous day Battle Group C-1 of Task Force C had been fighting in the Central Sector in the Nabatiye area. During the night of June 7/8, the force, its mission accomplished, moved westward and joined elements of Task Forces A, B, and C in the vicinity of Sidon. Early in the morning Task Force C crossed the Awali River and, following the armored Battle Group A-4 (now detached from Task Force A and a part of Task Force C), continued northward on the coastal plain toward Beirut. By evening the forward detachments of the task force reached a point about two kilometers south of Damour, where they were halted by strong PLO resistance, including ambushes and counterattacks. Liaison was maintained with Task Force B to the northeast. The advance from the south was effectively supported by air force strikes, and by naval vessels which shelled PLO targets.

Task Force D (Central Sector). In the early morning, the spearhead of Task Force D reached the Besri River bridge, where it clashed with a unit of the Syrian 85th Brigade, which had arrived from Beirut in BTR-152s. During a short but fierce engagement, the Syrians suffered heavy casualties

Israeli Invasion
Day Three — June 8, 1982

and were driven back. Following this clash Northern Command Headquarters ordered Einan to advance as rapidly as possible toward the Beirut-Damascus highway.

In order to speed up the advance, Einan split his force into two columns. Battle Group D-1 moved along the eastern road of the Lebanon Mountains toward Ain Zhalta. The other column, Battle Group D-2, advanced west of the crest toward Beit ed Dine. Both roads were typical Lebanon mountain roads, narrow, treacherous, easily blocked.

The decision to split into two columns enabled Task Force D to advance nearly 50 kilometers during the day, in spite of the nature of the roads. At about 6:00 P.M., the spearhead of the western column, Battle Group D-2, reached the outskirts of Beit ed Dine and the heights over the es Safa River, which form the main natural defense barrier of Beirut from the southeast. The spearhead of the eastern column, Battle Group D-1, approached Ain Zhalta, about ten kilometers south of the Beirut-Damascus highway.

At this point the Northern Command had to decide on one of three options for Task Force D: 1) turn all or part of the task force to the west toward Damour, via Deir el Kamar; 2) advance eastward toward the Bekaa Valley via Maasser ech Shouf and Kafraiya, where it would be behind the main Syrian deployment in the valley; 3) continue northward to cut the Beirut-Damascus highway.

General Drori decided on the third alternative and directed Einan accordingly. However, during the following 50 hours Task Force D, frustrated by terrain and fierce Syrian resistance, was able to advance only three kilometers.

The bottleneck was Ain Zhalta, a small village of stone houses, inhabited by several hundred people, in a valley between gorges of the es Safa River and Wadi Abu Kashkish. On June 7 the Syrians had deployed a tank battalion, reinforced by commando, artillery, antitank, and engineer elements, in the Safar-Shtaura sector. The commander of this force sent a detachment to Ain Zhalta, where it took up defensive positions. Shortly before nightfall on the 8th, as the spearhead of Battle Group D-1 entered the village along the narrow road, it suddenly found itself inside the Syrian defense position and taking very strong fire from all directions. The two leading tanks and several APCs were immediately hit and either destroyed or damaged. The Israeli advance was halted.

During the night the Nahal infantry attempted to penetrate into Ain Zhalta in order to extricate wounded IDF soldiers trapped in the village. The rescue operation failed. Not all wounded were taken out, and the road was not opened. Furthermore, the rescue effort caused additional Israeli casualties. The Syrians remained entrenched in and around Ain Zhalta.

Air Activities. In air battles over Lebanon, Israeli jets shot down six

Syrian MiGs. The first air battle started at 8:00 A.M., when two Mig-23s were shot down while trying to intercept Israeli fighters over Beirut. Around noon two other MiGs were shot down in a dogfight east of Sidon. At 1:15 P.M. one MiG was destroyed over Damour, and an hour later a sixth Syrian aircraft was shot down over Beirut.

Chapter XIV
Battle of
the Bekaa Valley:
The Onslaught

Syrian-Israeli Confrontation

The Israeli Government has steadfastly maintained that when the attack on the PLO began on June 6 there was no intention of attacking Syrian forces in Lebanon, unless Syria initiated hostilities. The Israelis continue to insist that they avoided combat with the Syrians until they were provoked by Syrian ground and air attacks late on June 8 and early on June 9. However, this assertion is difficult to reconcile with the offensive actions carried out by Task Force D on June 8, described in the previous chapter. Nor can it be readily reconciled with the activities of the various task forces of the Bekaa Forces Group, farther to the east. These operations clearly threatened the flanks of the main Syrian forces, enveloping them from west and east, and placing them in a very precarious situation.

It is not clear whether the confrontation with the Syrian Army that was in the making on June 8 was the result of a local decision within the guidelines provided to General Drori at the Northern Command, or of direct orders from Defense Minister Ariel Sharon, with or without the knowledge and approval of Prime Minister Begin. It is clear that Sharon not only wanted to get rid of Syrian SAM missile batteries in the Bekaa Valley, but had also sought vigorously to reduce the Syrian presence in Lebanon, because it tilted the internal situation in that country in favor of the PLO and the Muslim left. There is no evidence to suggest that the Israeli Cabinet had secretly approved such an operation in advance.

In any event, the evidence does indicate that by evening of June 7 General Ben Gal's Bekaa Forces Group had completed plans and was ready to move the next day against Syrian forces and remnants of PLO units in the Lake Karaoun area. What is not known is whether this was a contingency plan, or an already approved operation. The BFG apparently had a three-fold mission: 1) to break through the Syrian Army defenses in the Karaoun, Rashaiya areas: 2) to occupy the western slopes of Mt. Hermon and the Anti-Lebanon Mountains, which dominate the Bekaa Valley from the east; and 3) to seize the eastern slopes of the Lebanon Mountains which command the Bekaa from the west. The BFG would then advance through the southern part of the Bekaa Valley, to reach and cut the Beirut-Damascus highway.

The operational plan prepared by General Ben Gal, and approved by the Northern Command headquarters, called for: a) an attack on Syrian defenses in the Jezzine area with most of Task Force Z; b) committing Task Force V to make the main effort along the eastern slopes of the Lebanon Mountains and in the Bekaa Valley; and c) committing Task Force H to an enveloping maneuver from the east along the western slopes of the Anti-Lebanon Mountains. Battle Group Z-3, an armored battalion, was to be held in BFG second echelon.

The Third Day (June 8, 5:00 A.M.—June 9, 5:00 A.M.)

Task Force Z (BFG-West). In the morning, General Lev's Task Force Z, which on the two previous days had moved up close behind Task Forces C and D, launched an attack on the Jezzine defense system on the southern ridge of Jabal Barouk (1,500 meters above sea level), stretching from Kfar Houne in the south through Jezzine to Niha in the north. This was the western anchor of the Syrians' defense zone, where they had deployed one mechanized infantry brigade reinforced by artillery, tank, and commando units. An additional tank battalion arrived at sunrise June 8 from the Karaoun sector. South of Jezzine, defensive positions were held by the PLO Yarmuk Brigade, 600 strong, reinforced by Syrian tanks (T-55), artillery, commando, antitank, and engineer elements.

The attack of Task Force Z was facilitated by the success of Task Force D and some elements of Task Force C which had earlier passed along the western fringes of the Syrian defenses. En route, Task Force C had destroyed several Syrian ambushes and cut off elements of the PLO Castel Brigade to the west from Syrian forces in the east.

The Jezzine defenses were assaulted simultaneously from three directions. Units of the Golani Brigade, which had been transferred from Task Force C and attached to Task Force Z, attacked from the Niha area in the northwest. The armor of Battle Group Z-1 moved from the west along the road, while infantry units advancing from the Nabatiye area attacked from the south. Most of the Syrian forces in Jezzine had arrived in the area only a few hours previously, and had not had time to acquaint themselves with either the situation or the terrain. Nor had they been properly deployed to take advantage of their potentially superb defensive position. They were quickly defeated by the coordinated Israeli infantry and armor attack. By sundown, General Lev had captured almost the entire Jezzine defense zone. Syrian troops that were not killed or captured escaped northward. Thirty-two Syrian tanks were destroyed.

Occupation of the Jezzine defenses enabled the Bekaa Forces Group to prepare an assault on the Karaoun defense sector using a pincer attack from the west, along the Jezzine-Mashghara road, and the north, using the Maaser ech Shouf-Kafraiya-Joub Jannine road. During the night Golani troops began to advance to the north toward Maaser ech Shouf.

Task Force H (BFG-East). Sakel's Task Force H began its advance late in the morning. At noon Battle Group H-2 approached the village of Mimes, some seven kilometers north of Hasbaiya and defended by a combined Syrian and PLO force. After a short artillery shelling, Israeli troops assaulted and captured the village. Battle Group H-2 continued to advance, meeting only slight resistance. By nightfall it had advanced halfway toward the Syrian main defense zone in the Rashaiya area.

While Battle Group H-2 was engaged along the Hasbaiya, Mimes, Kfair, Ain Aata road, Battle Group H-1, reinforced by additional engineer elements, attacked a Syrian commando company at Wadi Shebaa in order to open the road to the north. Wadi Shebaa had been fortified with obstacles, mostly minefields, trenches, and earth dikes. A paratroop company which spearheaded the attack dislodged the Syrians, and occupied the ridges along the road. The Syrians suffered heavy losses; about 70 of the commandos were killed.

As the Israeli paratroopers and the Syrian commandos were engaged in combat, Israeli engineers cleared obstacles from 12 kilometers of the road, and prepared it for troop movement. However, Battle Group H-1 advanced only one kilometer before it stopped, its commander having learned from intelligence that a Syrian commando battalion had taken up well-prepared defensive positions at the northwestern exit from the wadi through which Battle Group H-1 was to pass. Realizing that he would have to engage the Syrian commando battalion under disadvantageous circumstances, the battle group commander, after consulting with General Sakel, decided not to use the Wadi Shebaa road. Instead, he turned around and moved his entire force along the Hasbaiya-Rashaiya road, the so-called "village" road, further west.

Task Force V (BFG-Center). During the day, Vardi's Task Force moved into the combat area, ready to jump off on June 9. The task force carried out only intelligence probings to the west and northwest of Kaoukaba.

PLO Bombardment of Galilee. Around noon on June 8, while the

Bekaa Forces Group was carrying out these limited operations against the PLO and Syrian forces, several Katyusha rockets were fired by PLO gunners at the Galilee panhandle from a Syrian-controlled area north of Hasbaiya. No casualties were reported.

The Fourth Day (June 9, 5:00 A.M.—June 10, 5:00 A.M.)

By June 9 the war in Lebanon had expanded into full-scale hostilities between Israel and Syria. Two days earlier, on June 7, the Syrian High Command, facing the possibility of a major confrontation between the two countries, decided to reinforce its troops in Lebanon, even though this would weaken the defenses on the Golan Heights, where for years large Israeli and Syrian forces had been facing each other. In addition to ground forces, the reinforcement included three more SAM batteries, bringing the number of these in the Bekaa Valley to 19. The missiles were so emplaced as to bring part of the air space over the Galilee panhandle within Syrian antiaircraft range.

Damascus hoped that these troop movements—particularly the SAM deployment—would serve as a warning and deterrence to Israel. The employment of the SAMs could cause heavy losses to the Israeli Air Force. The Syrian command assumed that this would force the IAF to limit its air operations in Lebanon, thus decreasing its commanding superiority in the air.

The Israelis, on the other hand, considered the deployment of the missiles a further flagrant violation of the tacit understanding reached in previous years, and decided that the time had come to knock out the much vaunted Soviet-made missiles. They evidently reasoned that unless these air defense weapons were destroyed or neutralized they would make a total victory difficult, if not impossible. It was further thought to be an ideal oportunity to humble aggressive Syria while it was almost completely isolated in the Arab world. When the Israelis made this decision is not clear. However, they had been training for such an operation for months.

Syria's election to shift more missiles and reinforcements into Lebanon was probably ill-advised, because it created a new and bigger threat to the entire Israeli operation. Instead of having a deterrent effect, it seems to have persuaded the Israelis that only force would solve the problem. It certainly provided an excuse—if one was needed—for Israeli operations against the Syrians. One cannot ignore the possibility, of course, that provocative maneuvering by the Israeli High Command on June 8 was designed to stimulate just such a Syrian reaction. By moving the IDF into the eastern sectors of Lebanon until the IDF virtually stood eyeball-to-eyeball with Syrian troops, and by sending other units in the central sector to

LEBANON

BEIRUT

BAABDA

JAMHUR

ALEY BHAMDOUN

CHTAURA ZAHLE

KHALDE

SOUQ EL GHARB SOFAR

Ain Dara

DAMOUR

Ain Zhalta

Kfar Matta

Barouk

BEIT ED DEIN

Besri

Joub Jannine

SIDON

Lake Karaoun

JEZZINE

MAGHAR

Kfar Meshgi

Zaharani River

Rashaiya

Sarafand

LITANI RIVER

Aadloun

Al Hilwe

Kaoukaba O HASBAIYA

Nabatiye

MARJAYOUN

BEAUFORT O

Litani River

SYRIA

TYRE

JOUAIYA

Rachidye

METULLA

Qana

ROSH HANIKRA Baranit

ISRAEL

Israeli Invasion
Day Four — June 9, 1982

cut the Beirut-Damascus highway, the Israeli command seems deliberately to have made the Syrians feel threatened and menaced by encirclement.

For the first three days of hostilities, Syria appeared to be heeding Israeli warnings to stay out of the fight, and clearly demonstrated its unwillingness to be dragged into confrontation with Israel. The isolated aerial and artillery engagements were just token gestures designed primarily to silence its even more inactive Arab critics and show them that Syria was doing something practical to help the Palestinians, while they themselves were sitting on the sidelines. The ground combat near Jezzine had all been at Israeli initiative.

In fact, at the outset, Israeli attacks had been clearly directed solely against the PLO, scrupulously avoiding the Syrian-held areas, despite the dilemma posed by the presence of the PLO units interspersed among Syrian occupation forces within range of Israeli territory, and well inside the presumed 40 kilometer-deep *"cordon sanitaire"* between northern Israel and PLO artillery. But after the fall of Hasbaiya on June 7, and the extension of Israeli control over most of the Arkub region, so-called Fatah-land, at the foot of Mt. Hermon, hundreds of PLO fighters fled north into Syrian-held territory from where they continued shelling advancing Israeli troops and even towns and villages in the Galilee panhandle.

This, of course, prompted Israeli artillery to silence the sources of such fire. In turn, the Syrians perceived this counterbattery fire as an Israeli attempt to challenge the Red Line, long tacitly accepted by Damascus and Jerusalem as a line neither side would cross. This perception appeared to be confirmed on Tuesday, June 8, by the Israeli attack on the southernmost deployment of Syrian troops at Jezzine. At this point the Syrians concluded that the Israeli thrust had become a threat, not only to their already shaken credibility as the sole protector and ally of the PLO, but also to Syria's vital national security interests in the area. They now had evidence that Israel would not honor its pledge not to attack Syria in South Lebanon unless its own forces had been attacked first. A full-scale IDF onslaught seemed imminent to the Syrians.

Air Activity. The Syrian SAM complex was centered in the Zahle area. The planned Israeli air attack on the complex was not a simple raid. The Syrians had deployed a dense air defense system which included the most advanced and sophisticated weapons and radar that they had received from the Soviet Union. In addition, hundreds of Syrian MiGs were available and ready to engage any attacking Israeli planes. Nevertheless, the Israelis were confident. Their air force had trained and prepared for such a possibility ever since Damascus first moved air defense missiles into Lebanon.

The Israeli air attack on the SAM batteries commenced at 2:00 P.M.

on June 9. It was carried out under the direct command of Major General David Ivri, Commanding General of the IAF, who controlled operations from his command post near Tel Aviv. The Israelis used F4-E Phantoms, A-4 Skyhawks, F-15 Eagles, and Israeli-made Kfirs. As the Israeli planes appeared over the Bekaa Valley, Syrian interceptors from nearby bases attacked them. Soon a tremendous air battle developed, with over 50 Syrian and nearly a hundred Israeli planes engaged in dogfights. In the next three hours, the IAF shot down 29 MiGs and destroyed 17 out of 19 Syrian missile batteries, without loss of a single Israeli plane.

The destruction of 17 Soviet-made SAM batteries was one of the most spectacular and impressive achievements of the Israeli Air Force during the war. The Soviet "Guideline" (SA-2), "Goa" (SA-3), and "Gainful" (SA-6) missiles deployed by the Syrians in the Bekaa Valley were all advanced types of Soviet antiaircraft guided-missile systems and had long been the bane of the Israeli Air Force. The missile range of close to 60 kilometers (SA-6) effectively covered all of the southern half of Lebanon, including a slice of the northern Golan Heights and the Galilee panhandle.

The Israeli achievement is in part explicable by the fact that Israeli pilots had been flying over Lebanon for years almost without constraints, and had thus become familiar with the terrain, and with the locations of Syrian antiaircraft systems. Experience in the 1973 war, and in occasional subsequent encounters, also enabled the Israeli pilots to learn the strengths and weaknesses of the Soviet-made systems. In addition, continuous realistic training and practice simulations of such attacks were also of significant help.

Nevertheless the attack posed difficult and complex problems. Specific details of the attack procedures are still secret, thus it is impossible at this time to discuss definitively the methods which led to the annihilation of the formidable Syrian air defense system. It can be assumed that the Israeli success was made possible by the integration of very careful advance planning, aerial surveillance (in part by drones, or remotely piloted vehicles—RPVs), precision strikes by highly trained pilots, a highly sophisticated system of command and control, coordination with surface-based long-range artillery and missiles, highly sophisticated air-to-surface and anti-radar missiles, equally sophisticated electronic countermeasures (ECMs), and (perhaps above all) preeminence in the air.

According to unconfirmed reports, some of the SAM systems were hit by the new Israeli Zeev surface-to-surface rockets. Zeev rockets, with a range of 40 kilometers, are designed to fire at air defense radar, using sensors to home on radiation emissions. Supposedly they knocked out surveillance and fire control radars used by SA-6 batteries and the deadly

ZSU-23-4 low-level antiaircraft guns. Unquestionably, long-range Israeli artillery, from positions south of Lake Karaoun, contributed to the highly-coordinated effort. Air-launched weapons included laser-guided bombs, and there were self-protection ECMs on each Israeli aircraft.

Task Force Z (BFG-West). During the day, Task Force Z advanced eastward from the hills of Jezzine along two axes toward the Karaoun defense zone. One element followed the Jezzine, Mashghara road, the other moved along the Kfar Houne, al Katrana, Maydun, Ain al Tina road.

The Israeli advance was slow, frequently interrupted by Syrian antitank ambushes, especially in the Mashghara and Ain al Tina areas. In the morning, Syrian aircraft and helicopter gunships launched strikes against the Israeli armored column in the Mashghara area, further delaying the advance. Israeli aircraft refrained from intervening against the Syrian air attack because the Syrian planes were operating within the envelope of SAM batteries deployed in the Bekaa Valley, which were not attacked until afternoon.

Task Force H (BFG-East). In the morning, Task Force H reached al Hilwe, where it encountered intense Syrian and PLO resistance. The battle for the village, which is dominated from Kfar as Zait, continued throughout the day. The terrain made it impossible to maneuver; the battle turned into a fierce house-to-house combat. By nightfall the village was captured, and the remnants of the Syrian tank brigade and PLO forces either surrendered or retreated northward. During the engagement four Israeli soldiers were killed and many were wounded.

Task Force V (BFG-Center). Task Force V was committed to combat in the center of the Bekaa Valley on the Kaoukaba-Kfar Meshki axis. It jumped off early in the morning from the Hasbaiya-Kaoukaba line, and shortly after cleared out Syrian and PLO units deployed in the defensive zone between the Litani River to the west and the Hasbani River to the east. After the Hasbaiya-Kaoukaba defenses were broken, the task force penetrated into the area southeast of Lake Karaoun, where it encountered increased resistance from Syrian tank and commando units. The Israelis nevertheless made considerable progress.

By nightfall, armored Battle Group V-2, reinforced by infantry and engineers, had advanced northward along the road Hasbaiya, Dhunaybah, Kfar Meshki to within one kilometer of Dhunaybah. At the same time, Battle Group V-3, composed of paratroops reinforced by tanks and engineers, opened the Kaoukaba-Karaoun road all the way to Zilaya. Armored Battle Group V-1, which was moving on the most difficult axis, along the trails of the Jabal bir ed Dahr ridge, nevertheless made the most spectacular progress and took the village of Lavi (Libbaya).

Summary

June 9 was the critical day of the Bekaa Valley battle, and of the war. Not only did the IAF gain complete control of the air, and eliminate the potential air defense threat to that control, but Israeli ground forces established a comparable preeminence on the ground. The forward Syrian defense line, along which Damascus seems to have expected to halt the Israeli onslaught, at least temporarily, was irretrievably shredded. This was accomplished in part by skillful maneuvering, which permitted the Israelis to enfilade the line from the west, and in part by brutal shock tactics, which demonstrated that the Israeli combat effectiveness superiority, so clearly displayed in the 1973 war, was at least as great as it had ever been.

Chapter XV
Battle of
the Bekaa Valley:
Denouement

The Fifth Day (June 10, 5:00 A.M.—June 11, 5:00 A.M.)

Bekaa Forces Group: Task Forces Z, V, H. During the previous two days the Bekaa Forces Group had overrun the forward Syrian security zone and by the evening of June 9 was approaching the Syrian main defense zone in the area between Lake Karaoun and Rashaiya. This defense zone consisted of several brigade-sized defense positions, built primarily in mountainous terrain along the eastern and western ridges of Jabal Aarbi and on the western slopes of the Anti-Lebanon Mountains. The principal Syrian force in the area was the 1st Tank Division, which was deployed in the areas of Lake Karaoun, Joub Jannine, and Rashaiya with nearly 300 tanks, including scores of T-72s, over 150 artillery pieces, and about the same number of antitank weapons mounted on APCs (BRDM-2).

At 6:00 A.M. on June 10 the battle for the main defense zone commenced. Task Forces V and Z attacked a Syrian tank brigade deployed on both sides of the upper Litani River south of Lake Karaoun. In the ensuing battle Vardi's and Lev's attack was supported by massive air strikes and artillery fire directed mainly at Syrian tank deployments and roads. Task Force Z attacked and defeated a reinforced tank battalion west of the Litani River in the Mashghara and Karaoun Dam area. At the same time, to the east, Battle Group V-3, composed mostly of paratroops advancing from Yohmor, and armored Battle Group V-1, coming from Wadi Hafufa, destroyed another Syrian tank battalion which was desperately attempting to hold both banks of the Litani.

The two Israeli task forces then continued northeastward to the vicinity of Kfar Meshki and Dhunaybah where at about noon, they ran into another Syrian tank brigade. This encounter also was fierce, but shorter, and the Syrians soon fell back. Task Force Z then moved north-ward along the road to Aitanit and Saghbine. Battle Group V-1 advanced with minor opposition from the center of the Jabal Aarbi mountains to Kamed el Laouz, about ten kilometers from the Beirut-Damascus highway. These successful operations by Task Forces Z and V enabled Task Force H to advance from Rashaiya north and eastward. Early in the evening forward elements of Task Force H, following a mountainous road through rugged terrain reached Kfar Quoq and Baka, each about five kilometers from the Syrian border. This advance sealed off Fatahland, formerly an autonomous PLO enclave, from the Syrian hinterland.

The Syrian command now decided to deploy what was left of its badly defeated forces along a new line of defense north of Joub Jannine, Kamed el Laouz, and Mdoukha. However, the Israeli Air Force com-menced massive attacks on Syrian deployments, making it very difficult for the Syrian troops to establish a new defensive line.

By nightfall of June 10 the general situation of the opposing forces was as follows:

Israeli Bekaa Groups

• Task Force Z was advancing along the "western" road (west of Lake Karaoun and Sahel el Karaoun). After encountering only weak resis-tance, it had taken Kafraiya, and was continuing northward toward Kabb Elias.

• Battle Group V-1 (armor) had taken up positions on the ridges to the north of Kamed el Laouz.

• Battle Group V-2 (armor) was deployed in the Kaoukaba, Ain Arab areas.

• Battle Group V-3 (paratroops) was deployed in the Karaoun sector.

• Task Force H was on the mountain road between Rashaiya and Aaiha. Forward elements of the task force had reached Kfar Quoq and Baka.

Syrian Forces

Faced with an imminent Israeli breakthrough of the Karaoun, Rashaiya defensive line, the Syrian command estimated that the Israelis had two possible courses of action.

• The IDF main effort could turn eastward and threaten Damascus, less than 40 kilometers away.

• The IDF could continue northward to block the Beirut-Damascus highway, and cut off the Syrian forces in the Lebanon Mountains and Beirut areas from the Bekaa Valley and Syria.

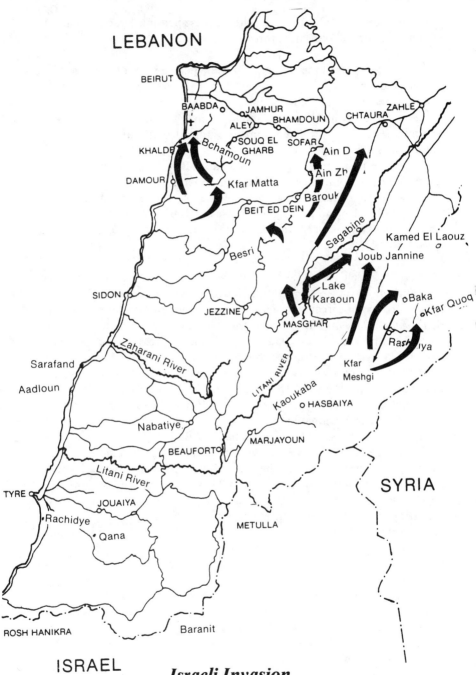

Israeli Invasion
Day Five — June 10, 1982

In order to be able to meet either of these possible Israeli actions, the Syrian command deployed its forces as follows:

- Remnants of the 1st Tank Division (elements of one tank and one mechanized brigade) were deployed in a half circle along the line Ain Arab-Kamed el Laouz, four kilometers northeast of Joub Jannine.
- The 3d Tank Division—moving into Lebanon from Syria—was to occupy a second line of defense in the Kabb Elias, Shtaura, and Jdeidet Yabus areas.
- The 47th Tank Brigade, in the Zahle, Rayak sectors, was to form a reserve ready to counterattack in case of an Israeli breakthrough.
- One additional tank brigade was deployed near the frontier, just west of the Mt. Hermon range, to repulse any IDF advance through Dir el Ashiyer and Kahle toward Katana (Syria), thus protecting Damascus from the southwest.

The Israelis were aware that the Syrian 3d Tank Division was rushing from Syria to take up its assigned defensive positions. The Bekaa Forces Group was directed to speed up its advance and attempt to reach the Beirut-Damascus highway before the 3d Tank Division should arrive. While Task Forces Z and H made considerable progress during the night of June 10/11, serious problems developed in the Task Force V sector.

Battle Group V-2 had been ordered to advance as fast as possible to Mazraat Azi (on the road to Anjar), and join Battle Group V-1 at the Kamed el Laouz crossroad. From that point it was to advance northward toward the Beirut-Damascus highway behind Battle Group V-1. At 1:00 A.M. on June 11, as the leading elements of Battle Group V-1 passed the crossroad at Kamed el Laouz and were approaching the village of Soultane Yacoub, they suddenly found themselves inside the defensive perimeter of the Syrian 1st Tank Division. Both sides were surprised. Syrian tanks, APCs, and other vehicles were parked along the road, and their crews were preparing meals. In the ensuing melee, two Israeli spearhead tanks were hit and started burning, blocking the road. The tanks behind them found themselves under fire from all directions. The advance was halted, and through the rest of the night Task Force V was engaged in extracting its elements trapped inside the Syrian lines.

The failure of Task Force V to break through on the Kamed el Laouz—Soultane Yacoub axis made it impossible for the Israelis to reach the Beirut-Damascus highway during the night of June 10/11. The Syrians succeeded in containing the Israeli forces and stabilized their defenses to the south of the highway.

At the time of the clash at Soultane Yacoub, the Bekaa Forces Group was deployed as follows:

- Task Force Z had bypassed the Aammik marshes, and its leading detachment was several kilometers south of Kabb Elias.
- Task Force V occupied the ridge of Jabal Aarbi to the line Kamed el Laouz, Joub Jannine.
- Task Force H was deployed along the line Kfar Danis—Kfar Quoq.

Air Activities. During the night of June 9/10 the Syrian Command had decided to move a tank brigade southwest from the Zahle-Rayak area, to block the advance of Israeli Task Force D toward the highway (see Chapter XVI). This move, however, would have seriously weakened Syrian defense over the eastern portion of that vital communication route, and so it was also decided that the area would have to be secured by another tank brigade, shifted to the Bekaa Valley from Homs, in central Syria. The movement began later than intended, and the brigade from Syria was still on the road, just west of the Lebanon-Syria border, shortly after sunrise on June 10. It was immediately attacked by the IAF, which was interdicting all roads leading from Syria into Lebanon. The brigade lost more than 20 tanks, and most of its vehicles. However, the remnants of the brigade grimly continued their movement, and reached Zahle and Rayak later in the morning of the 10th.

The destruction of the Syrian SAMs in Lebanon, as well as the absolute air superiority enjoyed by the IAF, coupled with the deep penetrations achieved by Israeli troops, had broken land lines of communication between many Syrian units. A number of them were virtually isolated, and all were cut off completely or partially from reinforcements and supplies. All routes through which the Syrians could bring in fresh troops and supplies were now vulnerable to Israeli attacks from the air, and in many cases from the ground.

The Sixth Day (June 11, 5:00 A.M.—June 11, 12:00 noon)

The Israeli and Syrian commands agreed to a ceasefire starting at noon. However, the Israeli government excluded the PLO from this agreement, and reiterated its pledge to continue operations against the PLO, until its destruction. (A unilateral ceasefire with the PLO was declared by Israel late the next day, June 12, at 9:00 P.M., but it was broken on the 13th. Each side accused the other of breaking it.)

Bekaa Forces Group: Task Forces Z, V, H. At sunrise, Task Force Z turned southward toward the Aammik marshes. By mid-morning it had reached Mansoura, where it clashed with the Syrian 82d Tank Brigade of the 3d Tank Division. During the fight several T-72 tanks were destroyed.

By morning Task Force V, supported by heavy artillery barrages and air strikes, succeeded in extricating its troops from behind Syrian lines at Soultane Yacoub. In view of the forthcoming ceasefire, no serious efforts were made to break through the formidable Syrian defenses.

Task Force H jumped off early in the morning, but was stopped by elements of the Syrian 3d Tank Division along the line Baka–Jabal Damduna. In the ensuing battle a number of T-72 tanks were either destroyed or damaged.

Altogether, according to Israeli reports, in encounters between Syrian and Israeli armor, nine Soviet-made T-72 tanks, the most advanced tanks in the Soviet arsenal, were knocked out by Israeli Merkava tanks, without the loss of any Merkavas. Merkava, the Israeli-designed and built tank, is equipped with a fire combat system that includes a laser range-finder and an ultra-sophisticated night vision system. It has a better engine than other tanks used by the IDF, which gives it greater maneuverability. Its fire-extinguishing system is activated the moment the tank is hit. The Merkava seems to be better protected than the Soviet T-72, the US M-1 or German Leopard II. It also has a greatly improved system to protect its crew.

Shortly before noon, as the ceasefire hour was approaching, the Bekaa Forces Group took up defensive positions along the line Mansoura–Joub Jannine–Kamed el Laouz–Kfar Danis–Jabal Damduna.

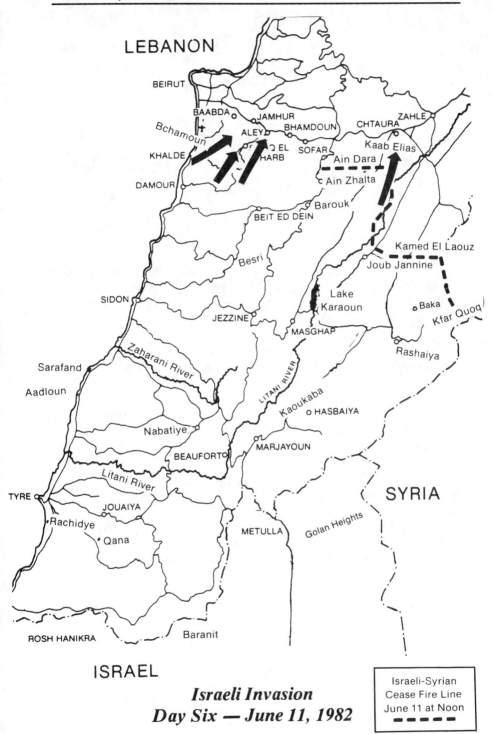

Israeli Invasion
Day Six — June 11, 1982

Israeli-Syrian
Cease Fire Line
June 11 at Noon

Chapter XVI
Mop-up in the West:
Advance on Beirut

Although on June 9 the main focus of the war shifted dramatically from the Israeli operations against the PLO in the western and central regions of southern Lebanon to the engagements with Syrian forces in the Bekaa Valley, nevertheless those operations did not slacken.

The Fourth Day (June 9, 5:00 A.M.—June 10, 5:00 A.M.)

Task Force A (Western Sector). Mopping-up operations continued by General Mordechai's battle groups between the Awali river and the Israeli border. The entire city of Tyre was cleared. In the Rachidiye refugee camp only a few strongpoints remained in PLO hands.

The battle for Sidon was still in progress. The PLO was holding several blocks in the center of the city close to the port area where the PLO headquarters were located, as well as a few strongholds in other sectors. Mordechai postponed an attack on the huge refugee camp el Hilwe, because a large number of civilians were being forcibly held by PLO fighters in well-prepared, fortified areas, schools, and mosques.

Task Force B (Western Sector). At sunrise Task Force B attacked Damour. Initially, at the outskirts of the town, PLO resistance was light. However, as elements of the task force approached Damour proper, the resistance stiffened. Israeli forces encountered many ambushes, which were particularly difficult to deal with under conditions of urban warfare. Pressing forward, the paratroops reached the center of the town, where George Habash's PFLP main defenses were located. A determined assault took several strongpoints and broke the defenders' will to resist. The PFLP defense collapsed. The Israelis began mopping-up operations, and by evening Damour was in their hands. During the night Task Force B got a needed night of rest, their first in 96 hours.

Task Force C (Western Sector). During the day, Task Force C, together with elements of Task Forces A and B, fought its way along the Coastal Road toward Beirut. Progress was slow because of numerous PLO counterattacks and ambushes. By evening, the Israeli forces were halfway between Damour and Khalde, approaching the southern suburbs of Beirut. The Syrians recognized that the capture of Damour put the Israelis at the gates of Beirut. The Syrian command decided to fight a decisive battle for Beirut south of the city and quickly took up defensive positions along the line Khalde-Ain Aanoub, with forward outposts at Duha and Bchamoun. These defenses were manned by the Syrian 622d Independent Infantry Battalion, one commando regiment, engineer and antitank units, and one PLA tank regiment. All approaches to the defense line were mined and other obstacles set up.

Task Force D (Central Sector). Throughout June 9, Task Force D was busy extracting casualties from the village of Ain Zhalta, and made no progress. In the evening armored Battle Group D-1 was reinforced with infantry. Before sunrise June 10, after a night-long flanking march, infantry units reached the rear of the Syrian Ain Zhalta defense system, ready to attack in the morning, while the tanks were prepared to attack from the front (south).

The Fifth Day (June 10, 5:00 A.M.—June 11, 5:00 A.M.)

Task Force A (Western Sector). Fighting continued in the center of Sidon, where the PLO held several blocks. The area was heavily shelled by artillery and naval guns and bombed by the Israeli Air Force. The Israelis, trying to minimize casualties—their own and civilian—advanced very slowly. A large group of PLO fighters converted the city's main hospital into a fortress. Others barricaded themselves in separate houses.

From the military point of view, of course, the city was already taken; the few areas controlled by the PLO were isolated. Nevertheless the capture of these urban strongpoints posed a dilemma for General Mordechai, since he could see that it would be difficult to take the PLO positions without civilian casualties. The Israelis geared themselves for a costly and possibly protracted struggle, involving house-to-house and block-to-block battles with elusive PLO combatants who merged into the civilian population and who knew the city better than the IDF. This was also the situation at the refugee camp of el Hilwe, at the outskirts of Sidon, which the PLO had turned into a stronghold, keeping thousands of Palestinian civilians as hostages. The PLO expected that the Israelis would not mount an assault which could cause heavy non-combatant losses. All attempts to negotiate with the PLO extremists holed up in two of the camp's mosques and neighboring buildings failed. The answer to local Lebanese emissaries sent by the Israelis to mediate was always the same: "We will fight to the death."

To the south and southeast of Sidon, as far back as the Israeli border, Task Force A continued mopping up remnants of the PLO forces, and tightening the noose around the few remaining strongpoints. Progress was slow, as the Israelis continued their efforts to safeguard civilians.

Task Force B (Western Sector). After a night's rest, paratroops of Task Force B commenced their advance eastward along the mountainous road toward Kfar Matta and then turned northward, heading for Baissour and Bchamoun. During the day, Syrian and PLO commandos ambushed the advancing Israeli force several times, but were unable to halt the advance. By evening forward elements of the paratroops approached the village of Bchamoun, where a reinforced Syrian commando battalion was deployed. The Israeli task force commander decided to regroup, bring up his reserves, and attack the Syrian positions the next day.

Task Force C (Western Sector). During the day Task Force C, including Colonel Geva's 211th Armored Brigade (formerly Battle Group A-4), advanced along the Coastal Road. The Israelis overcame numerous PLO and Syrian ambushes and counterattacks, and by evening had reached the southern outskirts of Khalde. The advance was supported by Navy gunboats which shelled PLO strongpoints and other targets. From Khalde the Israelis could overlook and control the Beirut International Airport, about four kilometers to the north, and could clearly see the tall buildings in the center of Beirut, less than ten kilometers away.

At this point General Kahalani decided to envelop the PLO and Syrian forces deployed in the western and southern suburbs of Beirut, and cut them off from the Beirut-Damascus highway. He ordered his forward elements to strike eastward into the mountains just east of the coastal plain. This maneuver would also assist Task Force B, since the Syrian commando battalion at Bchamoun facing that task force would be in danger of encirclement.

Task Force D (Central Sector). In the morning, Task Force D carried out a coordinated assault on Ain Zhalta from the south and north. The Syrians were unable to cope with attack from two directions. They withdrew in confusion, and Ain Zhalta was finally captured by the Israelis. Battle Group D-1 then continued northward toward the Beirut-Damascus highway. However, at the approaches to Ain Dara, the Israelis again met strong Syrian resistance from well-prepared defensive positions. General Einan called for several air strikes and tank-killing helicopter sorties, causing heavy Syrian losses. Nevertheless, recognizing that a frontal attack on Ain Dara could result in many casualties, the battle group commander decided to forsake the attack and instead to occupy the hills around the village, giving him a commanding view and field of fire over the Beirut-Damascus highway, only three kilometers away.

The Sixth Day (June 11, 5:00 A.M.—June 12, 5:00 A.M.)

The ceasefire in the Bekaa Valley, which commenced at noon June 11, didn't include the western sector. There the Israeli forces continued their operations against PLO fighters and Syrian units, whose forces were intermingled.

Task Force A (Western Sector). Most of the PLO fighters encircled in the center of Sidon surrendered during the morning, leaving the entire city, except for a handful of PLO strongpoints, in Israeli hands. The refugee camp at el Hilwe remained surrounded. Intermittent shelling of areas occupied by the PLO continued during the day as Israeli troops slowly squeezed the PLO fighters into the center of the camp.

Task Force B (Western Sector). In the morning Task Force B attacked and captured the village of Bchamoun, defended by Syrian commandos and PLO units. The fighting in the area continued throughout the day.

Task Force C (Western Sector). Early in the morning, Task Force C took Khalde, where it encountered only limited resistance. During the night of June 11-12 most of the PLO and Syrian troops withdrew to Beirut, leaving only rear guards who were no match for Israeli forces. The 211th Armored Brigade came close to the southern edge of the Beirut International Airport, where it was halted by PLO and Syrian antitank detachments and artillery and Katyusha fire. Israeli troops took up positions on the hills overlooking the airport from the south and southeast.

Task Force D (Central Sector). Reinforced by infantry elements of the Golani Brigade, which had arrived during the night from Jezzine, Task Force D started to advance along several mountainous roads and trails toward the Beirut-Damascus highway. Under Israeli pressure Syrian troops withdrew slowly northward. In compliance with the ceasefire, the Israelis stopped their advance at noon. At that time, Task Force D was only a few kilometers away from the Beirut-Damascus highway, and in fact could control the road from the dominating hills.

Chapter XVII
Ceasefire
and
Consolidation

The Encirclement of Beirut, June 11-13

On June 11, General Drori ordered Task Force B to take Ain Aanoub in the Shouf Mountains and open the road to Kfar Shima, a Christian village held by Phalangists. The sector, which included a number of fortified villages, was defended by a Syrian commando battalion reinforced by tanks, artillery, and antitank weapons and by several PLO units. The engagement that ensued developed into one of the fiercest battles fought by Task Force B. Israeli attacks and Syrian-PLO counterattacks lasted for the entire day (June 12). The Syrian commandos resisted stubbornly and the Israelis had to fight from house to house, and from hill to hill. The battle ended after 14 hours when the Syrians and the PLO withdrew, leaving on the battlefield over 100 men killed, and many more wounded. Some 25 Syrian tanks and numerous APCs were destroyed.

Meanwhile, recognizing that active field operations against the PLO had virtually come to a halt, the Israelis declared a unilateral ceasefire at 9:00 P.M. on the 12th. This was tacitly accepted by the PLO. Although the ceasefire was broken the following day, with each side claiming that the other had broken it, the general situation around the periphery of Beirut remained unchanged.

On Sunday, June 13, at 11:00 A.M., exactly one week after the operation started, Israeli paratroops under Colonel Yair Yarom linked up with Lebanese Force (Phalangists) troops at a roadblock near Basaba, closing the ring around Beirut. Meeting the Israeli troops was Fadi Frem, Bashir Jemayel's deputy, who exchanged friendly handshakes with Yarom and other paratroopers. The PLO and Syrian troops in Beirut found themselves in a pocket, totally encircled by the IDF and the Phalangists.

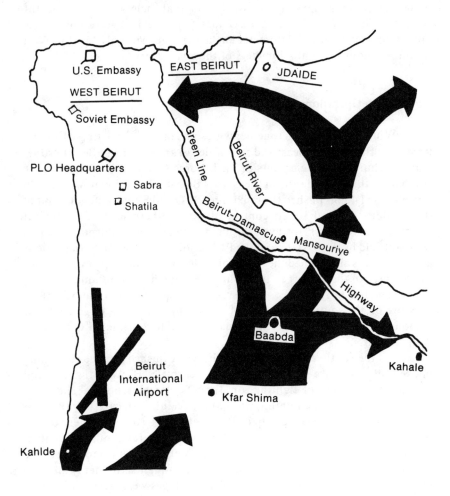

Israeli Advance in Beirut Area
June 12-14, 1982

Task Force B, in conjunction with elements of Task Force C, continued to advance. By the morning of June 14, the Israelis had occupied the Beirut suburbs of Jdaide, Mansouriye and Baabda, which dominate the Lebanese capital from the mountains to the east and southeast. They also penetrated into some urban areas of greater Beirut, namely Bourj Hammoud, Tel Zaatar, part of the Ain Rummanah neighborhood, and the Ashrafiya area. The encircled PLO and Syrian forces were completely bottled up in a 25 square kilometer enclave, in the primarily Muslim West Beirut, including several kilometers of the coastal strip.

Mopping-up Operations

While Task Force B, together with some units of Task Force C, were fighting in the hills southeast and east of Beirut and in parts of Beirut proper and its suburbs, main elements of Task Force C were engaged in intense combat north of Khalde and at the nearby Beirut International Airport. On June 14, the Israelis pushed the remaining PLO and Syrian defenders out of the Khalde area and seized control of the southern part of the Beirut International Airport. However, the main runways and the airport terminal were still held by the Syrians and the PLO until June 20, when Syrian troops and PLO units abandoned the terminal building and took up new positions to the north of the airport in the Bourj el Barajneh refugee camp.

The Israeli Air Force, and Israeli artillery and naval guns kept up pressure on the southern districts of West Beirut. Among targets hit and demolished was the six-story headquarters building of the PLO at Bourj Abu Haydar.

To the south, elements of Task Force A flushed out the remaining pockets of resistance in Sidon and the nearby el Hilwe refugee camp. During the last day of fighting, on June 14, Israeli troops shelled and bombed the camp. The fighting was hand-to-hand with carefully targeted artillery support. The last group of PLO defenders, some 500 men strong, barricaded itself in two mosques, along with several thousand civilian hostages. The PLO troops declared that they were determined to fight to the death. On June 15, however, they had second thoughts. Suddenly all PLO resistance ceased, and most of the civilian hostages were freed unharmed.

By June 17 Israeli casualties had risen to 214 killed, 1,176 wounded (76 severely, 237 moderately, and 863 lightly), 23 missing in action, and one pilot taken prisoner by the PLO. The highest ranking Israeli officer to fall in battle was Major General Yekutiel Adam. As Israeli troops were approaching Beirut, Adam, former deputy Chief of Staff, was inspecting the progress of operations for the Chief of Staff. He entered a house in Duha, overlooking the area of the Beirut International Airport. Having seen everything he could from an upstairs veranda, he came down the staircase, accompanied by Colonel Haim Sela, to be shot at pointblank range by seven PLO guerrillas who were hiding under the stairs. The PLO men then fled. Israeli soldiers present on the scene gave chase, killing three and capturing two of the assailants. Other officers lost included 1 colonel, 2 lieutenant colonels, 65 majors, 16 captains, 28 lieutenants, and 14 second lieutenants. Among the wounded, 194 were officers, and 982 NCOs and privates.

The IDF held 149 Syrian prisoners, of whom 16 were officers. The highest ranking prisoner was a lieutenant colonel. Many hundreds of Syrians had been killed and several thousand wounded.

PLO losses were about 1,000 killed, some 2,200 wounded, and over 5,000 prisoners of war. Not all prisoners of war were Palestinians. Among the captives were men from Austria, Germany, Syria, Jordan, Egypt, Bangladesh, Yemen, Kuwait, Iraq, Pakistan, Niger, Algeria, Libya, Saudi Arabia, Sri Lanka, Iran, Somalia, and Mali. The status of the PLO prisoners presented a legal problem to Israeli authorities. Israel is a signatory to the 1947 Geneva Convention, which defines a prisoner of war as someone serving in the army of a recognized state. A POW enjoys privileges, such as visits from the International Red Cross, and may not be put on trial. Israel does not recognize the PLO and has, in the past, prosecuted anyone suspected of belonging to it as being a member of a hostile organization. Foreign nationals among the prisoners, including citizens of non-Arab countries, presented special problems.

In a legal sense captured PLO guerrillas were not entitled to treatment as prisoners of war because the PLO is not a national fighting force under international law. The Israelis decided, however, to accord most of them all the privileges due to POWs. They, and some Lebanese suspected to be involved with the PLO, were sent to a specially built POW camp at Ansar, approximately 15 kilometers northeast of Tyre. Only those PLO leaders, and other individuals determined by the Israelis to have been involved in serious terrorist acts, were sent to Athlit, an Israeli prison near Haifa. Most of the foreign nationals, after close interrogation, were returned to the countries of their origin.

Although Beirut was encircled, the deployment of Syrian and PLO forces at Aley, Bhamdoun, and other sectors of the outer defense of the city not only limited the freedom of movement of Israeli troops, but could provide a springboard for counterattacks aimed at breaking the siege of Beirut. The Syrians were entrenched in positions which blocked all roads to Beirut from the east, and had within artillery range the Lebanese Ministry of Defense at Yarzeh, the Presidential Palace at Baabda, the Phalangist Headquarters in East Beirut, and Israeli Forward Headquarters. In addition, the dominating features of the Aley area enabled the Syrians to bring direct fire against the Israeli troops at Baabda and Kfar Shima. Because of this situation, General Drori decided to force the Syrians out of the Aley and Bhamdoun areas, to tighten the siege of Beirut, and to occupy a stretch of the Beirut-Damascus highway between Beirut and Sofar. The plan called for Task Force D to advance northeast on Bhamdoun from the Mansouriye area, and for Task Force B to attack southeast toward Aley from the Baabda area. Syrian forces in the Aley and Bhamdoun areas consisted of two commando regiments, two tank battalions, one artillery battalion, engineer elements, and PLO units.

Tightening the Grip on Beirut

On June 22, the ceasefire broke down as the Israelis commenced their planned operation. At first, Syrian and PLO troop concentrations at Bhamdoun, Aley, Sofar, Kahle and other towns and villages came under heavy artillery barrages and air strikes. Syrian SAM batteries, which were endangering Israeli planes, were hit and destroyed by artillery fire. Artillery bombardment and air strikes were followed by the attack of mixed armor and infantry battle groups which advanced along the assigned axis. Heavy fighting raged for every village and hill leading to the Beirut-Damascus highway.

In the morning of June 23, to the north of Mansouriye additional Israeli planes, artillery, and tanks were called into action to repel a Syrian commando counterattack against Einan's troops approaching the Beirut-Damascus highway from the south. The Syrian counterattack was backed by artillery, mortars, and antitank fire. As the Israeli fighter bombers approached to give support, they were intercepted by a number of MiGs of the Syrian Air Force. In the air battle two Syrian planes were shot down without any Israeli loss. This brought the number of Syrian aircraft destroyed since the start of the war to 87.

On June 24, Syrian and Israeli tanks fought a seesaw battle close to the highway for some 16 hours, while artillery guns from both sides pounded each other.

By noon, June 25, Aley and Bhamdoun were in Israeli hands and Task Forces B and D had succeeded in taking most of the ridges to the north and south of the highway. In Bhamdoun and Aley alone, the Israelis destroyed 15 Syrian tanks and captured intact a similar number abandoned by their crews. The Syrian lines were broken and Syrian forces retreated eastward toward the Bekaa Valley. By evening the entire outer defense perimeter of Beirut was held by the IDF, including a 15-kilometer stretch of the Beirut-Damascus highway from East Beirut to Sofar. A new ceasefire was arranged and went into effect at 6:00 P.M., June 25. Only the Dahr el

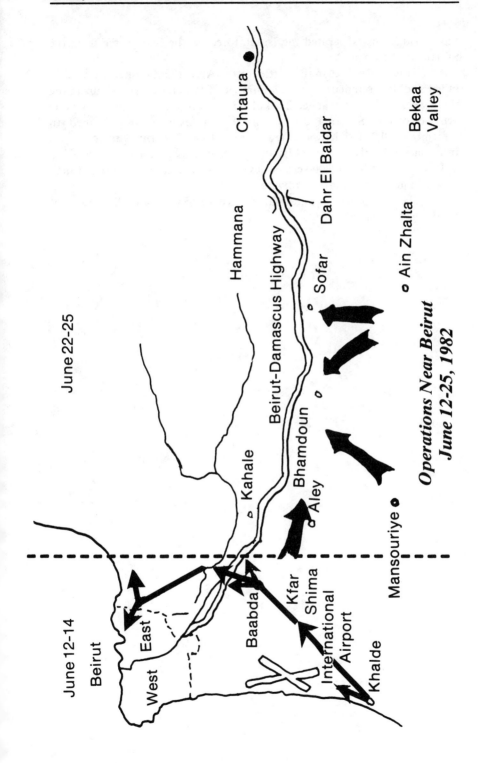

*Operations Near Beirut
June 12-25, 1982*

Baider ridge now separated the Israeli forces in the Beirut area from the Syrians in the Bekaa Valley.

Israeli casualties in the battle for the Aley, Bhamdoun area were 30 killed and 95 wounded. The total number of Israeli casualties during the three-week operation reached 260 killed in action, 1,270 wounded, and one prisoner of war. Syrian and PLO casualty figures were not published. In December 1982, the Kuwaiti newspaper, *Al Rai al Am*, quoted Syrian Information Minister Ahmed Iskander as stating that "the Israeli invasion of Lebanon cost Syria 5,000 casualties and several billions of dollars worth of warplanes and military hardware."

The battle for Aley and Bhamdoun ended Syrian and PLO hopes of breaking the siege of Beirut.

Chapter XVIII
A Military Assessment

General

With the ceasefire agreement with the Syrians in effect, and the PLO swept away from its strongholds in southern Lebanon and encircled in Beirut, the first and the second phases of the Israeli campaign came to an end. From a strictly military point of view it was a brilliantly executed military operation, carried out with precise coordination between major branches of the Israeli Armed Forces—infantry, armor, artillery, engineers, Air Force, Navy, and vital supporting elements. Meticulous planning and execution accounted for the lightning advance into Lebanon's difficult, mountainous terrain, often ahead of schedule.

The logistical problems of sustaining this thrust of over 100 kilometers were tremendous. Ammunition, fuel, and food had to follow advancing troops; ground forces needed the constant cooperation and support of the Air Force; the Navy had to coordinate with the Army; amphibious landings were made far behind the front lines; artillery and engineers had to work in tandem with speeding infantry and armored spearheads. All these were accomplished because communications was instant and the necessary intelligence was usually available on call.

In less than three startling weeks the PLO war machine in South Lebanon and in Beirut, with its modern weapons and equipment, and an immense quantity of ammunition, was destroyed. Although in several places PLO resistance was fierce, PLO fighters were no match for the IDF, which quickly achieved the officially declared aim of the operation, and much more. According to unofficial figures nearly 1,200 PLO guerrillas were killed in action and some 3,700 wounded.

Syria, too, had to bow to the superb performance of the Israeli forces, especially its Air Force and armor. In intense fighting Syrian troops suffered heavy losses and retreated along the entire front. Unconfirmed Syrian losses were about 1,000 killed and nearly 3,700 wounded. The Beirut-Damascus highway was cut, and the Syrian garrison in Beirut encircled. Nineteen Syrian SAM batteries and at least 87 aircraft were destroyed, leaving the Israeli Air Force master of the air.

Ground Operations

The 1982 War in Lebanon was the only Arab-Israeli war which was fought exclusively against Arab forces occupying the territory of an independent Arab state, and not against that state. It was also the only war in which the PLO was engaged against the IDF as a major participant. For the Israeli Army, which was used to fighting regular armies, the encounter with an essentially guerrilla force was a challenge which it successfully met. An especially difficult problem for the Israelis to solve was the intermingling of the PLO fighters with the civilian population, Palestinian and Lebanese alike, during combat in densely populated urban areas.

The Syrian Army, although not totally defeated, had been severely jolted and its self-confidence shaken. Had it not been for the pressure by the United States for a ceasefire, which was declared on June 11, the IDF might well have driven the Syrian Army from Lebanon in three to four more days of combat. The Lebanese Army assumed a position of "friendly" neutrality toward Israel, while the Phalangist Christian militia openly welcomed and cooperated with the IDF.

The war in Lebanon was the first in Israel's history in which objectives were determined from the beginning to the end in a master military plan prepared well in advance by the General Staff and not made known to the public nor presented in detail to the Cabinet. The initiative was in Israeli hands, and was used to the full. Considering the scope and objectives of the operation, the IDF achieved a total strategic surprise.

The Israelis could have mobilized and committed more troops, but a larger force would not have provided any tactical advantage. The IDF had enough troops available to hit the enemy hard and to maintain ever-increasing pressure. They did not move in piecemeal fashion or in stages, as they had during the Litani operation. Instead they struck with the entire force and chose the pace which suited them best. The Israeli planners were strongly opposed to movement in stages. They were afraid that in such a controversial war each follow-up step would be subject to external and internal political pressure, which could doom the entire offensive. Not only the drive to Beirut and the Beirut-Damascus highway, but even the highly publicized mission of 40 kilometers, which would have halted the Israeli advance approximately at the Zahrani River south of Sidon and the Karaoun Lake in the Bekaa, might have failed.

The arrival of Israeli spearheads at the gates of Beirut took place generally in accordance with the plan. The intention was to reach Beirut and to leave the battle for the city to the Phalangists. However, Northern Command contingency plans foresaw the possibility of a siege of Beirut and the need for the IDF to enter the city to render assistance to the Phalangist allies.

In the logistical area, the lessons of the 1973 War had been learned, and the Israelis were well prepared. In previous wars, the IDF—except for the Navy—had depended mainly on imported major weapon systems. In the Lebanese War the Israelis, for the first time, relied largely on their own weapon systems, developed and produced by the Israeli armament industry. Major breakdowns were infrequent, indicating a high level of equipment maintenance and preparedness. All weapons and equipment left the depots in combat-ready condition. In the 1973 October War over 100 tanks had been left behind at mobilization because of various deficiencies, and some 15 percent of other equipment was not combat-ready. In the Lebanese War, on the other hand, not one tank or other major weapon system remained behind because of unserviceability, an impressive administrative and logistical achievement, with far-reaching beneficial effects on the conduct of the war. In the first line units equipment was modern and new. In later wave units, although some "hand-me down" armament and equipment were used, they were in perfect condition. Of course, it must be remembered that in 1973 the Israelis were surprised, whereas in 1982 they had had adequate time to bring everything to a state of full readiness.

Difficult mountainous roads in the operational area forced the Israelis to use unorthodox and improvised methods of delivering supplies to the combat zone. Armament, ammunition, equipment, food, and fuel were often delivered by air drops, by helicopters, or by landing craft along the beaches.

Introduction of protective measures for soldiers, such as fireproof clothing, flak jackets, and protective glasses, saved many lives, and assured lighter wounds. The protective clothing was the result of one of the lessons learned from the October War. Doctors were particularly enthusiastic about the merits of the fireproof coveralls and gloves worn by tank crews, which saved many from grave injuries and burns. Over 90 percent of the casualties were evacuated by air directly to civilian hospitals in Israel, and this also saved lives.

The timing and circumstances of the war also were advantageous to the Israelis. The war was fought on only one front, not against a coalition of Arab states on two or three fronts, as in previous wars, thus providing the IDF with more freedom of action. Cairo was bound not to intervene because of the peace accord. Jordan and Syria were engaged in an acrimonious dispute and on the brink of open hostility; it was most unlikely that King Hussein would get involved on the side of his bitter enemy, Assad. Iraq, which in 1973 had sent about 500 tanks and nearly 20,000 troops to reinforce the badly shaken Syrians, was itself involved in a deadly war with Iran.

To Israel, the war was not a life-or-death struggle, and the Israelis had ample opportunity to battle-test many weapons. Among these were the TOW antitank missile; the Merkava tank; the HETZ (arrow) armor-piercing, fin-stabilized, discarding-sabot (APFSDS) ammunition; and certain types of artillery and reconnaissance systems.

Air Operations

Whereas the Israeli ground forces started the Lebanese campaign on June 6, the Israeli Air Force commenced continuous operations over Lebanon in the afternoon of June 4, with an attack on PLO targets in West Beirut and South Lebanon. Operations of the IAF were not opposed by the Syrian Air Force until June 7 when, in an air battle over Beirut, one Syrian MiG was shot down. The next day, on June 8, Syrian air activities increased, and the IAF destroyed six Syrian aircraft in air encounters.

Up to June 9, all of the IAF close air support operations were directed against the PLO. Up to that time, the IAF was strictly limited to defensive operations against Syrian planes, and was forbidden to cross the Syrian border. On June 8, when the first serious clashes between Syrian and Israeli ground troops occurred, the ground forces requested close air support, but the Air Force—following explicit orders from the Israeli government—declined, and continued only authorized reconnaissance flights over Syrian positions in Lebanon. At noon on June 9, the IAF received permission to attack Syrian ground targets. This change was triggered by two events: the arrival of new Syrian SAM batteries in the Bekaa Valley on June 7 and 8, and Syrian air attacks against Israeli ground forces on both days.

IAF operations on June 9 were directed essentially against the 19 SAM batteries in the Bekaa Valley and against Syrian Air Force planes which engaged the attacking Israeli aircraft. The Israelis had been preparing for the attack on the SAMs and other air defense installations in the Bekaa since the spring of 1981 when the Syrians first deployed their missiles in Lebanon. The situation was not substantially changed, although the threat was increased, when the Syrians moved an additional air defense brigade from the Golan Heights area to the Bekaa early in June.

It took the Israelis less than three hours to destroy 17 of the 19 missile batteries. At the same time 29 Syrian aircraft were downed in air battles without any loss to the Israelis. This number does not include several Syrian MiGs which were apparently hit by Syrian SAMs. Although all SAM batteries were manned by Syrian troops, many foreign observers believed that Soviet advisors were present at the firing positions and control centers. This has been denied by the Syrians and there is no hard evidence available to refute the denials.

The destruction of the Syrian air defense system on June 9 assured the IAF total air supremacy over Lebanon. Nevertheless, the Syrian Air Force continued to fight. On June 10, despite the heavy losses already suffered, courageous Syrian pilots once more challenged the Israelis. The effort was unsuccessful, and the Syrians lost 35 more aircraft, bringing the total number of planes lost to 71. On June 25, when the second and final ceasefire with the Syrians came into effect, total Syrian aircraft losses in the war had reached at least 87 aircraft, including several advanced MiG-23 fighters. Also destroyed were six Gazelle attack helicopters. During the same period, the Israeli Air Force had lost only one Skyhawk, shot down on June 6 by a PLO SA-7, one attack helicopter, and one medical evacuation helicopter.

Israeli air operations and command and control procedures were centrally controlled and highly successful. Senior commanders could take personal control of each engagement, and even of individual aircraft, at any time.

A brief survey of the air war indicates that the principal advantages of the Israelis over the Syrians were: the IAF ability to coordinate the activities of all aircraft, the quick reactions of the pilots and ground controllers, and the ability to exploit to the maximum the capabilities of their equipment. The Israelis believe that the human factor (personnel as opposed to hardware) is more important than ever in the conduct of modern warfare. Thus they believe that high technology cannot be decisive without the trained ability to use it. And here apparently lies one of the major superiorities of the Israelis over their enemies.

The main air battles, in which tens of aircraft on both sides took part, as well as individual air duels, revealed consistently superior performance on the part of Israeli pilots. This Israeli preeminence was due, among other things, to the following factors: high degree of readiness; high combat effectiveness; familiarity with the combat area; confidence in the electronic control and communications systems, based upon many hours of training; knowledge of Syrian methods of air combat and air defense; initiative; well-prepared and well-executed plans; somewhat better equipment; better coordination with ground forces; and a psychological edge because of the history of the previous wars.

While the data is still classified, in spite of the close coordination there were apparently several cases when, in the heat of the battle, the IAF struck its own troops. The most widely known accident happened on July 10 in the Bekaa Valley at the crossroad near Kfar Meshki, when IAF planes attacked an Israeli tank column destroying several tanks and killing 13 men.

Close air support helicopters were attached to, and were under the command of, ground forces, and their survivability was higher than expected. Helicopter-mounted TOWs were very effective against tanks. Because of controversies with ground forces in previous wars regarding the results of air attacks, the IAF used video tapes to confirm destruction of ground targets, particularly tank hits. The IAF claims that it can prove that it destroyed at least 100 Syrian tanks, and is convinced that it hit many more.

The Naval War

The Syrian Navy did not enter the battle during the Lebanese War. There seem to have been valid reasons for this. In the first place, the Syrians did not perceive a threat from the sea comparable to that from the Bekaa Valley. Furthermore, credible deterrence posed by the Israeli Navy, which had badly battered the Syrians in the 1973 October War, kept the Syrian Navy close to port. The Israeli Navy, on the other hand, played a vital and unique role in the war by carrying out combined operations with the ground and air forces.

Landing operations and other means of support to ground operations had been planned and rehearsed for two years preceding the war. Combined training exercises with armored units and paratroops were carried out in order to assure the highest degree of cooperation. Special forces units (frogmen, commandos) often preceded the advancing ground forces, landing in the coastal area, delivering surprise blows to pockets of resistance. Fighting for the crucial Coastal Road, Israeli Navy commandos on several occasions achieved surprise in place, timing, and scope of operation. In the opening stages of the campaign, in a classic envelopment maneuver, the Israeli Navy executed a major amphibious landing deep behind the PLO front lines and seized a beachhead north of Sidon. The PLO units in Sidon found themselves cut off and in imminent danger of being surrounded at the very outset of the fighting.

The Navy transported and landed scores of tanks, other armored vehicles, artillery, and hundreds of troops to the battle front. Such landings demonstrated Israeli capabilities for seaborne invasion operations and logistical competence. The Navy also provided fast, and often massive, accurate fire support to the ground forces. Missile boats and seaborne 76mm naval guns knocked out PLO strongpoints in the western sector along the Coastal Road, often reaching targets inaccessible to ground fire.

The Israeli Navy cut off Beirut from the sea. Israeli warships stopped and searched various vessels, not only in order to prevent supplies from reaching the PLO still in Lebanon, but also to apprehend PLO fighters trying to flee the area. The Israeli Navy also closely controlled the approaches to Jounie, Lebanon's only active port in the conflict region, even though that part was held by the Phalangist Lebanese Forces. During the campaign, Israeli ships were occasionally shelled by PLO artillery, but no craft or men were lost. There were no serious mechanical breakdowns of equipment.

The Israeli Navy used a higher proportion of Israeli-designed and manufactured armament than did either of the other services. This included the Reshef class of missile boats, Gabriel missiles, electronic equipment, and computers. Although almost everything in the Navy is controlled by computers, the Israelis are convinced that it was the training of the men which gave their technology an extra dimension. They believe that in the final reckoning it is the fighting seaman who must analyze, evaluate, react, and make the crucial decision. However, from a naval point of view, the war in Lebanon was a very limited operation. The Navy was never under great pressure, and was able to carry out its assigned missions in an orderly fashion in accordance with the plans. Every action carried out by the Navy was examined by commanders, staffs, and analysts just as soon as it was completed. Some conclusions were drawn on the spot and, if necessary, mistakes were rectified immediately. Other problems were passed to special "think tanks" for analysis and recommendations for the future.

Among the lessons learned were: a need for more landing craft; a requirement for hydrofoil missile boats, much faster than the existing boats; and a need for more attention to electronic countermeasures against missiles, in order to be able to face not only Soviet but also western technologies. The sinking of HMS *Sheffield* by a single air-to-sea French-made *Exocet* missile during the Falkland War did not escape the attention of the Israeli Navy, and the possibility that a hostile state might acquire such a missile remains a constant concern.

Chapter XIX
The Siege of Beirut

General Situation

The ceasefires that ended Israel's initial hostilities with Syria and with the PLO completed one phase of the military operation, but it was soon evident from the situation in Beirut that there was an ongoing war. The IDF had encircled more than 14,000 Arab combatants in West Beirut. Of these about 10,000 were PLO fighters (approximately half of whom had fled from the south), plus a Syrian-supported PLA brigade of about 2,000 men, and a Syrian brigade of 2,300 men. These troops were well armed, adequately supplied for a long siege, and well entrenched. They were determined to fight, and had no qualms about using the nearly 350,000 civilians in West Beirut as their shield.

The question that faced Israeli political and military leaders was: what to do next? Any military decision had to be weighed against the ramifications that a military action would have, both internally in Israel and internationally. The Israeli national consensus which had been so evident at the outset of the campaign was beginning to dissipate. Internal cohesion and public identification with the war became weaker as the number of Israeli casualties mounted. A final thrust on West Beirut would undoubtedly increase the Israeli death toll.

Earlier Israeli expectations that the Phalangist militia would play the main role in cleaning up West Beirut were dashed by Bashir Jemayel, the Phalangist leader, despite his previous commitments to the contrary. He considered himself a potential presidential candidate, and was unwilling to harm his political future by alienating most of the Muslims in Lebanon by an attack on Muslim West Beirut. Furthermore, his fighting forces were relatively small, and he felt that their primary goal should be to conserve their strength as much as possible, so as to be in a position to take over control of Lebanon after the Palestinians were driven out and all foreign occupation forces withdrawn. Thus he would not commit himself to a battle which could seriously damage his power base, so necessary for the future.

A major consideration for the Israelis was the danger of inflicting many civilian casualties. To keep such casualties to a minimum, the Israelis would have to limit their use of artillery and air support, which in turn would mean the likelihood of more Israeli fatalities. It was, of course, the PLO realization of Israeli concern over their own and civilian casualties which had led the PLO leaders to integrate their military installations into the civilian community. It is easy to be critical of the PLO for this deliberate violation of the Geneva and the Hague conventions. However, given the desperate nature of their cause, and the overwhelming military power of their enemy, this callous disregard of the laws of war is at least understandable.

Foreign governments, including the United States, were warning Israel not to push further. They argued that Beirut was the capital of Lebanon, and must remain inviolate, regardless of the fact that its western part contained a huge Palestinian armed camp over which the Lebanese government had no authority. In addition, world public opinion had become extremely sensitive to civilian casualties, and any attack on Beirut would necessarily mean more civilian losses, no matter how careful the IDF might be.

Obviously the war machine which so effectively defeated the PLO in South Lebanon had stalled. The Israeli government had to decide whether Israel could afford to restart it. To the General Staff, which had planned the campaign, the operation could not be considered a complete success if the remnants of the PLO were to escape intact. The organization's command structure, its leadership, and thousands of its men, were still alive and showing signs of recovering from the shock of the initial Israeli blitz. The Israeli leadership and the people were divided. Many urged that military action should be temporarily suspended, while efforts were made to encourage as many civilians as possible to leave the city. These people believed that the siege should remain tight, however, and that the PLO should be kept on the defensive. Other Israelis advocated that an immediate assault be mounted on the city, while the iron was still hot and the PLO still demoralized.

The Phalangists preferred an even more radical solution to the PLO and the Palestinian problem than any proposed by the most militant Israelis. They were less sensitive to civilian casualties than Israel. After all, they had known nothing but civilian casualties for the past seven years, and this had been the history of the Lebanese Christian community for centuries. They wanted the Palestinians and their military organization wiped out. Only reluctantly did they agree to grant free passage to any Palestinian civilian wanting to leave West Beirut. However, they agreed to do so, only under Israeli pressure, providing that the fugitives were not armed and moved directly north to Tripoli, which was under PLO control.

By June 25, when a ceasefire was reached with the Palestinians, the IDF had deployed a sizable and varied force around Beirut and the Beirut International Airport, just south of the city. To the east, the IDF controlled the Beirut-Damascus highway, and the strategically important Bhamdoun-Aley-Jamhour triangle. Access to Phalangist-controlled East Beirut was under Israeli supervision. To the south, all approaches to the Beirut International Airport and the capital itself were sealed by the main Israeli ground forces. To the west, the Israeli Navy blockaded the coast, while in the north, the Phalangists and the Israeli Army controlled access to and from the city.

Arafat Decides to Fight

On Sunday, June 27, the Israeli government proposed a solution that it hoped would be acceptable to the PLO and Syria. The Lebanese Army would enter West Beirut to accept the arms of the PLO. The armed Syrians and the disarmed PLO fighters and leaders would then be permitted to leave the city under the protection of the International Red Cross, and to go along the Beirut-Damascus highway to Syria. The Israeli Army would insure safe passage in the section of the highway under its control. In case the PLO preferred an alternate route, this would also be made possible by the Israel Defense Force. The Israeli government rejected unofficial proposals which would allow any PLO political organization, or symbolic or token military presence, in Beirut. General Eitan, Chief of Staff, warned that the IDF would use military means to increase political and diplomatic pressures on the PLO if it did not accept the Israeli proposal.

Meanwhile Palestinian leaders—from PLO Chairman Yasser Arafat to the leftist radical George Habash—reaffirmed their determination to take on Israel in West Beirut and to fight to the death, unless they achieved an honorable settlement that would leave some form of PLO presence in Lebanon. Capitulation to the Israeli terms was considered treason. The PLO had two main demands: to maintain a political presence in Lebanon, and to negotiate a new military arrangement with the Lebanese government which would give it the right to remain in the country. Taking advantage of the ceasefire, the Palestinians were bolstering the defenses of West Beirut. They mined the southern approaches to the city, booby-trapped junctions, placed explosives in buildings so that they could be blown up to collapse on advancing forces, dug trenches, and fortified bunkers. PLO engineers built earth ramparts, reinforced with bridging girders, in a ring around the western part of Beirut. In the center of the city they had drilled holes into street surfaces, ready for new mines which would be laid if the PLO fell back to a second or third line of defense.

The Israeli Blunder

Possibly one of the greatest blunders in the short military history of modern Israel was the failure of the IDF to take Beirut between the 11th and 15th of June 1984.

One may argue the legality or morality of the Israeli decision to invade Lebanon, and whether the provocations which triggered that decision were commensurate with the implications of the decision. Nevertheless, from the standpoint of the national interests of Israel, the decision was probably reasonable, and also was probably sound, so long as the objectives were directly related to those national interests, and the war was conducted in accordance with the objectives. However, there is no doubt that from the beginning of the operation the objectives set by the Defense Minister, Ariel Sharon, and the Chief of Staff, Rafael Eitan, differed from those agreed on by the Israeli Cabinet. Sharon and Eitan had as their prime objective the destruction of the military capability and political effectiveness of the PLO, without regard to any territorial limits on the scope of the operation. Most members of the Cabinet, however, believed that they had approved a limited operation which would not extend more than 40 kilometers north of the Israeli frontier.

Sharon's and Eitan's second objective was to inflict a punishing defeat on Syria, whom they considered Israel's principal enemy. While the Israelis made much of their intent to avoid hostilities with Syria unless the Syrians attacked them, in fact they demanded that Syria accept terms so humiliating that even the most naive person could not have expected Syrian acquiescence. Damascus would have to stop harboring PLO fighters in the ill-defined zone 40 kilometers from the Israeli border, withdraw its troops from the southern part of the Bekaa Valley, and withdraw its SAM missiles from Lebanon. The advance of Israeli troops along the eastern slopes of Mount Lebanon and in the Lake Karaoun areas would be so threatening to the Syrian Army that they could only choose either to retreat without opposition, or stay and fight, despite a very unfavorable ratio of forces. That the Israeli General Staff from the outset expected that, faced with this choice, the Syrians would fight was evident from the IDF deployment in the Bekaa area. The Cabinet never received a briefing on the full implication of the 40-kilometer zone objective. Although the advance was directed officially and nominally against the PLO, hostilities with Syria were inevitable.

Thus, on June 9 and 10, as the operations rapidly swept well north of the 40-kilometer line, and as Israeli troops approached Beirut and drove the Syrians back toward the Beirut-Damascus highway, Cabinet members struggled with conflicting emotions. They were—like all Israelis—elated by the success of the operation, but becoming increasingly concerned by the implications of the success, and angered that they had been misled by Sharon. They had approved a quick, short, low-intensity military operation, and found themselves presiding over a substantial war in which Israeli casualties were mounting. Under these circumstances, by June 11 the Cabinet was bringing substantial pressure on Sharon to bring the war to a conclusion and to limit casualties. Cabinet members were particularly alarmed by the international implications of the expanding war in light of the worldwide condemnation of the Israeli invasion of Lebanon. Even more, perhaps, they were troubled by the prospect that the Israeli Army might enter Beirut, and the consequent possibility of heavy Israeli casualties in street fighting in that city.

Two things must be remembered about Sharon's situation at this time. In the first place, since he was one of the most senior generals of the Israeli Army (albeit in Reserve or Retired status), and at the same time the Minister of Defense, he was virtually the commander in chief of an army at war; he acted that way, and his military subordinates accepted it. Second, he was only one minister in the Cabinet of a democratic country. While he exercised exceptional power, he was not a dictator, and could not act dictatorially. This, of course, is why he seems deliberately to have misled his colleagues, and even the Prime Minister, about the true objectives of the operations he was directing. Given the situation as it existed on June 11, with immense political pressures on Israel to accede to a ceasefire and not to enter Beirut, and tremendous pressures on Sharon to accommodate his operations to the will of the Cabinet, he seems simply to have given up the idea of a direct assault on Beirut. Sharon resigned himself to forcing the besieged Syrians and PLO guerrillas to surrender by low-level military pressure including air raids, artillery bombardment, and limited ground attacks. An all-out attack on Beirut to destroy or evict the PLO by force would have required Cabinet approval, which under the prevailing circumstances probably seemed to him most unlikely. In the first place, the Cabinet would have feared heavy casualties from street fighting. Furthermore, it had long been an Israeli article of faith that IDF troops should not occupy an Arab capital. Thus, possible opportunities to reach Damascus in 1967 and 1973, and Cairo in 1973, had deliberately been avoided.

However, the traditional Israeli reluctance to occupy an Arab capital did not necessarily apply to Beirut, where a majority of Lebanese— Christians and Muslims alike—at least in the summer of 1982, considered the Israelis liberators from the oppressive rule which had been imposed on them by the PLO. Furthermore, a prompt Israeli sweep into Beirut on or about June 11 or 12 could not possibly have been seriously opposed by either the PLO or even the Syrian elements of the West Beirut garrison. The city was far from fully prepared for defense, and could have been taken with relative ease. In a candid conversation with the authors a number of

Palestinians conceded that the PLO fighters and the Syrian troops were demoralized, dispirited, and panic-stricken as a result of the crushing defeat they had suffered in the previous week. It is doubtful if they could even have been as effective as the defenders of Tyre and Sidon, who—after all—had been able to inflict some minimal casualties on the Israeli attackers. The ceasefire on June 25 gave the PLO fighters a valuable breathing space to beef up their defense, and their diplomats enough time to muster world sympathy for the Palestinian cause.

We don't know whether Sharon tried to use this line of argument to persuade his reluctant colleagues in the Cabinet to agree that Israel should not miss the opportunity to destroy the PLO, an opportunity which might never occur again. But if he tried, he obviously was not successful. Of course Sharon could have continued his high-handed treatment of the rest of the Cabinet, confusing their deliberations, misadvising them on the real situation at the front, and sending the army in to take the city without Cabinet approval. The Israelis had enough troops outside the city to accomplish this. During the 48 hours after the ceasefire with the Syrians on June 11—when fierce fighting was still going on in the Shouf Mountains over-looking Beirut—it would have been possible for the IDF to occupy West Beirut under the guise of local combat necessity. It is doubtful whether the mostly civilian members of the Cabinet could have seriously objected to such an interpretation of "combat necessity."

In light of the fact that Sharon had not shrunk from misleading the Cabinet at the outset of the war, and that a few weeks later he had no qualms in breaking the ceasefire with the Syrians in order to improve Israeli positions in the Aley and Bhamdoun areas, it is somewhat surprising that he did not use such an option as well to take West Beirut.

The possibility that Sharon lost his nerve when facing the Beirut issue cannot be ignored, particularly when one considers the contemptuous assessment of his highly publicized performance in the 1973 War by a well-known Israeli general who fought beside him in that conflict. "It is one thing to talk aggressively, as Sharon did," the general remarked in a private conversation with one of the authors.[*] "It is another thing to be aggressive when it really mattered; Sharon was not." Perhaps such an assessment is too harsh, taking into consideration Sharon's record as a decisive and coura-geous military commander in all of Israel's previous wars. Nevertheless the fact is that militarily the IDF lost an unparalleled opportunity to enter Beirut, when the city could have fallen into its hands like the proverbial ripe plum, and destroy the PLO. An observation by Dennis Hart Mahan, one of America's greatest military theorists, comes to mind: "The very elements of nature array themselves against the dilatory general."

[*] Trevor Dupuy

An objective assessment cannot ignore the fact that Sharon was more responsible than anyone else for initiating the war that most damaged Israel's international reputation. Nor can it be ignored that he did this deliberately because he thought the objectives and the potential damage to Israel's enemies were worth the risk. But, when the objectives were clearly within his grasp, he shrank—for whatever reasons—from seizing the historical opportunity to assure their achievement.

The Consequences of the Blunder

But what was a military blunder was a political disaster. The virtual destruction of the PLO had been in Israeli hands. The potential gain for Israel would have warranted at least as many casualties as had already been suffered in the campaign—even though in fact casualties would have been little more than negligible. The objectives for which Israel had incurred grave political and military risks would have been more than fully achieved. Even if Syria were allowed to retain a foothold in eastern Lebanon, Assad would have had little possibility of influencing future Lebanese governments, and a real peace treaty between Lebanon and Israel would have been a well-grounded hope. There would, unquestionably, have been at least some possibility of a significant move toward improved peace and stability in the Middle East.

As it was, militarily Israel had won another war, a clearcut and overwhelming victory on the battlefield. But politically Israel had, as would become evident in the following months and years, lost the war. Whether the sacrifice of Israeli lives was in vain or worth the benefits only the future can tell. The Israelis are divided on this question. The attitude of the majority could best be described in the old maxim—"If you find yourself in a hole, for heaven's sake, stop digging." The euphoria of the first days of the invasion, when nearly 90% of the population supported the operation, had long gone. Menachem Begin, who could have taken a place in Israeli history as a leader worthy of comparison with Ben Gurion, stepped down as Prime Minister and faded from public view. Future historians may well castigate him as a man who did not seize an opportunity and flawed a potential triumph.

The PLO, although badly beaten and weakened by internal dissensions and splits, still remained a political force to be reckoned with. Jerusalem's expectations of installing a friendly government in Beirut did not materialize. Vanished were Sharon's hopes that the Christian Phalangists would be able to whip Lebanon into a unified country, tied to Israel by a peace treaty. Early in 1985, after two and a half years in Lebanon, Israeli casualties reached over 600 killed and nearly 4,000 wounded, practically double the losses suffered during the actual combat operations in the summer of 1982. During the first months of the war most of the Lebanese Muslims and Druze, while never close to Israel, had welcomed the IDF with flowers, as liberators from Palestinian occupation. But, as time passed, they became more alienated and some of them, especially the Shiites, began to wage a guerrilla war against the IDF in South Lebanon.

Only President Assad of Syria, despite his military defeat, emerged as a prime winner. With Soviet help he was able to rebuild his armed forces and remained no less—and no more—of a threat to Israel than before the war. He revived his influence, and used it successfully to enhance Syria's standing throughout the Middle East. He holds the key to any new regional developments, including a settlement in Lebanon. He showed himself as a skillful opportunist and diplomat, and a strong leader worthy of comparison with Kemal Ataturk.

Continuing Pressure

On July 3, Israeli and PLO forces traded artillery fire along Beirut's southern flank, threatening to undermine the eight-day-long ceasefire. PLO antitank fire was directed at Israeli armor and infantry advancing toward Bourj el Barajneh camp in the southern part of the city. Other Israeli armored units moved into Christian East Beirut, and closed the main crossing points along the 5-kilometer "Green Line" that divided the Lebanese capital into Christian and Muslim sectors. Israel also kept up pressure on the beleaguered PLO, by sending jets to drop flares at night and to make sonic booms. PLO antiaircraft artillery batteries and SAMs launched a heavy barrage at the planes but none were hit. Leaflets were dropped, and loudspeakers blared warnings in Arabic, urging the civilian population of West Beirut to flee the city.

Israeli Centurion Tank at Outskirts of Beirut

In the developing war of attrition Israeli tanks and PLO front line troops at the southern outskirts of the city were deployed less than 300 meters apart. After July 3 the IDF units at the Beirut International Airport and at the nearby university inched forward a bit, but the PLO remained in place, with an apparent resolve not to budge. On July 5 there was intense Israeli shelling of PLO targets in the Fakehrani district and at the Arab University compound housing the PLO communication center and Arafat's Command Headquarters. The PLO responded with fierce Katyusha, mortar, and 130mm gun barrages, and very heavy rifle grenade and antitank fire. These prolonged duels did not facilitate the diplomatic efforts of Ambassador Habib to work out a package deal under which Yasser Arafat and his men would evacuate West Beirut to avert a possible Israeli onslaught.

On July 7, after a quiet day, as the Lebanese and the PLO leaders pondered an American offer to evacuate PLO fighters from the besieged city, artillery and mortar exchanges between Israeli and PLO gunners resumed in the southern suburbs of Beirut. Tanks on the front line, and 175mm and 155mm guns in the hills above Beirut, bombarded the PLO-held stronghold of Bourj el Barajneh and the area east of the Beirut airport. A number of Palestinian ammunition depots were hit and huge fires burned out of control in several of them. The Soviet Embassy and the Soviet Trade Mission were slightly damaged, but there were no casualties among the staff members. The PLO troops responded with antitank missiles and artillery fire at IDF positions close to the front line. The shelling was most intense around the airport and in nearby hills, which the Israelis had captured in mid-June. Shells fell in suburban Yarzeh, close to the residence of the US Ambassador. The PLO Command and the Syrian garrison in Beirut did not release casualty figures for this fierce battle, but their losses were undoubtedly high. Israeli Headquarters reported four of its men killed during the exchanges of fire, bringing the official toll for the entire operation by mid-July to 281 killed and 1,570 wounded in action. Of the wounded, 404 were still in hospitals, 383 were recuperating at military rest homes, and 783 had been sent home. There were 11 men missing and one known prisoner of war.

In the weeks that followed there were more intermittent breaches of the ceasefire as negotiators tried to find a formula to get the PLO out of West Beirut. The Palestinians were, of course, playing for time in order to wrest political victory from military defeat. They had regained enough confidence to believe that they would not have to withdraw from Beirut. The PLO leaders hoped that diplomatic pressure from various sources, especially from the United States, would dissuade Israel from attacking them in their strongholds. The Israeli government, on the other hand, emphasized that, although its aim was to get the PLO out of West Beirut by political means, it would not hesitate to turn to military options. Both sides were seriously considering a proposal for the Israeli troops to withdraw about five kilometers from their existing lines, and to be replaced by a multinational force. The PLO would then agree to leave if land passage to Syria were assured.

Syria, however, refused to accept the PLO fighters, despite a Saudi Arabian promise of billions of dollars in assistance programs. Damascus announced that it was prepared to admit only the PLO leadership, not the rank and file fighters and their families. Syrian internal security forces were already busy enough dealing with Muslim Brotherhood turbulence; President Assad had no desire to add to his security risks by hosting nearly 10,000 dejected and frustrated Palestinians. They would have arrived armed with their personal weapons, and Syrian attempts to disarm them could have triggered violence. In fact, President Assad regarded with equanimity the idea of Israel attacking West Beirut and physically deposing Arafat and the existing PLO leadership. Assad had never had a cordial relationship with Arafat, and his elimination would enable Assad immediately to produce an alternative Palestinian leadership, which he had waiting in Damascus for such an event. Then Syria would emerge as the undisputed master of the Palestinian destiny.

Flare-up in the Bekaa Valley

While the diplomatic activity to break the statement in the Beirut crisis continued, and the fighting in and around the city did not abate, there was a sudden eruption of warfare in the Bekaa Valley. On July 21 an Israeli truck convoy was ambushed east of Lake Karaoun, and five Israeli soldiers were killed. Next day Israeli planes, tanks, and artillery attacked Syrian and PLO targets along the 40-kilometer ceasefire line stretching from a point northeast of Beirut to the eastern edge of the Bekaa. On July 23, in a response more symbolic than martial, Syria deployed three Soviet-made SA-8 "Gecko" missile batteries in Lebanon south of Shatura near the village of Bar Elias. This was a challenge to the long-standing Israeli warning that no Syrian surface-to-air missiles be deployed on Lebanese territory. Unlike the SA-6 "Gainful" missiles which Israel destroyed on June 9, the SA-8 "Gecko" missiles are fully self-contained and do not depend on central tracking and a radar control system. Although their range is only 13 kilometers, they are highly mobile. On July 24 Israeli jets attacked these missiles, and in less than an hour destroyed all three batteries.

After that raid, Syria threatened that it would retaliate with all types of weapons if Israel again violated the ceasefire in Lebanon. Damascus even hinted at use of SCUD surface-to-surface missiles at targets in Israel, but these threats were not taken seriously by Israel. However, a few days later

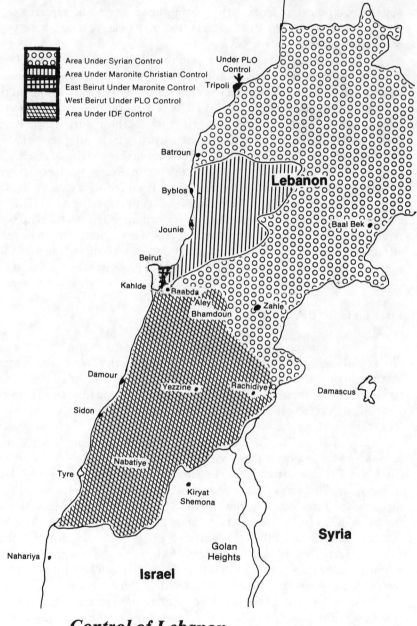

Area Under Syrian Control
Area Under Maronite Christian Control
East Beirut Under Maronite Control
West Beirut Under PLO Control
Area Under IDF Control

Under PLO
Control

Tripoli

Batroun

Byblos

Lebanon

Jounie

Baal Bek

Beirut

Kahlde

Baabda
Aley
Bhamdoun

Zahle

Damour

Yezzine

Rachidiye

Damascus

Sidon

Nabatiye

Tyre

Kiryat
Shemona

Syria

Nahariya

Golan
Heights

Israel

Control of Lebanon
End of July 1982

an Israeli Phantom, flying on a reconnaissance mission in the northern sector of the Bekaa, was shot down by a Syrian SA-6 missile fired from Syrian territory close to the border. One of the pilots was killed, and the other taken prisoner. This was the only Israeli plane lost to the Syrians.

Guarded Optimism Inside a Tightening Noose

As Israel maintained daily military pressure on Beirut, there were fierce exchanges of fire between the Israeli forces and the PLO and the Syrian contingents in the western sector of the beleaguered Lebanese capital. Between July 23 and 29 Israeli planes mounted daily attacks on PLO and Syrian targets in West Beirut, destroying ammunition dumps, troop concentrations, and command headquarters. Air strikes were preceded and followed by artillery, tank, heavy machine gun, and light arms fire. Israeli naval guns and missiles were brought into action, shelling Palestinian targets from the sea. The PLO and Syrians responded with fire from artillery, tank guns, and multiple rocket launchers. Palestinian-operated Soviet-made Grad missiles were fired from West Beirut at the Christian town of Jounie, just to the north of the capital, causing slight damage.

Despite these long-range exchanges, there was guarded optimism that a political solution was in sight. Israel had granted US Ambassador Habib more time to negotiate a resolution to the crisis. The IDF, which had cut off water and electricity to the area under siege for several days, restored the services. The Arab League Committee on Lebanon, after a two-day meeting at Jeddah, Saudi Arabia, on July 28, announced a plan which included the removal of the PLO forces from Beirut on condition that the safety of all Palestinians living in Lebanon be guaranteed. Syria modified its position slightly, and agreed to accept a few hundred SAIQA troops and the PLA. Jordan agreed to take nearly 2,000 of its nationals serving with the PLO. Egypt would accept about 500 of its citizens.

The PLO leaders began to lose some of their new-found confidence. They realized they were facing a choice between a voluntary exit arranged in diplomatic negotiations and a tightening siege amid Israeli pressure, with a final Israeli assault which would destroy the organization and its fighters. It became apparent to them that the more the PLO's position improved in terms of international sympathy and support, the more violent was the Israeli military reaction. Israel clearly would accept nothing less than an unconditional PLO surrender. Hopes that Washington would contain the Israelis were fading.

In the first week of August, the IDF advanced all around West Beirut. The movements were modest, but significant, some three kilometers from south to north, and few hundred meters from east to west. All ground attacks were backed by air, artillery, and shelling from the sea by gunboats. On August 1 Israeli forces captured the entire area of the Beirut International Airport and approached the Hai el Saloum district to its north, which they took the next day. The Israelis now held an east-west line from the sea up to Baabda, an East Beirut suburb.

Very heavy fighting developed on August 4 long before sunrise, as the IDF continued to push deeper into West Beirut. PLO responses with Katyusha rockets had little effect. In the southern sector, the Israeli forces took el Duazi, and threatened the PLO troops in the Bourj el Barajneh district from south, east, and west. Also the PLO-controlled districts of Sabra, Shatila and Fakehrani were threatened from south, east, and northeast. Farther east, Israeli infantry in about 100 armored personnel carriers, supported by an armored battalion and intense artillery fire—but without air support—advanced about 400 meters across the Green Line dividing the city into Christian and Muslim sectors, and captured the National Museum and the Hippodrome. To the north, they also made headway in the port area. Although the progress was small, these moves had considerable psychological and tactical consequences, shattering the PLO illusions that the Green Line was sacrosanct. The IDF was now in an excellent position from which to cut off the PLO-dominated southern part of the city from the northern downtown area, by pushing down the Boulevard Saeb Salaam through the Corniche Mazraa to the sea. The general siege of West Beirut could then be transformed into smaller sieges of isolated PLO pockets of resistance, allowing the Israelis to exert greater psychological and military pressure. The new IDF line in the northeast corner of West Beirut, perched directly above the Palestinian forces in the Fakehrani and the Beirut Forest of Pines areas, gave the Israelis a clear view of almost all of the PLO and Syrian artillery and tank deployment.

The fighting on August 4th cost 19 Israeli soldiers killed and 84 wounded, the single most costly day of the siege, bringing the total number of Israelis killed in action from the start of the operation to 318. No casualty figures for that day of the PLO and Syrian troops were given, although there were unofficial estimates of about 500 killed and wounded. Arafat called the Israeli advance very serious, and urged all citizens in West Beirut to take up arms to fight the modern Israeli war machine.

Tightening—and Loosening—the Screw

The fighting continued along the periphery of West Beirut through the following week despite some progress in diplomatic negotiations. (In fact, the progress was in large part due to the fighting.) The Israelis retained the initiative. They had obviously decided to send a message to the PLO that it should leave Beirut "or else." The increasing pressure demonstrated that the IDF was prepared to take whatever steps were necessary to evict the Palestinian fighters. It was, in fact, this repeated pounding of PLO targets which convinced Arafat that he must accept an agreement, being worked out by Ambassador Habib, for PLO and Syrian evacuation of West Beirut under the supervision of a multinational force.

During the latest round of fighting the Israelis again cut off most of the water supply to West Beirut. Then Prime Minister Begin—more for diplomatic than humanitarian reasons—ordered the IDF to reopen the flow of water to West Beirut. He also permitted fuel to get through so that electric power could be restored.

With Israeli tanks and troops massed near the Beirut port district, at the National Museum, and near the Gallerie Semaan crossing, and with IDF reinforcements arriving in the airport area, an Israeli assault on the city seemed imminent. The Israeli military spokesman in East Beirut disclosed that Israeli forces were very seriously preparing for military action in the event that diplomacy failed. Few doubted that Sharon, the architect of the operation, recognizing the opportunity he had missed two months earlier, was again eager for a military solution to the West Beirut stalemate that would annihilate the PLO leadership and cause many Palestinian guerrilla casualties.

Sporadic fighting—at Israeli initiative—continued for several days, close to the racetrack, where Israeli forces inched one more block into Palestinian-held West Beirut. In the center of the city, the Israeli Air Force hit and destroyed the apartment building that housed the PLO operations center, the backbone of Arafat's control and communications system. Bombs were dropped and artillery rounds fired at PLO troop entrenchments and bunkers in the badly battered refugee camps of Bourj el Barajneh, Sabra, and Shatila. The Palestinians responded with artillery, mortar, Katyusha, Sagger, and small arms fire directed at Israeli infantry and tanks. Both sides suffered losses. Israeli jets also attacked Syrian and PLO positions east of Beirut along the Beirut-Damascus highway, and destroyed a Syrian SAM missile battery in the eastern Bekaa Valley.

In the first ten days of August there were new landings of Israeli troops in the port city of Jounie, a Christian enclave just north of Beirut. An armored battalion of some 40 tanks moved into the Lebanese interior just to the east of Jbail—better known from ancient history as Byblos. In the deepest Israeli push into Lebanon since the start of the war, an armored brigade was deployed on the bluff of the Harkoura River just south of the Syrian lines northeast of Beirut. These Israeli landings and troop movements to the north and northeast of Beirut were taken by Damascus as an indication that Israel was contemplating a campaign against Tripoli, then defended by an assortment of PLO fighters, Syrian troops, and leftist

Lebanese guerrillas. Another possibility was that the Israelis might be preparing to outflank the Syrians in the Bekaa Valley. However, Jerusalem insisted that it was deploying its forces in the Jounie area in anticipation of the arrival of multinational contingents. The Israelis said that they wanted to be sure that no unauthorized landings were made at the same time.

On August 10, the Israeli Cabinet conditionally accepted the Palestinian withdrawal plan worked out by Habib. As a condition of acceptance, Israel demanded a list of Arab countries which would admit the PLO fighters and a precise tally of how many of them would go to which country. Another Israeli requirement concerned the timing of the PLO departure, and the arrival of the American, French, and Italian contingents of the Multinational Force (MNF). Israel insisted that the PLO drop its demand that the evacuation be supervised only by the French contingent of the MNF or by UN forces. Israel continued to reject any increased UN presence in Beirut, contending that the PLO might use either the French or the UN force as a shield to forestall the guerrillas' departure.

Early in the morning of August 12, as Habib was ironing out the final details of the evacuation agreement, and the PLO had already agreed in principle to leave, the Israelis commenced a sustained air and artillery bombardmant of West Beirut, lasting almost ten hours. While probably the most extensive Israeli bombardment to date, its intensity was highly exaggerated by press, radio, and television reports.

The heaviest bombing was directed at PLO headquarters offices, bunkers, and artillery positions, and in and around the Sabra, Shatila, and Bourj el Barajneh refugee camps and the Fakehrani district. Four headquarters buildings were destroyed and several Katyusha and gun emplacements hit. With gunboats participating, Israeli artillery shelled the Rawshah seaside district, the PLO strongholds near the port, and the Manara Lighthouse region several blocks to the west of the American University campus. Shells and bombs also raked buildings along the Corniche Mazraa, an area inhabited mostly by Lebanese.

Palestinian gunners fired surface-to-air missiles and modern anti-aircraft guns at the planes, but neither was an effective threat to the Israeli jets, which were trailing thermal balloons to deflect the heat-seeking missiles. By midday the Palestinians stopped firing, because either they ran out of ammunition or they had given up in futility. There were skirmishes in the National Museum area, where, in the morning, some Israeli infantry and a few tanks advanced several hundred meters, taking several buildings used as PLO firing positions. They withdrew under heavy pressure in the afternoon. During the day-long combat the IDF lost one man killed and ten wounded. According to Lebanese police reports, the Palestinian and Lebanese toll—military and civilian—was about 130 killed and nearly 400 wounded.

While the attack on August 12 may not have been a military necessity, it obviously helped the Israeli negotiators to have the last word. When the Arab states refused to take the Palestinians, Sharon went on bombing, and the Arab states changed their minds.

Minister Sharon, who personally ordered the attack of the 12th, explained that it was in response to PLO shelling of Israeli forces during the previous 48 hours which had killed 2 Israeli soldiers and wounded 37. He insisted that all the IDF was doing in Beirut was acting to protect the lives of its soldiers from the PLO fire. Sharon declared that bombing and shelling had sped up peace negotiations, and that this was also in accordance with government instructions authorizing response to truce violations. It was Sharon's belief that without such military pressure, the PLO might continue to drag the negotiations on indefinitely, since otherwise time was in the Palestinian favor. Historical examples, the latest being communist procrastination in Korea and Vietnam, certainly support this thinking.

President Reagan and other world leaders expressed shock at the Israeli bombardment of August 12, which came at the moment when Habib's efforts at mediation seemed to be at the brink of success. Israeli opposition leaders were also critical and requested that the prime minister put an end to the strikes. The Israeli Cabinet rebuked the Defense Minister, and ordered a halt to air attacks on Beirut unless specifically authorized by Prime Minister Begin. A ceasefire was declared late in the afternoon.

—

PART THREE
The Lingering Crisis

Chapter XX
Journalism And
The Conduct
Of War

Responsibility of the News Media

At this point it seems to us worthwhile to digress from the battle narrative to discuss the general coverage of this war, and the presentations of fact—the raw stuff of history—by the news media of the world. It is the western, democratic tradition that a free press has a moral responsibility to present facts truthfully and objectively. Instead, press, radio, and television reports on the war in Lebanon were, in general, slanted, biased, and hostile to Israel. What we saw in Lebanon during our visits in August and October, 1982, and later in March of 1983 confirmed this.

Let us make clear that we do not defend the Israeli initiation of the war. (Nor, given the complexity of the issues, do we necessarily condemn it.) We merely assert that the public should be able to expect that facts be presented as facts, and that news reports be objective.

Reporting the August 12 Israeli Bombardment

According to large front page newspaper headlines all over the world, and breathless lead stories in many languages on radio and television, on August 12 the Israeli Air Force launched its most devastating attack to date on West Beirut. It was reported that entire areas of the city were covered by clouds of black smoke, hundreds of buildings were destroyed, and nearly a thousand people were killed or wounded.

At this time, the authors of this book were travelling in South Lebanon, visiting many towns and villages, and talking to soldiers and local people. On August 12 we spent about five hours observing the Israeli aerial bombardment of West Beirut. Part of that time we were in an abandoned house in Deir Qoubil, on high ground overlooking West Beirut from just south of the airport. Then we drove along the narrow, winding road between Deir Qoubil and Aley, on the hills high above Beirut and Baabda, stopping frequently to watch the bursts and wisps of smoke curling up to form a haze over the city. Then, for more than an hour, we were in Beirut at the Gallerie Semaan checkpoint, the only crossing over the Green Line (dividing East and West Beirut) that the Israelis allowed to remain open (to one-way traffic—refugees from West Beirut).

During those five hours it was apparent from our observation that probably about 150 bombs were dropped on various targets in Beirut by Israeli aircraft. We have no basis for estimating how many rounds of artillery ammunition were fired, but in light of the limited activity in the many Israeli artillery positions we saw in and around Beirut, the shelling could not have been heavy. Certainly we saw fewer shell bursts than bomb explosions during the time we were there.

Of course, it must have been unendurable, extremely unsafe, and frightening for people in West Beirut during that time. The refugees streaming through the crossing point by car and on foot—one car with several recent shell-fragment holes, including one in the windshield—were obviously happy to be out. However, to any veteran soldier who has been under air or artillery attack in a combat situation, as the authors had been earlier in their lives, this was a relatively modest bombardment.

Therefore, we were astonished to learn from a BBC radio broadcast that night that this was the most intensive strike that the Israelis had yet inflicted on West Beirut. It was so intensive, according to the report, that President Reagan had telephoned Prime Minister Begin of Israel to express his outrage, and to threaten to call off United States involvement in negotiations for the PLO evacuation of West Beirut. King Fahd of Saudi Arabia was said to express his concern about the Israeli bombardment.

Our surprise turned to bewilderment when we read in the August 14 issue of the *International Herald Tribune* that "PLO communiques said that warplanes dropped 44,000 bombs and that at least 600 houses collapsed in the Shatila and Bourj el Barajneh Palestinian camps, and [that] Beirut radio station said that more than 100 buildings were destroyed in the city itself." The dispatch did not comment on these statistics, nor did it present any differing assessment of intensity of the bombardment or the damage it caused. So the reader could only conclude that the *Herald Tribune* believed that something like 44,000 bombs had devastated Beirut that day, destroying about 100 buildings. We later discovered that the *Washington Post* of August 13, 1982, reported a statement made by the PLO representative in New York to the UN Security Council that "1,600 bombs and rockets were dropped [on West Beirut], and 42,000 shells fired by land and sea-based

Israeli artillery." Again without comment.

Reports in both papers, as well as similar ones in many others, along with radio and television broadcasts, were obviously totally inconsistent with what we had seen that day. We were in and around Beirut for over five hours of the eleven during which the Israeli attack was reported as having taken place, and saw perhaps 150, certainly fewer than 200, bombs dropped on the city during that time. But let us suppose that we were not careful observers and that instead of 150 bombs, 2,000 or even a few more were dropped in those five hours. That means—if one accepts the *Herald Tribune* report—that about 42,000 more bombs must have been dropped in the remaining six hours of the period. This is 7,000 bombs per hour, or more than 100 per minute. No air force in the world could drop 42,000 substantial bombs on one target the size of Beirut in six hours, or drop 44,000 bombs in eleven hours (4,000 per hour; 70 per minute) for that matter.

The Israeli Air Force had fewer than 600 combat aircraft. In a maximum effort it might have been able to commit as many as 300 of these to such a bombardment mission. And these could probably have flown three combat sorties each during an eleven hour period. This is a maximum potential of 900 sorties. If each plane carried four bombs on each sortie, that would be an absolute maximum of 3,600 bombs, less than one-tenth of the number that the *Herald Tribune* reported. However, we stick to our on-the-spot observation that the actual intensity was probably one-tenth of that theoretical maximum, and thus less than one-hundredth of the reported intensity.

As to the *Washington Post* report, the figure of 1,600 bombs was, as we have seen, theoretically possible, but suggests an intensity at least four times greater than what we saw. The reported 42,000 rounds of artillery fire would have required a bombardment averaging nearly 4,000 shells per hour; in other words, almost continuous firing by at least 100 guns. On the basis of our observation, there could not have been more than 50 to 60 shells per hour fired from a few batteries. There was absolutely no firing being conducted at any of the several Israeli artillery positions we saw while travelling in the area that day.

We were visiting South Lebanon because we were gathering materials for this book so as to be able to present authoritatively and truthfully how the war was carried out. We travelled at our own expense; there was no invitation—direct or indirect—from Israeli, Lebanese, Muslim, Christian or Jewish sources. In other words, we were doing our best to remain scrupulously neutral in this phase, as in previous phases of the Arab-Israeli conflict. As historians, it seemed to us too early to judge whether the Israeli operation in Lebanon in the summer of 1982 was warranted for national security. Nor had we yet seen or learned enough to make up our minds on the justification of the Israeli advance to the gates of Beirut. We were

determined to retain open minds, and to write objectively about all aspects
of the conflict.

Contrasting Reports and Reality

The sensational reports of tens of thousands of civilian casualties,
some asserting that there were 60,000 in South Lebanon alone, were clearly
false, and should have been recognized as such by the newsmen and news-
women who made the reports. It should have been equally evident to these
reporters that their stories of 600,000 homeless refugees in the wake of the
Israeli invasion were impossible. This was, at the very least, equal to the
total population under Israeli control in South Lebanon. Reports published
after the war in Lebanese papers about total military and civilian casualties
of 17,825 dead and 30,102 wounded among Lebanese and Palestinians are
obviously grossly exaggerated, if not impossible, even if we ignore the
question of how the figures could be so precise.

In November 1984, there were Israeli-Lebanese negotiations in
Naqoura on the withdrawal of the Israeli forces from South Lebanon. The
Lebanese delegate requested from Israel indemnities in the amount of $10
billion for loss of property and 1,000 people killed during the Israeli
operation in South Lebanon. Without taking into consideration civilian
casualties in West Beirut before the PLO exodus, because it is almost
impossible to verify them, we had previously estimated fewer than 2,500
civilians—Lebanese and Palestinians—were killed and wounded in South
Lebanon from June to mid-August. The Lebanese estimate of 1,000 dead is
not inconsistent with our estimate.

In contrast, nearly 100,000 civilians were killed, and over 250,000
wounded in the seven prior years of civil war in Lebanon. In 1981, Syrian
shelling alone killed over 400 Lebanese civilians and wounded 800, primarily
in Zahle and East Beirut. Since 1975 no fewer than 150,000 men, women, and
children had fled the PLO rule of terror in southern Lebanon.

There could have been no more than 20,000 refugees, many of whom
we saw returning from the north to their homes in southern Lebanon in
August of 1982. Most of these had become refugees before the war, when
they were forced from their homes by the PLO occupation of South
Lebanon in the late 1970s.

Stories of harsh occupation policies and Israeli atrocities, which
have been sometimes eagerly compared to the Nazi Holocaust of World
War II, could have been reported only by those who had no idea of what the
Nazi extermination of six million Jews was, and who have not been in South
Lebanon since the beginning of the Israeli operation. Our own investigation
on the spot has led us to conclude that there was nothing that could be

termed either genocide or massacres committed by Israeli troops, as reported by some western journalists. There was no evidence of indiscriminate bombing and shelling, although Israeli commanders and soldiers admitted that innocent bystanders were sometimes killed or wounded. There obviously was no reign of terror in the territories overrun by the Israelis. Tales of wanton destruction and devastation of such cities as Tyre, Sidon, Damour, and Nabatiye are contrary to what we saw in those places.

On August 16, 1982, the *Los Angeles Times* correspondent in Beirut, Michael Kennedy, wrote in the *International Herald Tribune*: "In a little more than two months the Israelis have inflicted damage on West Beirut and southern Lebanon to a degree that makes the year and a half civil war 1975-76 seem almost minor." One wonders if Mr. Kennedy ever visited Damour—once one of the most beautiful cities in Lebanon and now largely a ghost town. Much of it was totally destroyed and many of its Christian inhabitants were killed by the PLO guerrillas in 1976. Kennedy writes further: "The horror of this war is matched only by the fear of tomorrow or the day after, should the Israelis, as many here still fear, decide to wipe out mostly Muslim West Beirut." We don't know with whom Mr. Kennedy talked, and who were those "many here." However, at that same time we talked extensively with a random selection of people—selected by us—Lebanese Christians, Muslims, and Druze, throughout South Lebanon. What these people feared—and they were almost unanimous—was the possibility that the PLO might make a suicidal decision not to withdraw from West Beirut but to stay and fight to the end. This, these people believed, would cause the Israelis to evict the PLO by force, and this would cause casualties to many innocent civilians. Nobody mentioned "wiping out" the city. But many Muslims did fear reprisals from Christian Lebanese militia against the Palestinians and also against Lebanese Muslims, a fear well known to the Israelis.

Whatever the Israeli responsibility may have been for the tragic massacres in the Shatila and Sabra camps—and this is discussed in a subsequent chapter—this issue must not be confused with the early press accusations against Israel for its conduct of the war in Lebanon in June, July, and August. To do so would be a grave injustice, because the record reveals that, prior to the Sabra and Shatila disasters, the Israel Defense Force did in fact demonstrate a commendable concern for the safety of civilians—Palestinians as well as Lebanese—in the war zone. The Israelis operated with punctilious respect for the laws of war, and the precepts of international morality in time of war.

Early in June the *New York Times* reported that Nabatiye, a town of some 50,000 inhabitants not far from the Israeli border, had been destroyed during the fighting. On August 10, when we drove through, and spent some time in, Nabatiye, there were no signs of war damage, save for bullet scars on some of the buildings on the southern edge of the city. That many other buildings could have been destroyed or damaged during the few hours' fight for the town is most doubtful. Combat could not have been heavy, for the defending Palestinians suffered only about ten casualties.

While the PLO resistance in Nabatiye was almost negligible, the fight for Sidon and the nearby Palestinian refugee camp el Hilwe was fierce and lasted several days. Press and television reports of the total destruction of Sidon were widespread. We had seen television shots of terrible damage and destruction. Thus, when we approached Sidon early in August we expected to see a ghost town with remnants of leveled houses and rubble everywhere. To our surprise only some five or six blocks near the center of the city were totally destroyed, and a number of houses along a 200-meter stretch of the waterfront were seriously damaged. (All of the television pictures were taken in that limited area.) We estimated that this amounted to less than 5% of the city's dwellings. A number of office buildings had suffered minor damage; some had shattered windows, some were pockmarked by bullets, but most were intact and untouched. The city of 200,000 people was teeming with life, with thousands of shoppers in stores full of goods. Movie theaters were open, and the traffic was at least as bad as in New York during rush hour. This was exactly two months after the first Israeli soldiers started the battle for Sidon with the PLO. (We did not have time to visit the el Hilwe refugee camp on this trip. However, we learned from the Lebanese and Palestinians we talked with that the destruction there was substantially greater than in Sidon.)

The image of the horrors of this war which we had seen between commercials on television screens in the United States were quite different from the actual scene we saw on the ground in Lebanon. By focusing their television cameras exclusively on selected destroyed buildings, without showing untouched neighboring structures on the same street, the electronic journalists dramatically exaggerated the degree of devastation and failed to provide balanced and comprehensive coverage.

Israeli Performance and the Laws of War

The IDF has been accused of brutality in its treatment of both Lebanese and Palestinian civilians on a scale comparable to the Nazi genocide of Jews of World War II. We have seen on our television screens visual "evidence" of the Israeli brutality in pictures of dead or maimed women and children, and stark pictures of damage and destruction. One example of misrepresentation in the media is a picture of a woman at a graveside in Beirut mourning the death of a beloved one, which, among other photographs depicting the miseries of war-torn Beirut, appeared in the August 2, 1982 issue of *US News and World Report*. Those who read Arabic could see from the words on the tomb that this was the grave of Halad Belaty who died on 29 Ramadan 1400, that is, on August 10, 1980, almost two years before the Israeli invasion.

It is not the authors' purpose here to suggest why these television images and other reports have been false or misleading. In fact, a number of other writers have already pointed out that the truth of what happened in Lebanon is quite different from the sensational image the public received through television, radio, and the press. Yet, despite these fairly extensive efforts to set the record straight, some still tend to equate the performance of the IDF in Lebanon to the practices of the hordes of Attila the Hun, Tamerlane, and Himmler. And although some of these efforts to indict press coverage of the war can be discounted to some extent because they came from sources with an obvious pro-Israeli bias, it is nevertheless clear that the media was more interested in reporting unverified inhumane performances by the Israelis than verifiable atrocities committed by the PLO. There was a clear double standard in the press attitude toward the behavior of the two sides.

It is interesting to look at the military aspects and implications of the Israeli performance in Lebanon in terms of the laws of war as generally recognized internationally.

Section 41 of the US Army Field Manual on *The Law of Land Warfare* (FM 27-10), in the paragraph entitled "Unnecessary Killing and Devastation," summarizes the intent of Article 25 of the Hague Convention of October 18, 1907, on "Regulations Respecting the Laws and Customs of War on Land" and Article 147 of the August 12, 1949, Geneva Convention "Relative to the Protection of Civilian Persons in Time of War," in the following words: "Loss of life and damage to property must not be out of proportion to the military advantage to be gained." As military historians we can think of no war in which greater military advantages were gained in combat in densely populated areas at such a small cost in civilian lives lost and property damaged. And this despite the PLO's deliberate emplacement of weapons in civilian communities, and in and around hospitals, in violation of those provisions of the Geneva Convention regarding obligations to locate weapons and military installations so as to endanger civilians and populated communities least.

However, it must be remembered that the PLO was not bound by the provisions of the Hague or Geneva conventions, which it had of course never signed, and was struggling for its survival. Although the less rigorous "customs of war" were presumably binding on PLO belligerents, under the doctrine of "military necessity" it could possibly be considered imperative for them to violate the customs regarding protection of civilians, thus forcing the Israelis to invoke the much more constrained "military necessity" guidelines of the conventions in order to defeat the PLO. We are not justifying what the PLO did, but merely pointing out that there was a propaganda advantage to be gained, and the PLO gained it. This fact should be recognized and remembered before unjustly criticizing the Israelis for doing what (under the circumstances) they had to do, and in the process causing losses and damage that were unavoidable and were truly minimal.

The PLO gained a propaganda advantage by forcing the Israelis to fire on military targets in civilian environments that should have been protected under the conventions. Two points are worth noting. First, a propaganda victory was won in the western world, and even in Israel, because of the double standard applied by the news media, which—on balance—grossly distorted the facts, and failed to present all of the considerations affecting the civilian loss of life and private property damage.

Second, the Lebanese people, both Muslims and Christians, were for the most part unimpressed by the news stories. They had suffered severely for more than six years from virtual PLO occupation of most of southern Lebanon. Thus, they were prepared to welcome the Israelis as "rescuers." They could see for themselves how the PLO had used innocent civilians as hostage shields around their weapons sites and other installations, and they could see the moderation exercised by the Israelis in dealing with this situation.

Initial Reaction of the Lebanese

As a result the Israeli Army was able to operate in Lebanon in an essentially friendly environment rather than in the hostile environment of an occupied enemy country. As combat operations continued, local Lebanese authorities were allowed full responsibility for local affairs, and law and order were maintained by local police forces. Even in towns and villages immediately behind Israeli front line positions there was no occupying force dominating the townspeople with emplaced weapons. In these towns, the only signs of an Israeli military presence was an occasional passing truck or jeep, or one or two soldiers strolling through teeming outdoor markets. At the same time farmers tilled the fields and harvested crops all around Israeli positions and even in no-man's land between Israeli and Syrian lines, which they entered through a small gap in the antitank barrier erected by the Israelis. An IDF soldier standing guard checked credentials as they went in and out.

One Israeli brigadier general told us somewhat wryly that his troops were paying a small price for this deliberate policy of "non-occupation." He said that the PLO "terrorists" occasionally infiltrated through the lines, and then worked their way to attack the rear of Israeli positions by going through villages. But these incidents were so few, and the Israeli local security measures so effective, that the IDF believed that it gained in the long run by avoiding the imposition of a military-occupying presence in Lebanese communities.

Assertions that the Israeli occupation of southern Lebanon was marked by a harshness matching the Nazi Holocaust of World War II would be laughable were it not for the tragic and brutal enormity of the comparison. The situation in Lebanon in 1982 and early 1983 was completely different from what we had been led to believe by many a news report. Nevertheless, any army on foreign soil eventually wears out any welcome it may have enjoyed, and—as we shall see—events in South Lebanon in late 1983 and 1984 finally indicated that time for the Israelis had run out.

Chapter XXI
Enter the Multinationals;
Exit the PLO

Habib's Evacuation Plan

During the week following the August 12 ceasefire there were only
minor small arms fire exchanges in the Beirut area. During the lull, Ambassador Habib hammered out the last details of the agreement for the evacuation of the Palestinians and Syrians trapped in besieged West Beirut.

On August 13 the PLO delivered to Habib a report of nearly 9,500
fighters to be evacuated from Beirut, showing their destinations in Jordan,
Syria, Algeria, North and South Yemen, Sudan, and Tunisia. However, the
PLO still insisted that it would not provide the Israelis with the names,
passport numbers, and organizational affiliations of the men being evacuated. The next day the number of evacuees was increased by some 50
percent, as Syria committed itself also to withdraw from West Beirut 2,700
men of the 85th Brigade, and 2,000 troops of the Syrian-controlled Palestinian Liberation Army.

Both the Lebanese government and the PLO gave their formal
assent to the Habib evacuation plan on August 18, and the Israeli Cabinet
followed suit the next day. The agreement paved the way for the early
Palestinian and Syrian departure from Beirut under the supervision and
protection of a three-nation Multinational Force (MNF) deployed in the
city. The Multinational Force, composed of units from France, Italy, and
the United States, was to be formed at the request of the Government of
Lebanon, to assist the Lebanese Armed Forces in assuring the safety of the
departing PLO personnel and of the Palestinians remaining in the Beirut
area, and in furthering the restoration of the sovereignty and authority of
the Lebanese government over the Beirut area.

According to the understanding, all of the PLO leadership, officers,
and troops would leave Lebanon peacefully for prearranged destinations in
other countries, in accordance with departure schedules. Military forces

present anywhere in Lebanon, whether Lebanese, Israeli, Syrian, Palestinian or any other, were in no way to interfere with the safe, secure and timely departure of the PLO members from Beirut. Palestinian noncombatants left in Beirut, including the families of those who had departed, were to be subject to Lebanese laws and regulations.

The MNF was to depart from Lebanon no later than 30 days after arrival, or sooner at the request of the Government of Lebanon, or at the direction of the individual governments involved. In case the departure of the PLO personnel did not take place in accordance with the agreed schedule, the MNF would be terminated immediately, and the contingents would leave Lebanon.

The departure period for the PLO and the Syrians was to be as short as possible, and—in any event—no longer than two weeks. On their departure, each PLO man would be allowed to carry with him one individual small arms weapon and ammunition. The PLO was to turn over to the Lebanese Armed Forces all heavy weapons and all other excess weaponry and ammunition. Prior to its departure, the PLO was also to provide the Lebanese Armed Forces full and detailed information as to the location of this military equipment left behind.

Through the International Red Cross, the PLO was to turn over to the IDF all Israeli nationals whom they had taken into custody, and the remains—or full and detailed information about the location of the remains—of all Israeli soldiers who had died inside the defensive lines of Beirut. The PLO was also to turn over to the Lebanese Armed Forces all other prisoners whom they had taken into custody. All arrangements for such turnovers were to be worked out with the Red Cross prior to the departure day.

Syrian and PLA troops deployed in Beirut were officially designated elements of the Arab Deterrent Force. According to arrangements made between the governments of Syria and Lebanon, all Syrian military personnel in Beirut were to return to Syria during the departure period. These forces would be allowed to take all their equipment and weapons with them. All elements of the Palestinian Liberation Army also were to withdraw from Lebanon to Syria.

Arrival of the MNF Contingents

On August 21, the first contingent of 397 Palestinians left Beirut by ship for Cyprus, starting the two-week evacuation process. Just before the 397 embarked at the port of Beirut, a force of over 300 French paratroops arrived to monitor the departure. The remaining elements of the Multinational Force were to arrive in increments a few days later. The total MNF was to consist of 800 American, 800 French, and 400 Italian troops. The MNF was to be assisted by some 3,000 Lebanese soldiers and security men.

On August 20, President Reagan had ordered a battalion of 800 US Marines to Beirut to participate with French and Italian forces in supervising the withdrawal of the Palestinian and Syrian troops. The Marines, from the 32d Marine Amphibious Unit, commanded by Colonel James M. Mead, were already at sea in the Mediterranean as part of the US Sixth Fleet. At 5:00 A.M. on August 25, the first elements of the battalion landed at the port of Beirut, quickly followed by other units. The battalion secured its positions in the port area, and replaced the French paratroops deployed there. By that time the French had already assisted in evacuation of 2,465 men of the PLO. Additional French forces landed at the port on August 26, and moved to the southern section of the city. They were followed by an Italian Bersigliari Battalion, which took up positions in the Gallerie Semaan area, close to the Green Line. The Italians were given the responsibility of monitoring and securing the departure of the Syrian, PLA, and PLO forces to Syria via the Beirut-Damascus highway.

During the evacuation period Colonel Mead and his men supervised the evacuation of 6,436 PLO men and their families to ships for transport to other countries. In general, the evacuation went smoothly and according to schedule. At the beginning there were some hitches and delays, particularly when Israel objected to PLO jeeps being loaded on the ships, claiming this was a breach of the Habib plan. In response to this protest, 21 jeeps were unloaded from the ship *Sol Phryne*, at Limassol, Cyprus, so that the evacuation could proceed.

Land evacuation to Syria started on August 27 after delays caused by fighting between Syrian troops and Christian militia near the Beirut-Damascus highway. Four convoys daily were planned for the overland transport during the period August 27-31. Each convoy was over a kilometer in length and included combat equipment, troops, and families of the evacuees. Israeli troops and flags were clearly visible only a very short distance away from the highway, creating a highly volatile environment. Nevertheless the Italian commander, Lieutenant Colonel Tosetti, and his troops handled the situation well, and 6,219 evacuees were escorted to Syrian lines without incident.

The 2,700 Syrian army troops (by Israeli count 3,500), part of the Arab Deterrent Force, were the last to leave on August 30 and 31. They left in about 250 trucks and buses, taking with them ten Soviet-built T-55 tanks, several other armored vehicles, and a number of artillery pieces. They withdrew, as agreed, only to the Bekaa Valley in eastern Lebanon rather than to Syria.

Departure of Arafat

On August 30, Palestinian Liberation Organization Chairman Yasser Arafat gave up his base in Lebanon and sailed to Greece. In an emotional farewell he vowed to continue the struggle against Israel for a Palestinian state, and decried the lack of support from Arab governments. Arafat, who expected to establish a new base in Tunisia, was accompanied by two senior PLO officials, bodyguards, and family members. There was great concern for Arafat's safety, and increased security measures were instituted by the Marines and the Lebanese Army. Beirut's crumbling port, shattered by seven years of civil war and the recent Israeli bombardment, was a scene of chaos, as hundreds of Arafat's supporters surrounded him seeking to get a last look at their leader before he boarded the Greek passenger ship *Atlantis*.

By September 3, all PLO fighters and Syrian troops had been evacuated without major incident. The Palestinians left Beirut for a number of different countries, but Syria took by far the largest number of them, about 8,100 by Lebanese count, or 7,400 by Israeli count. Tunisia accepted the second largest contingent—some 1,000. Between 700 and 1,000 left for South Yemen, between 550 and 700 went to Algeria, and lesser numbers went to Jordan, Iraq, Egypt, and North Yemen.

According to the Lebanese, the number of evacuees—including women and children—totalled 14,656. The Israelis counted 14,614. Both figures include Syrian troops.

While the evacuation was in progress, Israel complained that the PLO was turning over its heavy weapons, tanks, artillery, mortars, and ammunition to the left wing Muslim militia, and specifically to the leftist Mourabitoun organization, a PLO ally. This, of course, was a violation of the withdrawal accord negotiated by Habib, which required that the PLO leave its heavy arms to the Lebanese Army. There is little doubt that the Israeli charge was correct, but nothing was done about it.

On August 31 Israeli pilots shot down a Syrian MiG-25 jet aircraft, near Jounie, just north of Beirut. This brought the number of downed Syrian planes to at least 88. The MiG-25 was probably on a reconnaissance mission. A week later, on September 8, Israeli aircraft knocked out four Syrian SA missile batteries near Dahr el Baider, about ten kilometers east of Bhamdoun. A day later Israeli jets destroyed four more SA-9 launching pads in the same area.

After the departure of the PLO and the Syrians the situation in the Beirut area improved considerably. However, violations continued to jeopardize the already shaky ceasefire on the eastern front. Tension in the

Bekaa Valley was rising as each side accused the other of breaking the truce. Palestinian guerrillas operating from behind Syrian lines near the town of Rashaiya fired light weapons several times at Israeli positions. On September 4, eight Israeli soldiers were kidnapped in the Bhamdoun, Sofar area by a PLO raiding group and taken to Syrian-controlled territory. This brought to 17 the number of Israeli soldiers in PLO and Syrian hands. Both Syria and Israel started to send reinforcements to the area to beef up their forces.

On September 10 the 800 US Marines who participated in the Multinational Force turned over control of the port area to the Lebanese Army, and left Lebanon. They had not fired a shot. Most of the French and Italian troops departed during the following two days.

Chapter XXII
Assassination
and Massacre

Death of Bashir Jemayel

On the afternoon of September 14, a bomb demolished the headquarters of the Lebanese Christian Phalangist Party in the Ashrafiya district of East Beirut. This occurred as President-elect Bashir Jemayel, who was to assume office on September 23, was addressing several hundred of his followers at a weekly meeting in the building. Jemayel and several of his close associates were killed in the explosion. The bombing was the work of skilled professionals who obviously had access to the heavily guarded building.

Jemayel's death created a power vacuum in Lebanon. It also inevitably exacerbated the existing polarization between the Lebanese power groups. It seriously increased the difficulty of a mutual settling of accounts and caused general deterioration of the political situation which threatened to develop into a new civil war.

The President-elect, in his capacity as the Phalange leader, had been secretly working with Israel since 1976. The partnership had been growing over time as PLO and Syrian violence against the Lebanese Christians increased. As the presidential elections approached, however, Jemayel realized that, even though the Israeli invasion greatly boosted his presidential aspirations, close identification with Israel could undermine his bid to build a unified Lebanon by effecting a reconciliation with his Muslim foes. Thus he had since June been increasingly distancing himself personally from the Israelis, even though close collaboration continued between his Phalangist militia and the IDF.

Israelis Move Into Beirut

Confirmation of Bashir Jemayel's death reached Israel at about 11:00 P.M. on September 14. Prime Minister Begin immediately sum-

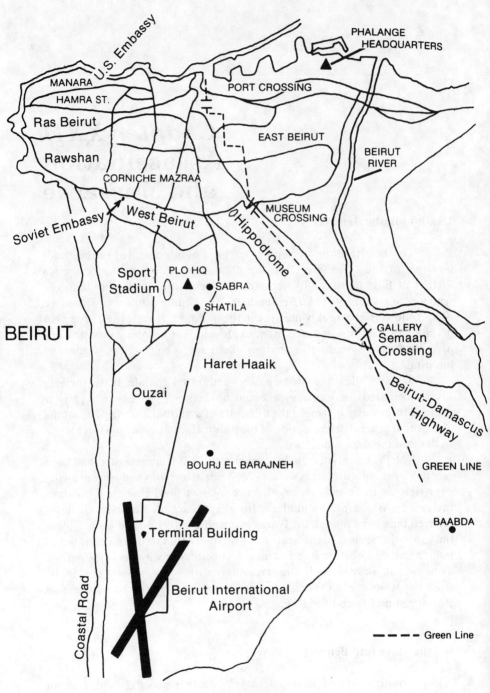

Beirut

moned Defense Minister Sharon and Chief of Staff Eitan to an emergency meeting. They decided that, because of the volatile situation, the IDF should at once enter West Beirut to preserve order. Directives for action were instantly sent to the Northern Command. One of these directives instructed that the Palestinian refugee camps in West Beirut were not to be entered by Israeli troops; searching and mopping-up of the camps was to be done later either by the Phalangist forces or by the Lebanese Army, or both. The instructions added that the Lebanese Army was entitled to enter any place in Beirut upon its request.

The Israelis justified their occupation of West Beirut by the necessity of forestalling the danger of violence, bloodshed, and chaos following the assassination of Bashir Jemayel. They asserted that some 2,000 PLO fighters, equipped with light and heavy weapons, had remained in Beirut in flagrant violation of the evacuation agreement. In fact, the IDF entry into West Beirut was perceived by many Christians and Muslims as the only action that could prevent bloodshed and protect the Muslims from the vengeful Phalangists, and it was hailed and praised accordingly on all sides.

Before dawn on September 15, General Eitan flew to Beirut, where he met Major General Amir Drori, commander of the Northern Command, and Brigadier General Amos Yaron, commander of the 96th Division deployed around Beirut. Afterward, General Eitan went to the Phalangists' headquarters. There he met with senior officers of the Phalangist Command and requested that they order a general mobilization of their forces, impose a curfew on all areas under their control, and be ready to join the IDF if fighting broke out. At the meeting the Phalangists were told that the IDF would not enter the Palestinian refugee camps in West Beirut. Supposedly, Eitan mentioned that the Minister of Defense and he had agreed the previous evening that the Phalangist forces should check the Sabra and Shatila camps for PLO fighters. Both camps were essentially residential neighborhoods with low permanent structures along narrow alleys and streets. Their borders were not exactly defined. The Sabra camp extended over an area of approximately 330 × 200 meters, and Shatila covered about 500 × 500 meters.

Firing From Sabra and Shatila Camps

The IDF entry into Beirut began shortly after 6:00 A.M. on September 15. Israeli infantry and armor advanced into West Beirut along several routes. During the first hours after the IDF entry, they encountered no armed resistance. The various well-armed Palestinian and leftist Lebanese guerrilla groups that remained in West Beirut were evidently taken by surprise. Within a few hours, however, some shots were fired at the Israelis, causing a few delays and changes in the routes of advance. Later, heavy fire was directed at the Israeli troops advancing east of the Shatila and Sabra refugee camps. The Israelis responded with artillery and offshore gunboat shelling of the Muslim leftist militia positions within the city, from which the firing had come. In the course of the fighting three Israeli soldiers were killed and about 100 wounded. There is no reliable data on casualties incurred by the Muslim leftist guerrillas or the Palestinians, but they were not high. Soon after this Phalangist officials suggested that their troops should occupy the Sabra and Shatila camps.

At 8:00 A.M. on September 15, Israeli Minister of Defense Sharon arrived at the forward command post of Brigadier General Yaron's division, located on the roof of a five-story residential apartment building some 200 meters southeast of the Shatila camp. Although it was possible to have a general view of the camps from the roof, it was impossible to see what was happening within the alleys and narrow streets. General Eitan joined Sharon at the command post and reported to him that he agreed with the Phalangists that they should move into the Sabra and Shatila camps. General Sharon then went to the Phalangists' headquarters, where he conferred with senior Phalangist officials and allegedly assented to their request that Phalangist forces enter West Beirut. They were to maintain contact with Major General Drori regarding their actions. From there Sharon went to the Jemayels' home in the village of Bikfaya to pay a condolence call on Bashir's family.

General Drori met with the Phalangist commanders in the evening of September 15 and told them that their entry into West Beirut would take place the next day. However, he was uneasy about the plans to allow the Phalangists into the camps, and he decided to ask the commander of the Lebanese Army to send his forces into the camps instead. The Lebanese Army leadership, however, declined.

By Thursday morning, September 16, West Beirut was completely in Israeli hands. There was no more fighting, and everything was quiet and calm. The Fakehrani, Sabra, and Shatila refugee camps were closed and surrounded, and the Phalangists were ready to move in. At about 11:00 A.M. several senior Phalangist officers met with General Drori at the headquarters of Yaron's division. There it was agreed that the Phalangists would coordinate their move into the camps with Brigadier General Yaron. It had been decided that one company of about 150 Phalangist troops would go through the Sabra and Shatila camps from south to north and from west to east. A Phalangist liaison officer with a radio set would be present at all times at Yaron's forward command post, and a liaison officer from the Israeli Mossad, officially known as the Intelligence and Special Projects Agency, would be at the Phalangist headquarters. The Phalangist company that was to enter the camps was an intelligence unit headed by Eli

Hobeika, chief of Phalangist intelligence. This unit was specially trained to flush out guerrillas who tried to hide among the civilian population.

General Yaron had doubts about the Phalangists' combat methods, and apparently had had arguments with them over these issues in the past. He spoke with the Phalangist commanders and warned them that their task was to clean out the camps of the terrorists and not to harm the civilian population.

The Phalangists Enter the Camps

The Phalangists began to move into the camps at about 6:00 P.M. on September 16. Israeli and Phalangist sources insist that at that time there were about 2,000 Palestinian guerrillas in the camps, armed with light and heavy weapons. The Palestinians have denied this, and they are undoubtedly right. It would have been suicidal for the Phalangists to have sent in only 150 men against such a large, well-armed force. On the other hand, there is no doubt that as the Israelis were advancing into West Beirut they had received considerable fire from the area of the Sabra and Shatila camps. It is also reasonable to assume that not all of the PLO fighters left during the evacuation but that some remained in the camp in order to renew underground activities at a later period, and to protect the civilian population which had remained in the camps. Keeping in mind the hostility prevailing between the various sects and organizations, it was not unreasonable for the PLO to provide such security to their families and fellow Palestinians.

The Phalangists entered the Sabra and Shatila camps in two groups, one from the west, and the other from the south. Once they passed the barrier surrounding the camps, their movements within the camps were no longer visible from the roof of the Israeli forward command post, either by Israeli observers or by the Phalangist liaison officer. Since the Phalangists started their operation after nightfall, they had requested that the IDF provide illumination. The Israelis complied and fired mortar illuminating shells over the camps intermittently throughout the night. Soon after they entered the camps, the advancing Phalangists were engaged by PLO guerrillas, and sustained several casualties.

At about 9:00 P.M. the Phalangist liaison officer received a report from one of the Phalangists inside the Shatila camp that they were holding 45 people. He requested advice from the liaison officer about what he should do with those people. The Israeli heard the liaison officer reply, "Do the will of God," which the Israelis interpreted as instructions to kill the prisoners. In another radio communication overheard by an Israeli officer, the commander of the Phalangist unit which had entered the camp told Eli Hobeika that he had captured 50 women and children, and asked what to do. Hobeika's reply over the radio was, "This is the last time you are going to ask me a question like that. You know exactly what to do." After hearing this, raucous laughter broke out among the Phalangists' liaison personnel on the roof of the forward command post. It was obvious to the listening Israeli officer that murder of women and children was being condoned. However, no matter how disgusted he may have been, he did nothing about it.

Shortly after this the Phalangist liaison officer entered the dining room at the forward command post building and stated in the presence of many IDF officers, including Brigadier General Yaron, that about 300 persons, including many civilians, had been killed by the Phalangists. Soon, however, the Phalangist officer corrected his statement to 120 killed. At about 10:30 P.M. the Deputy Intelligence Officer of the Northern Command received a report about the Phalangist officer's statement that either 300 people or 120 people had been killed in the camps. He transmitted this information to the Intelligence Branch of the General Staff in Tel Aviv, with the suggestion that this was an important and sensitive matter of personal concern to senior responsible officers, including the Director of Military Intelligence. The text of this report was distributed to various itelligence sections and reached the Director of Military Intelligence, Major General Yehoshua Saguy at his home shortly after 6:00 A.M. on September 17.

From the content of the report Saguy mistakenly determined that the source of the report was the Operations Branch and not the Intelligence Branch. Thus the intelligence personnel, following standard doctrine that unconfirmed reports not from intelligence sources are unreliable and therefore should not be circulated, did not disseminate the account. The report was transmitted verbally at about 7:30 A.M. to the Defense Ministry's situation room. There is no evidence that the report reached the Defense Minister, or came to his knowledge in any other way. Saguy arrived at his office about at 8 A.M. and ordered that more information be obtained immediately about what had happened in the Sabra and Shatila camps. Some clarifying information arrived during the morning hours, but no direct confirmation of the report and no further details were obtained.

Israeli Awareness of the Massacre Potential

Meanwhile, at 7:30 P.M. on Thursday, September 16, the Israeli Cabinet had met to discuss the situation in Lebanon in the wake of the assassination of Bashir Jemayel. Besides members of the Cabinet, the Chief of the General Staff, the Director of the Mossad, and the Director of Military Intelligence also were present. The Chief of Staff provided details about the IDF's operation and about his meetings with Phalangist commanders. He explained that that evening the Phalangists had already entered the Palestinian refugee camps, but that the IDF soldiers would not enter the camps and would not fight together with the Phalangists. General Eitan added that, with one minor exception, all of western Beirut was in Israeli hands.

There was considerable discussion at the meeting about the wisdom of entering West Beirut, but at the end the general opinion was that it was justified and correct. Deputy Prime Minister David Levy, while agreeing with the resolution justifying Israel's move, nevertheless warned that the argument that it had been done to prevent chaos could be criticized and disbelieved, since the Phalangists were permitted to enter the Palestinian camps. Israel would bear the blame for whatever might happen. It is interesting that Mr. Levy seemed to be under no illusions about what the Phalangists might do in the camps, nor do there seem to have been any illusions among those hearing his words, since no one contradicted him.

During the night of September 16/17, word about the excesses committed by the Phalangists in the camps was circulating among the IDF officers at the divisional forward command post. At one point the Phalangists in the camps complained that two of their people had been killed, and that the Israelis were not supplying sufficient illumination, which made the operation very difficult. When asked by the Phalangist liaison officer to increase the illumination, Lieutenant Colonel Triber of the Divisional Operations Branch responded that the Phalangists had already killed 300 people and he was not willing to provide them with illumination to kill more. Nevertheless, limited illumination was later provided.

At approximately 9:00 A.M. on Friday, September 17, Brigadier General Yaron met with representatives of the Phalangists at the divisional forward command post, and discussed with them their request that additional Phalangist units should be allowed into the camps. This issue had not been resolved when General Drori arrived at the divisional command post at 11 A.M. As soon as he learned about the events in the camps the previous night he ordered Brigadier General Yaron to halt the Phalangists' operations. They were to stop where they were, and not to advance any further. This order was immediately conveyed to the Phalangist commanders. At the same time Drori informed General Eitan that he had ordered the Phalangist operations to stop.

Rumors of murders being committed in the camps were already circulating among Israeli officers and soldiers in the Beirut area. At 8:00 A.M. the distinguished Israeli journalist Ze'ev Schiff received a call at his home in Tel Aviv from a friend in the Israeli General Staff, informing him that there had been slaughter in the camps. Mr. Schiff tried to check the report with Military Intelligence and Operations, and with the Mossad, but received no confirmation, except a comment that "something" was going on. At 11:00 A.M. Schiff met with Minister of Communication Mordechai Zipori at the minister's office and told him about the information he had received. Zipori, a prominent retired general, and former Deputy Defense Minister, tried to contact the Director of Military Intelligence and the head of the Mossad by phone, but could not reach them. Then he called the Foreign Minister, Yitzhak Shamir, told him about the report he had received from Schiff, and asked Shamir to check the matter with the proper authorities.

In the meantime, in Beirut, Brigadier General Yaron met with several Phalangist officers during the morning hours and agreed that an additional Phalangist force could deploy at the airport, but would not be sent into the camps until it was approved by General Eitan. General Drori met with the commander of the Lebanese Army again, and tried once more to persuade him directly and, through him, the Prime Minister of Lebanon, that the Lebanese Army should enter the camps. Drori's request once more was refused.

During the day on Friday, September 17, IDF troops stationed near the refugee camps became aware of continuing violence there. Crew members of a tank company deployed on an earth embankment some 200 meters from one of the buildings of the camp saw Phalangist soldiers taking men, women, and children out of the camp and leading them to the sport stadium. One officer, Lieutenant Avi Grabovsky, saw Phalangist soldiers killing a group of five women and children, and then he observed another incident of a Phalangist soldier killing a civilian man. Grabovsky reported what he had seen to his commander and to other officers of his unit. They suggested that he report this to the brigade commander. Other Israeli soldiers, from units stationed in the vicinity, related that they saw various acts of mistreatment by Phalangists of men, women, and children, who had been taken out of the camp. Stories about these murders circulated among the troops. One Israeli soldier, seeing a Phalangist who had just come out from a camp, asked him why they were killing civilian men and women. The Phalangist answered that women will give birth to terrorists, and that their children also will grow up to be terrorists.

The Involvement of Generals Eitan and Sharon

General Eitan arrived at the Khalde airstrip south of Beirut at 3:30 P.M. on September 17. He was met by generals Drori and Yaron. The three drove to the Phalangist headquarters in East Beirut. On the way Drori briefed the chief of staff on what he knew about the Phalangists' actions and atrocities.

According to one version, during the subsequent meeting the senior

Phalangist commander did not mention any atrocities committed by his troops in the camps, nor did General Eitan mention what he had learned from Drori. The discussion was relaxed, and supposedly there seemed to be satisfaction that the Phalangists had effectively carried out their mission in the camps. General Eitan apparently agreed that the Phalangists should continue mopping up the camps until 5:00 A.M. on Saturday, September 18, at which time, because of American pressure, they should stop their action. In another unconfirmed version of the meeting it was said that the Phalangists had reported to General Eitan that the operation was proceeding satisfactorily and that everything was all right. They complained that the Americans were pressuring them to leave the camps, which they would do by 5:00 A.M. the next day, after having carried out all their missions. General Eitan's reaction, according to this report, was: "Okay, all right, you did the job."

The Phalangist commander wanted to send more troops into the camps, but General Eitan did not agree, since the Phalangists were supposed to leave the camps the next day at 5:00 A.M. There is reason to believe that, in spite of Israeli disapproval, the Phalangists sneaked in some additional troops. These were not from the Phalangist detachment concentrated at the airport, since this unit was being observed by the Israelis.

During the meeting the Phalangists requested a few tractors or bulldozers from the IDF, in order to demolish illegal structures in the camp. General Eitan agreed to the request. However, at the conclusion of the meeting an order was issued to give the Phalangists only one tractor, after removing Israeli markings from it. The tractor was supplied too late to be used, and was returned immediately by the Phalangists, who, meanwhile, had brought in their own tractors, which they used in the camps during the night of September 17/18 and on the morning of the 18th.

After the meeting with the Phalangists, General Eitan returned to Tel Aviv, and at about 8:30 P.M. he called the defense minister to report on his visit to Beirut. Presumably he informed General Sharon that in the course of the action in the camps the Phalangists had harmed the civilian population. He allegedly stated that they had "gone too far," and that therefore their activities had been stopped in the afternoon. The entry of additional forces had been prevented, and an order had been issued to the Phalangists to remove their forces from the camps by 5:00 A.M. the following morning.

Apparently this was the first time that General Sharon learned about the killings in the camps—at least officially. There is no evidence that he had any previous specific official information concerning the massacres commited by the Phalangists in Sabra and Shatila. It also appears that even though these events were already known to many Israelis, including a few Cabinet ministers, there had been no reports on this to Prime Minister

Begin during those two days. Complaints had been received by the Foreign Ministry from American Embassy officials, but these were handled routinely by Foreign Ministry personnel, and a summary was sent to the situation room in the Defense Ministry to be brought to the attention of General Sharon.

The Evidence Accumulates

The Phalangists did not leave the camps as directed by 5:00 A.M. Saturday, September 18. Shortly before 7:00 A.M. several Phalangist soldiers entered the Gaza Hospital, run by the Palestinian Red Crescent, in the Sabra camp, and took a group of foreign doctors and nurses working at the hospital to a former UN building. As the group passed along Sabra Street they saw a number of corpses on both sides of the street, and groups of people sitting on the sidewalks with Phalangists guarding them. After arrival at their destination, some of the doctors and nurses were interrogated. But the interrogation was suddenly stopped short, and all the people were taken to an Israeli command post, where they were handed over to IDF officers. The Israelis released the prisoners immediately and transported them to another part of town.

Brigadier General Yaron learned at 6:30 A.M. that the Phalangists had not yet left the camps as instructed. He met immediately with the local Phalangist commander and ordered him to vacate the camps without any delay. The Phalangist forces left the camps at approximately 8:00 A.M. Afterward the Israelis instructed the inhabitants of the camps, over loudspeakers, to assemble in certain areas, and those who did were led to the stadium. There, the IDF gave them food and water and permitted them to return to their homes.

After the Phalangists left the camps, Red Cross personnel, many journalists, and other persons entered. It was immediately apparent that, particularly in Shatila, civilians, including women and children, had been massacred. It was equally clear that many of the dead could not have been killed in combat, but had been murdered. There was evidence of many acts of barbarism.

It is impossible to determine precisely the number of people who perished. The low estimates of some 300 people came from sources connected with the Lebanese Government and the Phalangists. Palestinian sources speak of thousands of casualties. The IDF estimated that the number killed in the massacre was between 700 and 800. The Lebanese Red Cross and the International Red Cross reported that 460 bodies were found and counted in the camps, including 328 Palestinians and 109 Lebanese. The remainder included Syrians, Iranians, and other foreign nationals.

Among the bodies there were 15 women (8 Lebanese and 7 Palestinian) and 20 children (12 Lebanese and 8 Palestinian). In addition several hundred people disappeared and presumably were murdered. Also, an unknown number of others apparently were buried by families before the Red Cross count. All together it would be reasonable to assume that the total number of victims of the massacre was close to one thousand.

Whereas the Minister of Defense and senior members of the Israeli defense establishment learned about the tragic events in the camps on Friday, September 17, no report of the slaughter was made to the Prime Minister even on Saturday, September 18. It is said that Mr. Begin learned about the massacres from a BBC radio broadcast Saturday evening and immediately called Sharon and Eitan requesting confirmation and explanation. They reported to him what had happened, and informed him that the actions had been halted and that the Phalangists had been removed from the camp. Begin had not been a party to the decision to allow the Phalangists into the camps, and he received no report about that decision until the Cabinet met on the evening of September 16. It will be recalled, however, that the results of that decision had been predicted quite accurately at the meeting by Deputy Prime Minister David Levy. Neither at the meeting nor afterward did the Prime Minister raise any objection to the entry of the Phalangists into the camps. Nor did he react to Mr. Levy's warning.

Direct Responsibility of the Phalangists

All the evidence indicates that the massacres were perpetrated by the Phalangists between 6:00 P.M. September 16, when they entered the Sabra and Shatila camps, and 8:00 A.M. September 18, when they left. The victims were found only in the areas where the Phalangist forces were in control. No other military or semi-military forces were in the camps when the massacre was committed. Although there were accusations that Major Haddad's Free Lebanon militia had participated, this is patently false, and was so proven in the subsequent Israeli investigation.

Following the massacre, the Phalangist commanders, in various interviews with the mass media, denied that they were responsible. Confronted on September 19 by General Eitan, who had visited the camps, the top Phalangist leaders seemed bewildered. It is possible that they did not know exactly what had happened in the camps and had no control over their people there. But their responsibility is unquestionable. Although there is no evidence to suggest that the Phalangists who entered the camps had received explicit orders from their top command to perpetrate acts of slaughter, the attitude of the field commanders was clear from the radio conversations overheard by the Israelis. The men who entered the camp

were consumed with hatred for all Palestinians, whom they blamed, and—
in a general sense—rightly, for atrocities and the many other calamities
brought upon the Christians during the civil war. Their hatred was com-
pounded by longing for revenge in the wake of the assassination of their
beloved leader, Bashir Jemayel, and scores of his and their close associates,
two days before they entered the camps.

It must not be forgotten that what the world saw as an atrocity was
just one more event in the tragic chain of murders, massacres, revenge, and
genocide which had been common occurrences in Lebanon for many centuries. Had the Phalangists who were in those camps failed to do what they
did, they would probably have been censored by their fellows. This is not to
justify what was done, or to suggest that the perpetrators of the atrocities
deserve sympathy because they were simply doing what had been done to
their families and compatriots by the PLO. Although in their minds they
seemed to rationalize what was done, nonetheless, it was an abominable
crime committed in cold blood.

Indirect Responsibility of Israel

The facts of life and death in Lebanon were well known to most
Israelis. This is evident from the words and actions of Israeli officers on the
scene before the massacres, and from the words of Deputy Prime Minister
Levy, and the reactions—or lack thereof—of his fellow Cabinet ministers.
Opposition leader Shimon Peres stated during the Knesset debate shortly
after the massacres, "Mr. Prime Minister, Mr. Defense Minister, I want to
ask you whose stupid idea was it to send the Phalangists to the refugee
camps in order to locate the terrorists? . . . Have you an answer, Mr.
Sharon? After all, you don't have to be a political genius or a famed
commander. It is enough to be a country cop in order to understand from
the outset that those militias, which were emotional more than ever following the murder of their leader, were likely to commit atrocities among
innocent people."

One cannot dismiss Israeli responsibility for the massacre by saying
that it was "indirect." The horrified reactions of most Israelis to the tragedy
make it clear that the Israeli nation and the Israeli people should not be held
responsible for what happened at Sabra and Shatila. But there were a
number of Israelis who—in the eyes of their countrymen, and probably in
their own consciences—had more than an indirect responsibility for what
happened, because they allowed it to happen. Strictly speaking, the indirect
responsibility lies with the Israeli Government in general, and with those
officials and officers of the IDF in particular who authorized the entry of
the Phalangists into the camp, disregarding the very possible danger—

almost the inevitability—of a massacre. Substantial indirect responsibility must also be assigned to those individuals who, when they received reports of what was happening in the camps, did not act to prevent the continuation of the Phalangist crimes, who did not do everything within their power to prevent or halt the slaughter.

An equally significant indirect responsibility falls also on the Lebanese Government and the Lebanese Army Command since they did not respond affirmatively to General Drori's urgent request that they enter the camps before, or instead of, the Phalangists. They entered the camps only on September 19, after the massacres had already been committed, and the Phalangists had left.

The decision to allow the Phalangists to enter the camp was unwarranted and unjustified. Those who made it were well aware that combat morality among various factional combat groups in Lebanon was much lower than that of the IDF, and that atrocities against civilians had been widespread in Lebanon. It was well known that the Phalangists harbored enmity toward the Palestinians, not only because they were considered to be the source of all troubles that afflicted Lebanon, but because the PLO had committed equally horrible massacres against Lebanese Christians.

Nevertheless, the decision to send in the Phalangists had not been made arbitrarily without consideration of certain military implications that could benefit the IDF. The entry of the Phalangists into Sabra and Shatila meant that the IDF could avoid possible losses in hazardous combat in built-up areas. The Israelis were using Phalangist expertise in identifying PLO guerrillas, which was better than that of IDF soldiers. In addition, the Israelis, by agreeing to the Phalangist request, were also giving them an opportunity to take part in an operation which they regarded as a move toward the restoration of Lebanese independence.

Although all these were valid considerations from a narrow, strictly military, point of view, those in the IDF who were responsible for this rationalization should have realized that by letting the Phalangists into the camps massacres were virtually inevitable. These massacres, in turn, besides being a human tragedy, would cause disastrous consequences for the Israeli government and the Israel Defense Force, as well as trauma for the nation.

At the inquiry into the events leading up to the massacre Brigadier General Yaron made a statement on the degree of Israeli indirect involvement and responsibility. He said: "On this point [the possibility of massacres] everyone showed insensitivity, pure and simple. Nothing else . . . On Friday (September 17) . . . I did badly, I admit. I cannot know how it is possible that a division commander—and I think that this applies to the division commander and up—how it is possible that a division commander in the field does not know that 300, 400, 500 or 1,000—I don't know how many—are being murdered here? If he is like that, let him go. How can such a thing happen? Why didn't he know? Why was he oblivious? That's why he didn't know, and that's why he did not stop it . . . but I take myself to task. I admit here, from this rostrum—we were all insensitive—that's all."

Return of the Multinational Force

On September 20, 1982, in the wake of the massacres in the camps, the Lebanese Cabinet asked the US, French, and Italian governments to return the Multinational Force to Beirut to maintain order. The three nations agreed to the request with the stipulation that they would do it only after the Israelis withdrew their forces from the city. On September 21, the Israeli Government accepted the redeployment of the Multinational Force, but did not make any commitments on when the IDF would withdraw. A day later, however, under heavy international pressure, the Israelis outlined a plan for a phased withdrawal from West Beirut, to be completed in four days.

The first contingent of the Multinational Force, 350 French paratroopers and infantrymen, returned to the city on September 24. The entire force was to be increased to 3,600 men, with each of the three countries contributing 1,200 soldiers. The Israelis completed most of their withdrawal from West Beirut on September 26, leaving only a token force in the port area and at the Beirut International Airport. On September 27, French and Italian members of the MNF entered the camps of Sabra and Shatila.

On September 29 the US contingent began landing at the Beirut port area and at the Beirut International Airport, and took up positions near the airport as the last of the Israeli troops were departing.

The Multinational Force divided West Beirut into three roughly horizontal zones. The French were responsible for the city area as far south as the refugee camps of Sabra and Shatila, the Italian zone encompassed the Bourj el Barajneh camp farther south, and the US Marines were to patrol the southernmost zone around the International Airport. There was no overall command or coordinating organization. During the following weeks the MNF consolidated and strengthened its positions, and cleared out thousands of pieces of unexploded ammunition that had accumulated during the seven years of the civil war and the recent fighting. A general feeling of safety and security was quickly established among the Muslim population of West Beirut. Most of the people felt that, at least for the time being, the horrors of a war lasting nearly a decade had finally ended.

One week after the assassination of President-elect Bashir Jemayel, on September 21 the Lebanese parliament elected his brother—Amin Jemayel—President of Lebanon by a sweeping majority. He was elected easily because he was supported by many Muslim delegates who had opposed Bashir. The Muslim legislators sensed that Amin was less pro-Israeli and more pro-Arab than his brother. They also believed that by ignoring the Phalange responsibility for the Sabra and Shatila massacres, they could not only strike a deal with Amin about an increased Muslim role in the future government, but that they could get Amin's assurances that the new government would keep Israel at arm's length, and would have closer relations with the Arab world.

On November 1, President Reagan, at the request of the new Lebanese President, agreed to expand the role of the US Marines in Beirut. President Reagan changed the role of the Marines from simple "presence" to "participation" with the other national contingents of the Multinational Force in limited patrols.

Chapter XXIII
Renewal of
Lebanon's Civil War

The hoped-for peace and reconciliation between the various Lebanese political and religious groups lasted for only a short time, despite the presence of the Multinational Force in Beirut. For a few months, however, much of Lebanon, including Beirut, enjoyed peace and tranquility, which had been unknown since 1975.

Israel-Lebanon Agreement

During this period of relative calm the Israeli and Lebanese governments attempted to normalize the new and peaceful relationship which the Israeli invasion had made possible. Negotiations between Israeli and Lebanese delegations began in a seacoast hotel in Khalde, south of Beirut, late in December 1982. Later sessions rotated between Israel and Lebanon. On May 17, 1983, the governments of Israel and Lebanon signed an agreement to end the war between their respective countries. They agreed to the existing international boundary as the inviolable border between the two states, and to mutual respect for the sovereignty, independence, and territorial integrity of each country.

Although this was the crowning achievement of the pact, in fact the state of war between Lebanon and Israel had been purely formal and theoretical. Lebanon had taken part only in the first Arab-Israeli War—1948-1949—and the entire negotiations were conducted not between belligerents, but between neighboring states which had no reason to fight against each other. Nevertheless the Lebanese, concerned about their relations with other Arab states, entered the agreement most reluctantly, and signed it only under considerable pressure from the United States.

The agreement, a complex package of formal documents, understandings, and memoranda, called for a simultaneous withdrawal of Israeli, Syrian, and PLO forces from Lebanon, despite the fact that Syria had not been consulted, directly or indirectly, during the negotiations. A security zone delineated by the Awali River, some 45 kilometers to the north of the Israeli border, was agreed upon. In this security zone Lebanon was to maintain specified limited forces.

Two Lebanese Army brigades were to be stationed in the security zone. One, a Lebanese Army territorial brigade, was to be stationed in the so-called zone "B", an area up to 15 kilometers from the Israeli border. The other, a regular Lebanese Army brigade, was to take over the remaining parts of the security zone, or zone "A", up to the Awali River. It was understood that Major Sa'ad Haddad's militia was to provide the nucleus of the territorial brigade. The regular and territorial brigades were to be equipped with their organic weapons and equipment, but no heavy weapons. Lebanese authorities were to enforce special security measures aimed at detecting and preventing hostile anti-Israeli activities and the introduction into the security region, or movement through it, of unauthorized armed men or military equipment.

The success of the entire agreement depended on Syria's attitude, and especially on its willingness to withdraw its forces from Lebanon, which under the prevailing circumstances seemed very doubtful. In Damascus, the agreement was considered anti-Syrian, anti-Arab, pro-American, pro-Israeli, and unacceptable as a warrant for the withdrawal of Syrian and PLO troops from Lebanon. Supported by the Soviet Union, Syria rejected the agreement, and demanded an unconditional withdrawal of Israeli forces from South Lebanon. Syria's rejection of the agreement, coupled with its support of armed opposition to the Lebanese Government, forced the Amin Jemayel government to abrogate the May 17 agreements less than one year later, and replace them with an uneasy alliance with Syria.

While negotiations with Israel were in progress, President Jemayel sought to achieve the following basic political goals: the removal of foreign forces from Lebanon, the extension of government authority over the entire country, dissolution of the various militia forces, and the rebuilding of the Lebanese Army. He failed utterly to achieve any of these goals. A year after he took office Syria and Israel continued to occupy almost 75% of the country, and PLO forces were still in Lebanon. The various independent Muslim, Druze, and Christian militias were in total control of their respective enclaves in the regions not occupied by Syria and Israel. The central government was unable to exercise its authority even over its own capital, and the Lebanese Army, which was to have been the backbone of the future Lebanese state, was approaching disintegration despite the arrival of a training mission from the United States.

Adversaries in the Renewed Civil War

None of the religious communities was ready to give up its narrow interests. Without a national consensus based upon compromise, new sectarian hostilities became unavoidable. The strongest and most influential forces that took part in the conflict that developed were:

The Lebanese Army, inactive since the 1975-1976 Civil War, was being rebuilt with US assistance. Eighty US advisors from different services were assisting in training, and the US Government committed over $150 million to equip the army with tanks, armored vehicles, artillery, mortars, machine guns, and other weapons. Early in the summer of 1983 the Army's strength was over 22,000 men, and it was planned to be enlarged to some 35,000. However, the paper strength of the Army was misleading. It was, in fact, a conglomeration of varied alliances split along confessional lines. This did not augur well for future cohesion, if the Army should be called upon to impose state authority by quelling fraternal fighting. About 30% of the enlisted men were Shiite Muslims; approximately 30% were Christians; the remaining 40% were divided between Sunni Muslims and Druze. However, the officer ranks were dominated by Christians, mostly Maronites.

The Christian Militia was comprised of several armed Christian organizations, the largest of them being the Phalange, founded by Pierre Jemayel, and the National Liberals, led by former President Camille Chamoun. The smaller groups included the Tanzine, Guardians of the Cedars, and the Maronite League.

The Phalangist organization of the Jemayel family had become the central core of the combined Christian militias called the "Lebanese Forces." Its strength was over 6,000 full-time soldiers and from 10,000 to 15,000 militiamen. The Lebanese Forces had a well organized Central Command, led by former Lebanese Army officers; its main centers of power were in Mount Lebanon and East Beirut. The link between the Christian forces and Israel had been established in the mid-1970s, and there had been many meetings between the Phalange leaders and representatives of the Israeli Government. The Israel Defense Force supplied the Lebanese Forces with weapons and uniforms, and offered officer training in facilities in Israel. The Mossad maintained close contact with the Phalangists and had a permanent office just outside East Beirut in the area controlled by the Lebanese Forces.

The Druze Militia was the military arm of the Progressive Socialist Party led by Walid Jumblatt. Its strength was about 4,000 men, heavily armed, with tanks and artillery. Jumblatt, who was closely associated with Syria despite the fact that his father Kamal was probably assassinated by Syrian agents, was receiving military aid from Damascus. Village and small town local Druze militia forces numbered about 5,000 additional fighters. Some of these could be mobilized in a matter of a few days to support the main militia force. The Druze center of power was in the Shouf Mountains south of the Beirut-Damascus highway.

The Amal, the militia of the Shiite Muslim el Amal movement was led by a Beirut lawyer and politician, Nabih Berri. The movement was organized in 1975 by Shiite Imman Moussa Sadr to unite the Shiite population of Lebanon in their struggle to end political and social discrimination against them, which existed even though they were a majority in South Lebanon and in West Beirut.

When the civil war erupted in 1975, the Amal became an ally of the PLO. Things changed in 1978 when, during the Litani operation in March of that year, local Shiite populations suffered casualties, and blamed them on the PLO. This led to violent confrontations between the PLO and the Amal. In August of that year Moussa Sadr disappeared while on a trip to Libya, and the Amal blamed PLO collusion, adding to the hostility between the two organizations. During and following the Israeli invasion of June 1982, the Amal was largely inactive. Like most of the Shiite population, members of the Amal were neutral or even friendly toward Israel, for they considered that the defeat of the PLO ended both the ruthless Palestinian occupation and the Israeli air raids in retaliation for PLO terrorism. Nabih Berri, who replaced Moussa Sadr at the head of the Amal, was a pragmatic politician. He saw in the Israeli invasion and destruction of the PLO benefits for the Shiites and even the possibility of sharing power with Jemayel. However, lack of progress in persuading the Jemayel government to give the Shiites a larger role in governing the country turned Berri toward militant policies. Meanwhile, the Amal was split by the defection of a small and fanatic faction led by pro-Iranian Hussein Mussawi. This group established its headquarters in Syrian-occupied Baalbek and organized the "Muslim al Amal" group. Its most fanatic members formed the Islamic Jihad, which claimed responsibility for numerous attacks on Israeli, US, and French forces, and foreign civilians residing in Lebanon.

The estimated strength of the Amal in 1983 was about 10,000 militiamen, armed by both Syria and the Iranian Shiite government of Ayatollah Ruhollah Khomeini. It controlled sections of southern and coastal Lebanon, most of West Beirut and—through Hussein Mussawi—Baalbek in eastern Lebanon.

Mourabitoun was the Sunni Muslim militia, commanded by Ibrahim Koleitat. It had a force of over 4,000 well-armed militiamen. Some of its weapons were acquired in August 1982 from the departing PLO guerrillas. Mourabitoun was leftist, pan-Arabic, and was originally inspired by former Egyptian President Gamal Abdel Nasser. Its main base of operations was in those areas of West Beirut where Sunni Muslims were in the majority.

Israeli Withdrawal from the Shouf Mountains

By mid-summer 1983 the Israeli government had decided to withdraw its forces from the Beirut suburbs and from the Shouf Mountains—where Christians and Druze were locked in a bloody conflict—and establish a new defense line along the Awali River to the north of Sidon. No withdrawal was planned in the eastern sector, where Israeli long range guns in the Bekaa Valley were positioned less than 30 kilometers from Damascus. The relocation operation was accomplished in two days, during September 2d and 3d, 1983. The Israeli decision had been prompted by internal political pressure, and by the hit-and-run attacks on the IDF in southern Lebanon. Between January and August 1983 Israeli forces in Lebanon were the target of over 260 attacks, in which some 200 men were killed or wounded. The United States, fearing escalation of sectarian strife, attempted to persuade the Israelis not to withdraw, but to no avail.

The new line followed the course of the Awali, Besri, and Barouk rivers for about 115 kilometers and intersected the old line at the northern tip of the Jabal Barouk, a north-south range of the Lebanon Mountains in central Lebanon. The line was made up of a number of fortified defensive positions and observations posts, all dug in along the steep cliffs of the rivers. The defense system included mobile patrols along the rivers, and roadblocks where traffic from south to north and north to south was being checked. The Israeli Navy patrolled the Lebanese coast from the Awali River to Rosh Hanikra (Israel), about 62 kilometers away.

The redeployment of the Israeli forces made life for the IDF somewhat easier, for it removed about half a million rather hostile civilians from Israeli responsibility. It also shortened lines of supply, decreasing the danger of attacks on the Israeli convoys. This enabled Israel to cut the strength of its forces in Lebanon to some 15,000 troops. Israel remained in control of a nearly 2,800 square kilometer area inhabited by approximately 270,000 Shiite and 60,000 Sunni Muslims, 65,000 Christians, 30,000 Druze, and 95,000 Palestinians.

Intensification of Violence

On April 18, 1983, a suicidal terrorist drove a truck filled with explosives into the driveway of the US Embassy in Beirut, hit the Embassy building and exploded his deadly load. In addition to the terrorist driver, the blast killed 63 persons, including 17 Americans, 32 local embassy employees, and 14 visa applicants and passersby. Responsibility for the attack was claimed by the Islamic Jihad organization.

Even before the attack on the US Embassy, there had been sporadic outbreaks of violence between Christians and Druze in the Shouf Mountains, a few miles to the east and south of Beirut. Low-level fighting between Druze and Christian militiamen started shortly after the Israelis occupied the Shouf area, in 1982. The IDF never allowed the fighting to get out of hand and if necessary intervened by either mediation or force. However, because of the intensity of the Christian-Druze hostility, the Israelis found that it was becoming an increasing burden to maintain peace in the region. Adding to Israeli frustration were isolated attacks on Israeli soldiers, several of whom were killed and wounded in the early months of 1983.

In the summer of 1983, in expectation of the forthcoming Israeli withdrawal from the Shouf Mountains south of Beirut to a new line along the Awali River, clashes between the Christian Militia and the Lebanese Army on one side, and the Shiite, Druze, and Sunni militias on the other increased. In August, on the eve of Israeli departure, fighting intensified to such a degree that in the heat of the battle artillery shelling occasionally spilled over into Beirut. Considering the Christian Militia and the Lebanese Army a common enemy, the Druze and Amal militias forged a strategic partnership and coordinated their military efforts.

While sporadic engagements were occurring in the Shouf Mountains, violence erupted in West Beirut on August 28. In three days of street fighting Muslim militia, primarily the Amal, seized control of West Beirut from the Army. During the fighting, on August 29, US Marine positions at the outskirts of the Beirut airport came under artillery and mortar fire for nearly six hours. Two Marines were killed and fourteen wounded. On August 31, some 6,000 Lebanese Army troops counterattacked, and by September 2 retook the city. Scores of Muslim militiamen were arrested.

In view of potential danger to the lives of the US contingent of the MNF, and to the very survival of the Jemayel regime, on September 1 President Reagan ordered an additional force of 2,000 Marines into the Mediterranean, to be based on ships off the Lebanese coast in the vicinity of Beirut, and directed that the aircraft carrier *Dwight D. Eisenhower* remain in Lebanese waters to protect the Marines and the concentration of vessels off the coast.

With the newly-arrived Marines, the United States contingent of the MNF increased to 3,500 men, of which 1,500 were on shore, and 2,000 afloat. The US Naval Task Force grew to 15 vessels. Although the French and Italian contingents of the Multinational Force were larger on the ground than the US, the United States had more troops in the Lebanese coastal waters, and its armada had the strongest firepower. France had 2,100 men stationed in West Beirut, and the aircraft carrier *Foch* was offshore. Italy had 2,050 troops stationed between the French and the

United States forces. Great Britain's small contingent of 100 men, last to join the MNF, was deployed just to the southeast of the US Marines, near the airport.

Increasing Involvement of the United States Forces

The US role in Lebanon's internal fighting expanded in the late summer when, on September 13, the US Government announced that the Marines were now authorized to call on US naval gunfire and air strikes for their protection. This escalation was the result of the steadily worsening situation in Beirut, and more Marine casualties: two killed and three wounded on September 6. On September 19, the Marines again came under heavy fire, and requested naval gunfire support. US ships fired more than 300 heavy rounds at the positions of the Druze and their allies in the hills overlooking Beirut.

Seeing no end of the fighting, and with civilian and military losses increasing at a frightful rate, the leaders of the warring factions, including President Jemayel, agreed to a ceasefire, which took place at 6:00 A.M. on September 26. The uneasy ceasefire was accompanied by the agreement of all major parties to convene reconciliation talks to hammer out solutions to all the differences among the factions.

PLO Civil War in Lebanon

Meanwhile, in May 1983, a group of Syrian-backed PLO officers and men, stationed in eastern Lebanon, had rebelled against Arafat. They accused the PLO leadership of incompetence resulting in the disastrous defeat in June 1982 and expulsion of the Palestinian fighters from Beirut. Arafat and his close associates were also accused of corruption, of an insufficient commitment to a continuous armed confrontation with Israel, and of selling out to the Americans. In a matter of a few weeks, the insurgents—led by Colonel Said Musa (Abu Musa)—captured a number of PLO bases in the Bekaa Valley, and surrounded the remaining "loyalist" fighters. Yassr Arafat, alarmed by the events, arrived in Syria to confront the rebel troops and talk them into submission. But the heated discussions led nowhere. Rebel leaders, with Syrian blessing, stood firm on their demand that Arafat resign. Furthermore, disagreements between Arafat and Syrian President Hafez Assad became so grave that, on June 24, Assad expelled Arafat from Syria.

In defiance of the Syrian Government's ban against his presence in Syria or in Syrian-held territory, on September 16, 1983, Arafat slipped back into Tripoli. He announced to his supporters that he would lead them in the confrontation with the rebel forces which were massing for an attack on Tripoli.

President Assad considered Arafat's return to Lebanon a challenge to him. Between September 24 and 29, Assad expelled the remaining loyalist PLO guerrillas from the Bekaa Valley and the Shouf Mountains southeast of Beirut. Those who resisted were arrested by Syrian troops, and the rest were either disarmed and permitted to return to their families, or left free to join the rebel PLO forces. Some, however, were able to deceive the Syrians and made their way to Tripoli to join Arafat, who was preparing his defenses in two Palestinian camps just north of the city.

The PLO leadership suffered another blow when, on October 18, SAIQA, the radical pro-Syrian faction of the PLO, announced that it no longer recognized Arafat as the legitimate leader of the PLO, and called on all Palestinians to reject the PLO leadership.

On November 3 Colonal Musa's rebel PLO forces, apparently backed by Syrian armor and artillery and by the Syrian-controlled Palestinian Liberation Army, launched an all-out attack to drive the loyalists out of the well fortified refugee camps outside Tripoli. Of these, the Beddawi camp where Arafat's command post was located was in the city's northern suburbs, and the Nahr al Bared camp was several kilometers farther north. There were nearly 15,000 Palestinians attacking the camps. The defenders were about 5,000 strong.

By November 9, the rebels had captured the Nahr al Bared camp where 16,000 Palestinians lived and agreed to a ceasefire. During the fighting at least 150 people were killed and over 500 wounded. Hundreds of people fled the embattled zone. The rebels began preparing themselves for an assault on the Beddawi camp and Tripoli proper.

Arafat charged that the attack had been planned by Damascus and carried out with the help of Syrian and Libyan troops. He appealed to the heads of all Arab states and especially to President Assad to prevent a massacre of the inhabitants of the camps and of the inhabitants of Tripoli. Arafat further accused Syria of trying to end the independence of Palestine and the PLO, and of a plot to create a new PLO that would be a Syrian puppet.

After a 24-hour lull, fighting resumed on November 10th with increased ferocity, accompanied by propaganda blasts, with each side accusing the other of breaking the ceasefire. The Beddawi camp fell on November 16, and Arafat moved his command post to downtown Tripoli, close to the port. Artillery and mortar shells rained on the city, and fierce street combat continued for several days. Rebel forces advanced steadily. By November 21 they were about one kilometer from Arafat's headquarters. The next day they declared a unilateral ceasefire and issued an ultimatum to Arafat and his troops to leave the city within three days.

The Second PLO Evacuation from Lebanon

Realizing that his situation was hopeless, and that further resistance would only end in his total defeat, and the likely death not only of hundreds of his loyalist troops but also his own, Arafat agreed. With Saudi Arabian mediation he started negotiations on the terms and methods of evacuation.

As soon as negotiations with Colonel Abu Musa's rebels and the Syrians started, an event indirectly related to the situation in Tripoli took place. On November 24, Israel and the PLO announced that they had agreed to an immediate prisoner exchange. This exchange ended long mediations in Geneva, Switzerland, arranged by the International Red Cross. The return of the Israeli-held POWs had acquired increased urgency to both the Israelis and Arafat because of the imminent takeover of Tripoli by the rebels, who were opposed to any deal with Israel. According to the terms of the agreement, some 4,500 Palestinian guerrillas and their Lebanese allies in the Israeli prison camp at Ansar in southern Lebanon, and about 100 Palestinian terrorists held in Israeli prisons, were to be exchanged for six Israeli soldiers captured by the PLO in September 1982. It was the largest prisoner exchange in the history of Israel and the PLO, and it was carried out without a hitch during the next several days.

In the meantime, in Tripoli, as negotiations dragged on, rebel and loyalist forces continued to exchange intermittent fire. The rebels hoped that by combining negotiations with sporadic military pressure they would have a better chance to force Arafat out without renewing major combat. A breakthrough came on December 3, when the United Nations Security Council agreed to Arafat's request that the UN flag be flown over the evacuation ships, thus placing the PLO loyalists under the protection of the international body. A few days later, the Greek Government offered to send ships to Tripoli to evacuate some 4,000 PLO fighters, and the French agreed to provide warships to escort the convoy out of Lebanese waters.

Nearly 16 months after his forced evacuation from Beirut, Arafat had achieved another political miracle. Only a few weeks earlier, when the rebels were moving in for the kill, his political and personal survival were in grave doubt. Now Arafat emerged relatively intact from another military debacle, ready to leave Tripoli with his political standing even enhanced to a certain degree. He continued to enjoy widespread support both among his fellow Palestinians and in Arab countries. Most Palestinians were solidly in support of a united PLO with Arafat at its top, and strongly condemned Syria and the rebels for resorting to arms instead of settling the differences through peaceful dialogue.

Then, on December 6, a Jerusalem bus was bombed, and six Israelis killed. Both the PLO loyalists and the rebels took credit for the attack. In reprisal, the Israeli government refused to give its consent to the evacuation, and expressed protest and dismay that the United Nations would give its protection to Arafat's ships. The Israelis were furious and called for total elimination of Arafat and his fighters. Defense Minister Moshe Arens suggested that if the western nations wanted to help Arafat and his followers to leave Tripoli, they should demand that the PLO lay down its arms and abandon terrorism. Said Arens in an Israeli radio interview on December 19, "When terrorists commit acts such as the attack on the bus in Jerusalem, and brag about it, civilized democratic countries cannot help them continue to do the same things. If a terrorist committed an atrocity, and a democratic country helped get him to a new location, so he could commit more such acts, that is not something which those of us who accept democratic values can accept."

For ten days following the bombing of the bus, Israeli gunboats bombarded the PLO loyalists' positions in the Tripoli area and blockaded the port to prevent Arafat from getting away. It was ironic that Israel—which went to war in June 1982 in order to rid Lebanon of the PLO guerrillas—was now preventing their departure.

Though not officially stated, the Israeli reason for the blockade was to perpetuate a situation in which the PLO loyalists and the rebels would continue to fight and kill each other, and to reduce the political prestige of Arafat. The Israelis would not have been sorry if, in the process, the PLO leader had paid with his life.

But keeping Arafat in Tripoli would have meant destruction of yet another Lebanese city, for which the Israelis would have been indirectly responsible. In addition, by trying to block Arafat's departure, Israel would have had to be prepared to take military action against French warships which were to escort evacuation ships flying the UN flag. If Israel was not ready to do that, then its talks of a blockade had no credibility. The rebels claimed that Arafat was deliberately exaggerating the Israeli threat, and making unnecessary arrangements to protect the evacuation in order to gain more press coverage and propaganda benefits from his departure. They announced that they held Arafat responsible for any further bloodshed caused by the delay of his exodus from Tripoli.

At this point the White House brought strong pressure on Israel to cease its obstruction of the evacuation. Jerusalem was not willing to jeopardize relations with Washington just to keep Arafat fighting for his life in Tripoli, and gave in.

The PLO Chairman and over 4,000 of his loyalist troops embarked from Tripoli aboard five Greek ships on December 20, 1983, ending PLO loyalists' rule of their last bastion in Lebanon. The rebels and Syria won the battle but not the war—at least not yet. Whatever political score President Assad and Colonel Abu Musa had to settle with Arafat would have to await a more opportune moment.

Chapter XXIV
Legacies of Hatred

Bomb Attacks on US and French MNF Contingents

During the summer and fall of 1983 the US contingent of the Multinational Force had received nearly 100 intelligence reports warning of the possibility of terrorist car bomb attacks. These warnings provided little specific information on how and when such attacks might be carried out, and were not taken seriously, despite what had happened at the US Embassy several months earlier. The Marine commanders considered terrorism only a secondary threat, and were more concerned with intermittent shellings of their deployment area by the warring militias. Then, early Sunday morning, October 23, 1983, the most serious terrorist attack ever perpetrated against a US combat force occurred.

At daybreak a large yellow Mercedes truck, loaded with some six tons of explosives, pulled into a parking lot in the Marine compound close to the Beirut International Airport. The driver circled the parking lot picking up speed, then crashed the truck through a barbed wire fence, rushed past two Marine sentry posts, smashed through an iron gate, drove over an 18-inch sewer pipe and through a row of sandbags, passed another sentry position, and hit the Marine headquarters building where some 400 Marines were living. There was a tremendous explosion. The building collapsed, killing 241 Marines and wounding over 100. At almost exactly the same time, another terrorist truck using similar methods smashed into the French compound, causing some 150 casualties.

Within minutes of the explosion, the British offered the use of their hospital at the Royal Air Force Base at Akrotiri, Cyprus. The offer was accepted by the US Command. Other offers of medical assistance from France and Israel were subsequently received, but they were deemed unnecessary, because of US medical capabilities on the spot and in Germany.

Circumstantial evidence points to Syria as having either engineered or permitted the attack by the pro-Iranian Lebanese Shiite Muslim organization Muslim al Amal, operating in Syrian-occupied Baalbek, where hundreds of Iranian Revolutionary Guards were headquartered.

Less than two weeks later, on Friday, November 4, a terrorist attack on a local Israeli headquarters compound at the outskirts of Tyre killed a total of 60 people: 28 Israeli military and security personnel, and 32 Lebanese and Palestinians in custody under suspicion of guerrilla and terrorist activities. At least 30 others were injured. The attack occurred at 6:10 A.M., when a terrorist drove an explosive-laden truck through a hail of fire into the IDF headquarters compound and blew up three buildings, which housed the General Security Services, a border police company, and Lebanese and Palestinian detainees. The explosion set off a chain reaction of detonations of small arms ammunition and hand grenades in the buildings, which continued for several hours, causing additional injuries among rescue personnel.

Within hours, Israeli Air Force planes attacked the areas of Mansouriye and Bhamdoun near the Beirut-Damascus highway, described by an IDF spokesman as "terrorist headquarters and facilities." According to Lebanese sources 69 people were killed and 120 wounded. Losses included three Syrian officers and 19 enlisted men. The Israelis insist that they have evidence that Syria was behind the car bomb attacks in Tyre and those against the US and French contingents of the Multinational Force in Beirut earlier in October.

Hostilities between Syria and the United States

On November 10 four unarmed US carrier-based F-14 reconnaissance jets were flying a reconnaissance mission over the area from which anti-government forces were shelling the positions of the Lebanese Army and US Marines, and came close to Syrian forces deployed in East Lebanon. The Syrians opened fire from antiaircraft batteries, but missed. All US planes returned safely to their carrier.

During the following weeks, US flights over Syrian-occupied territory continued, as did the hostile antiaircraft fire, but no planes were lost. Then, on December 4, the US Navy retaliated in response to another instance of Syrian antiaircraft fire at American unarmed reconnaissance planes on December 3. A strike force of 28 carrier-based US warplanes took off early in the morning and struck at Syrian antiaircraft guns at Hammana, in the mountains east of Beirut. Two of the planes were shot down. One, an A-6E jet attack fighter, crashed in Syrian-held territory, killing one crewman, Navy Lieutenant Mark A. Lange, and slightly wounding the other, Navy Lieutenant Robert O. Goodman, who was captured. The other plane, an A-7 Corsair, fell near Jounie. The pilot parachuted into the Mediterranean Sea and was rescued by friendly Lebanese forces. Later that day, eight US Marines posted in an observation bunker atop a building at the outskirts of the Beirut International Airport were killed when their position was hit by direct artillery fire from Syrian-backed militia guns.

On December 14, only minutes after Syrian antiaircraft batteries opened fire on two Navy F-14 reconnaissance jets, the battleship *USS New Jersey* shelled Syrian positions in the hills east of Beirut with 16-inch guns. Soon after, the *New Jersey* opened fire again, this time against the Druze militia who were shelling the Marines at the airport.

The United States Government tried to free Lieutenant Goodman through diplomatic negotiations with Damascus, but the Syrians were unwilling to release the American prisoner. Then, on December 29 Reverend Jesse Jackson, a Democratic presidential candidate, flew to Damascus to intervene personally with President Assad and win the release of the American flier. On January 3, 1984, after a dramatic appeal by Reverend Jackson, Assad—probably more for propaganda than humanitarian reasons—freed Goodman, who immediately returned to the United States.

During his flight back Goodman revealed details of his treatment by the Syrian captors. As soon as he was captured, the Syrians had interrogated him around the clock harshly for several days. He had been repeatedly beaten on the face and body. However, the beatings stopped as soon as officials of the International Red Cross visited him.

Collapse of the Lebanese Army

A new wave of very intensive fighting erupted early in 1984. Most of the fighting took place between Lebanese Army units and the Druze militiamen in the hills southeast of the capital, and in West Beirut between the army and the Shiite Amal militia. Artillery duels intensified, and the US Marine compound came under fire several times. As the street fighting in West Beirut reached its highest pitch, increasing numbers of Shiite soldiers deserted from the Army in response to an appeal from Amal leader Nabih Berri, who urged Muslim members of the Lebanese Armed Forces not to take up arms against their Muslim brothers, and to leave their units. A similar appeal a fortnight earlier by Walid Jumblatt had caused massive desertions of the Druze servicemen. Berri's and Jumblatt's calls split the Lebanese Army along sectarian lines. The Muslim members of the Jemayel government were also urged by Berri to resign, which they did.

On February 4 the commander of the Army's 1st Infantry Brigade, stationed in the Syrian-occupied Bekaa Valley, announced that he and his 2,000 men would no longer follow Army orders. It was obvious that the total disintegration of the Lebanese Army was imminent. A few days later the 6th Infantry Brigade, stationed in West Beirut, rebelled and put itself under the control of Shiite and Druze leaders. West Beirut was taken over by the Amal militia without any serious resistance.

The collapse of the Lebanese Army and the rapid deterioration of the Lebanese government forced President Reagan to order the withdrawal of the US contingent of the MNF in Lebanon from its base at the Beirut airport to the US ships offshore. This move, starting February 7, 1984, was to protect the Marines while retaining at least the facade of US involvement in the Multinational Force. US patrols could still have been sent into Beirut if the situation had required it.

In mid-February the Druze militia inflicted a serious defeat on the Lebanese Army at Khalde, and in the hills south of the capital. The Druze attacked a strategic crossroad just outside Khalde, not far from the airport, held by the Army's 4th Brigade. Wave after wave of Druze militia assaulted the brigade's lines, captured the crossroad, and advanced on Khalde. However, the brigade regrouped, counterattacked, and restored the situation. Then one of the battalion commanders, a Muslim, defected to the other side. His entire battalion panicked and scattered. Almost all of the Muslim soldiers deserted, and the defense collapsed. The remnants of the brigade, nearly all of them Christians, fled south to Sidon to find safety behind the Israeli lines. In less than 18 hours after the fight began, the Druze captured Khalde and occupied the entire coastal area to the Christian town of Damour some 12 kilometers to the south.

As a result of the capture of Khalde, the Druze and Amal militiamen completely encircled the Marine compound at the airport. Nevertheless, they did not interfere with the Marines' preparations for redeployment to the ships offshore. After their Khalde victory, the Druze militia continued to push the remnants of the Army and the Phalangists out of the Shouf Mountains southeast of Beirut, and took the critical town of Kfar Matta. Until the Israeli withdrawal in September 1983 this town had been divided between Christians and Druze, and after the Israeli pull-out it had been occupied largely by the Lebanese Army and Christian militiamen. The capture of Kfar Matta gave the Druze an unbroken line of communication between the sea and the Syrian Forces at the Beirut-Damascus highway and in the Bekaa Valley. As the Druze entered the area they discovered nearly 100 badly decomposed bodies, mostly women and older men. According to witnesses these were victims of a Phalangist massacre, probably in revenge for the killing of about 150 Christian villagers by Druze gunmen at al-Bira in September 1982.

The takeover of West Beirut by the Shiite militiamen, the rout of the Army in the Shouf Mountains by the Druze militia, and the desertion of entire army units, caused the virtual collapse of the Jemayel government. Amin Jemayel, never a strong leader, turned to Syria in the hope that Assad would be able to persuade the Druze and Muslims to let him stay on as the president, even if only as a figurehead. He was ready to pay whatever price Damascus might ask.

Departure of the Multinational Force from Lebanon

On February 8, Great Britain became the first member of the Multinational Force to withdraw its contingent—100 men—from Beirut. It was followed on February 20 by Italy, which withdrew almost all of its 1,400 men in a swift, two-day evacuation. With the US Marines preparing to leave for their ships, only the French contingent—1,600 strong—remained in Beirut.

The redeployment of the Marines began on February 21 and was completed five days later on February 26. The move involved about 1,300 troops who were evacuated by helicopters and landing craft from the beach south of Beirut. Some 300 Marines remained in Beirut to guard the US Embassy and the Embassy personnel. About 80 US military advisors also continued to train the severely depleted Lebanese Army. A small group of Marine and Army artillery observers—fewer than 20 men—took up positions in the village of Beit Meri, in the hills east of Beirut, to direct artillery fire from the US warships.

On March 30, President Reagan formally withdrew US Marines from the Multinational Force, and ordered the US Sixth Fleet to duties elsewhere in the Mediterranean. By that time the US warships in the Lebanese waters already had been reduced from 25 (at the peak of American involvement) to about 15.

The French Government began the withdrawal of its troops from Beirut on March 25, and completed it seven days later. The evacuation of the last 300 French soldiers on March 31 ended 19 months of existence of the MNF in Beirut.

Lebanon Reconciliation Conference

Although the warring factions had agreed on September 26, 1983, to convene a national reconciliation conference, it took the participants over a month to decide on the place for the talks and on a general agenda. Finally the long awaited conference opened in Geneva, Switzerland, on October 31, 1983.

The attending parties coalesced into two groups, representing different philosophies, political alliances, and religious affiliations. The first of these was the Lebanese Front, the main Christian coalition, represented by

Pierre Jemayel, President Amin Jemayel's father and the undisputed leader of the Phalange, and former president Camille Chamoun, leader of the National Liberal Party. Allied with this group were pro-government Shiite and Sunni Muslims represented by the former Sunni Prime Minister, Saeb Salam, and the Shiite Speaker of the Parliament, Adel Osseiran.

The second group, opposed to the government, was in turn divided into two blocs. One of these consisted of three leaders of the Syrian-backed National Front, a loose alliance of opposition forces organized on June 23, 1983. They were: the head of the Druze Progressive Socialist Party, Walid Jumblatt; former prime minister, Rashid Karameh, a Sunni Muslim; and former president Suleiman Franjieh, a Maronite Christian but an enemy of the Jemayel clan. Cooperating with this bloc in opposition to the government—but otherwise unaligned—was the radical Shiite Muslim Amal leader, Nabih Berri.

After weeks of angry and heated negotiations, the conference broke up at the end of December without any agreement, except for a face-saving decision to meet again soon. Obviously the participants had decided to seek to win in combat what they could not gain at the conference table.

After a suspension of over two months, the second round of the reconciliation talks opened on March 12, 1984, in Lausanne, Switzerland. This meeting became possible only after Jemayel's government abrogated its May 17, 1983, treaty with Israel, which Syria and the Syrian-backed block strongly opposed. Again the discussions were heated and the partici-pants showed no inclination for compromise. The statement issued at the end of the conference on March 20 by the Christian and Muslim leaders ignored all major points at issue, and called mainly for steps to be taken to consolidate the very fragile new ceasefire which had been declared on March 13. The leaders of the opposing factions agreed to set up a 32-member constitutional commission chosen by the President in consultation with the conference participants, which was to prepare a draft of a new constitution in six months. They called for an end of all defamatory media campaigns, and for continuous consultation.

There was no agreement on a new basis for power sharing among Christians, Sunni, Shiite, and Druze in a workable national unity govern-ment. There were no indications of any efforts to abolish the system based upon sectarian differences, or to delineate the precise powers and relation-ship of the president and the prime minister. While not a total failure, the results of the conference did not augur well for the future of Lebanon. The Lebanese Muslims would almost certainly have readily accepted a formula that redressed the grievances they had borne for decades. They would have been satisfied to have Lebanon remain an Arab country, committed to the Arab League Charter, and reflecting the Syrian attitude toward Israel. However, if such a deal had been made, the only losers would have been the

Maronites, who would have had to relinquish political power. Even though their position was increasingly untenable they were still unwilling to make such concessions.

Early in May 1984 President Jemayel appointed the strongly pro-Syrian Rashid Karameh to form a new cabinet. This marked a further step of surrender of the Lebanese government to Syrian domination and continuation of old rivalries, instead of giving new hopes to end sectarian conflicts.

Chapter XXV
Epilogue

What Does the Future Hold in Store?

Only the determined optimist can see the possibility of peace and tranquility in the Middle East in the proximate future. History suggests that there is never likely to be the kind of peace and tranquility in the Middle East that has been found for prolonged periods in some other regions of the world. But history also tells us that the present conflicts some day, somehow, will be resolved, even if they are only succeeded by new and as-yet-undreamed-of hostilities.

It is a brave, and probably foolhardy, person who attempts to forecast the course of events in the Middle East. The authors of this book hope that they may be considered brave—even bold—but not foolhardy. So we shall try to suggest only very tentatively how that troubled part of the world may at least get started from today to "some day, somehow."

There is a common belief—even among many inhabitants of the region—that if the Arab-Israeli conflict, and the future of the Palestinian people, could be resolved, peace would settle over the Middle East, with nations living side by side in quiet harmony. History, current relationships, and simple logic tell us that this is a totally unrealistic picture.

The Palestinian problem is unconnected with some of the gravest issues now facing the Middle East. If it were settled, the bloody struggle between Iraq and Iran would continue unabated. North and South Yemen would not stop their wary search for opportunities to sink daggers in each others' backs. Nor would the Soviet Union automatically abandon its bridgeheads in South Yemen, Ethiopia, or Syria. Libya would not stop being a haven for international terrorism, any more than its wild-eyed ruler, Qadaffi, would suddenly become an apostle of peace and international goodwill. And if the Israelis were to shake hands with the leadership of the PLO, there would still be a potential for bloody massacres of Sunni Muslims in Hamma, Syria, and equally bloody savagery among Muslims

Christians, and Druze in Lebanon.

Nonetheless, there can be no question that the Arab-Israeli conflict is the single most troublesome issue in the Middle East, and that it—in turn—revolves around the issue of Palestinian autonomy.

There are those who believe that the differences between the Israelis and the Arabs, and in particular the Palestinian Arabs, are intractable, and that the origins and nature of their hostility are such that a compromise and a negotiated end to the war is impossible. If those people—who include many Israelis—are right, the future of the region is grim, indeed.

Many Arabs compare 20th century Israel to the Crusader States of the 12th and 13th centuries. They visualize modern Israel as another such outpost of Western European civilization, which will eventually and inevitably be overwhelmed by the numerical superiority of the surrounding Arab population. Whether, in a very different international context, there is any validity to this comparison is unimportant. So long as this idea is held by a substantial number of the Arab intelligentsia, true peace between Arabs and Israelis will not be easy to achieve.

There are others in the region—Israelis as well as Arabs—who recognize that Israel is in a position to negotiate and compromise from a position of overwhelming military superiority. However, the issues to be negotiated—military, political, and economic—are both delicate and complicated, and the situation of Israel is such that it cannot afford to make any serious mistakes in the process of compromise. Nevertheless, it is possible that either a Palestinian state on the West Bank, or a Jordanian-Palestinian confederation (encompassing most of the West Bank and the kingdom of Jordan, established under terms which would guarantee Israel's security by a political treaty and Israel's own military might), could provide a basis for compromise and peace between Israel and its neighbors. From this could flow economic cooperation in the Middle East. The skill and vigor of the Israelis could assure them a position of equality, despite the overwhelming numerical superiority of the Arab population, and result in integration of national economies in such a way that cooperation would have to become the regional way of life.

These potential developments are as evident to Arabs as they are to Israelis. But reluctant as the majority of Israelis are to seek a resolution, the Palestinian Arabs are even more unyielding. The tragedy of the Palestinians and their leaders, from the time of the Grand Mufti of Jerusalem, Haj Amin el Husseini, to that of PLO Chairman Yasser Arafat, has been their refusal to talk to "the Jews," even to concede the right of existence to the state of Israel. This has caused them to miss a number of opportunities, and has led them from disaster to disaster. The PLO, for instance, has insisted that it would not sit down with representatives of Israel unless the Israelis accept in advance a number of preconditions. However, there is no historic example of a nation victorious in 35 years of warfare voluntarily accepting in advance of negotiations a wide range of obligations set by the defeated party.

Despite the evidence of their experience, the Palestinians have accepted at face value the emotional Arab rhetoric—some of it their own—to the effect that the cause of the Palestinians is the cause of the entire Arab "nation". This in turn has led them, time after time, to count on the solid support of all of their fellow-Arabs in all of their confrontations with Israel—and has led them to be disappointed each time. In fact, there is no Arab nation. The leaders of each sovereign Arab state will, when push comes to shove, put their sovereignty ahead of the interests of the Arab community as a whole, including that of the Palestinian Arabs.

The crushing defeat suffered by the PLO in Lebanon in 1982 for all practical purposes eliminated whatever credibility there was to a Palestinian military option. The PLO no longer has an independent or autonomous territorial base, and therefore can no longer maintain an independent standing army. The severely damaged Palestinian political movement has been split. Its rump military component's leader, Abu Musa, takes orders from Damascus, where the government has announced that "henceforth Syria will lead the Palestinian struggle." So desperate are Arafat and his largely demilitarized PLO that they are trying to find new patronage from old enemies: Jordan and Egypt. The PLO has no program. It has no military power. At least for the foreseeable future, the PLO has become a political football in the Arab world.

As for the plight of the Palestinian refugees, this must be analyzed from a historical perspective. The 600,000 Palestinians who left, or were forced in the 1940s to leave what is now Israel, and the 600,000 Jews who were at the same time expelled from various Arab countries and immigrated to Israel, were only a small percentage of the worldwide total of nearly 40 million refugees who were forced to find new homes in this same general time period. Of these, only the Palestinians have not yet been largely absorbed in their new homelands. They took refuge, of course, in fraternal Arab states. The fact that they have not yet been assimilated is in part due to their stubborn—and not unpraiseworthy—determination to retain a separate identity in anticipation of an eventual return to their former homes. Yet this lack of assimilation is certainly also reflective of mistrust on the part of the host nations where they have taken refuge, and unwillingness, because of political expediency, on the part of the hosts to accept the Palestinian refugees as fellow-citizens. In either explanation, the lack of assimilation of the Palestinians is another indication of the lack of substance to the concept of an Arab nation.

To achieve a settlement on the Palestinian-West Bank issue, both sides must be willing to compromise. The prospect of an interminable continuation of Israel's current situation as a beleaguered community should impel an Israeli willingness to compromise. The lack of response by the Arab states to Arafat's appeals for help during the 1982 war in Lebanon should convince the Palestinians that they will have to assume responsibility for their own destiny. No Arab coalition, nor even the Soviet Union, will assist in any fashion that does not further its own selfish interests. In addition to a willingness to compromise, there must also be an element of trust, which is totally lacking today on both sides. Developing such trust will be perhaps the most difficult task of all. Yet, as one of the authors of this book has pointed out, in an earlier publication,* one way of accomplishing this might be through the establishment of international trusteeships over the West Bank and the Gaza Strip. A trusteeship over the West Bank could even provide a starting point for a resolution of the most emotional issue of all: the future of Jerusalem.

It is not impossible to visualize Syria participating in a peaceful resolution of the Arab-Israeli conflict. To regain sovereignty over the Golan territories captured by Israel in 1967 might in itself be enough for President Assad to move toward compromise. If also he were able to play a leading role in negotiations leading to the establishment of a Palestinian state, so much the better. But President Assad will not be an easy negotiating partner, even if he can ever be persuaded to get to a bargaining table.

Assad, or his successor, will also have a major role in determining the future of Lebanon. On a smaller scale, the issues within Lebanon are perhaps equally as intractible as those that currently sustain general Arab-Israeli hostility. Those issues would exist even were there not an Arab-Israeli conflict. However, they will continue to be exacerbated by that conflict. And so it is likely that peace for Lebanon will be impossible until there is peace between Arabs and Israelis.

The history of Lebanon tells us that there is no assurance that Christians, Shiites, Sunnis, and Druze can live together, even without overlapping outside complications. Yet, once more, the historian can find a parallel that may be truly useful.

As noted at the beginning of this book, Lebanon was once falsely compared with Switzerland. But that need not be a false comparison in the future. The animosities that once existed among the German-speaking, French-speaking, Italian-speaking, and Romanche-speaking inhabitants of that tiny, mountainous country were not much different from those that have wracked tiny, mountainous Lebanon for many centuries. In fact one can still find occasional vestiges of those old internal Swiss hostilities. But the Swiss found a political method, based upon geographic, linguistic, and

* T.N. Dupuy, "A Proposed Step Toward the Middle East Peace," *Strategic Review*, No. 4, 1981.

religious regional divisions, and upon democratic goodwill, which resolved those ancient hostilities. A similar solution should not be impossible for Lebanon.

Peace will not come easily to the Middle East, nor to Lebanon. To curb current hostilities is easier said than done.

Appendix A
A Modified Quantified Judgment Model Analysis of the Bekaa Valley Battle

In the Six Day War of 1967 the Israelis inflicted crushing defeats on the Arab nations of Egypt, Jordan, and Syria. Then in the October War of 1973, after being overpowered in the opening stages by surprise attacks of the Egyptian and Syrian armies, the Israelis recovered and defeated the Arabs again. However, the initial Israeli defeats, and the stalemated end of the war, led most military analysts to conclude that between 1967 and 1973 the Arabs had done much to close the gap between their own capabilities and the military prowess of Israel.

Yet, careful quantitative analyses of the engagements of the two wars showed, quite convincingly, that the gap in military capability between the Israelis and the Arabs had actually widened between 1967 and 1973.[1]

The apparent anomaly is easily explained. Contributing to the overwhelming Israeli success against the Arabs in 1967 was the fact that the Israelis had had the advantage of surprise at the outset of that war, and the Arabs were never able to recover from their initial surprise and shock. In 1973, on the other hand, the Arabs had had the advantage of surprise. But in three days the Israelis had recovered from the shock of the initial surprise, were able to seize back the initiative from the Egyptians and Syrians, and were successful in most of the subsequent battles before the UN imposed a ceasefire.

Using data from the wars, and the Quantified Judgment Model (QJM)[2], it can be calculated that the average relative combat effectiveness value (CEV) of the Israelis with respect to the Arabs had increased from about 1.9-to-1.0 in 1967, to over 2.1-to-1.0 in 1973 (the Israeli-Syrian CEV was calculated as 2.5-to-1.0). What these CEVs mean, in simplified terms, is that, for example, 100 Israelis in a combat unit were the equivalent of about 190 Arabs in a combat unit in 1967, but that in the 1973 war, a combat unit of 100 Israelis was worth a similar combat unit of 210 Arabs. This does not mean that each individual Israeli soldier was, on the average, any smarter, stronger, braver, or more highly motivated than his Arab counterpart. It is simply that when organized, trained, and committed to battle in combat units, the Israelis were much more effective than the Arabs.

There have been recent comments by both Israeli and American military commentators suggesting that the events of the 1982 war in Lebanon demonstrated that the Israeli combat effectiveness superiority over the Syrians had declined since 1973. Qualitative analysis of the operations in the Bekaa Valley made us doubt if there had been any such decline in the Israeli CEV with respect to the Syrians between 1973 and 1982. In operations against the Syrians in the Bekaa Valley of eastern Lebanon, Israeli forces encountered substantial, and sometimes difficult, opposition. Although we do not have data about those operations adequate to perform a full QJM analysis, there is enough general information about the forces engaged, the losses incurred, and the advance rates of the Israeli troops, to perform a useful, although qualified, analysis of the combat of Israeli and Syrian forces, using a modified Quantitative Judgment Model approach.

Unfortunately it is not possible to undertake that kind of QJM analysis of the operations against the PLO in Lebanon, because the requisite statistical data for discrete engagements is still not available, and probably never will be. The Israelis overwhelmed the Palestinians in all field operations, and from the sketchy evidence available to us, the Israeli CEV against the PLO can be estimated to have been greater than 4.0-1.0; i.e., a unit of 100 Israelis had the same effectiveness as a unit of 400 PLO fighters, comparably equipped.

The deployments and approximate strengths of Israeli and Syrian forces, and their combat operations in the Bekaa Valley battle, are described in Chapters XI, XIV, and XV, earlier in this book. The basic data for the following modified QJM analysis of the battle is derived from that information.

Lacking detailed order of battle information, and precise combat statistics, a meaningful analysis is possible only if we assume that the relative combat effectiveness value of Israeli forces with respect to the Syrians was at least comparable to the CEV values calculated from the 1967 and 1973 war data: a CEV of 2.5-to-1.0. This means that in general Israeli combat effectiveness was 150% higher than Syrian, or that 100 Israeli soldiers in combat units were the equivalent of 250 Syrian soldiers in comparably equipped combat units.

If we apply the QJM factors to the battle and terrain circumstances in the Bekaa Valley and the adjacent mountains, where most of the fighting took place, we can derive the following specific factors for this battle: The Syrian combination of fortified, prepared, and hasty defenses can be represented by a multiplying factor of about 1.4. The rugged terrain enhanced the Syrian defensive capability by a factor of about 1.5. These same considerations—Syrian defensive posture, and the terrain—degraded the Israeli advance rates by factors of .7 and .6 respectively.

Based on our past analyses, we assumed that the combat value of modern main battle tanks, of the sort with which both Israelis and Syrians were equipped, is the equivalent of a 100-man "slice" of the non-armor elements of the engaged combat units. (Such a slice would include infantry weapons, artillery, anti-armor weapons, and air defense weapons.) Similarly Israeli close support aircraft were assumed to be the equivalent of a 250-man slice; Syrian close support aircraft were worth a 200-man slice; and Syrian SA missiles were also considered to be the equivalent of a 200-man slice.

Figure 1
Estimated Syrian and Israeli Force Strengths
Bekaa Valley Battle, June 8-11, 1982

	Israeli	Syrian
Troops	35,000	30,000
Tanks	800	600
Aircraft Available for Close Support	275	225
Non-Organic Air Defense Missile Launchers (SAMs)	—	120*

* There were 76 launcher units, some with single launchers (SA2), some with double launchers (SA3) and some with triple launchers (SA6).

Figure 1 shows the estimated Israeli and Syrian forces that took part in the Bekaa Valley battle. On the basis of these figures, and the assumptions presented, we can calculate the force strengths and combat powers of Israeli and Syrian forces for the period June 8-11 as follows:

	Israeli manpower equivalents	Syrian manpower equivalents
Troops	35,000 × 1 = 35,000	30,000 × 1 = 30,000
Tanks	800 × 100 = 80,000	600 × 100 = 60,000
Aircraft	275 × 250 = 68,750	225 × 200 =45,000
Air Defense Missiles	none	120 × 200 = 24,000
Force Strength (total)	183,750	159,000
Terrain	—	× 1.5
Posture	—	× 1.4
Combat Power (without CEV)	183,750	333,900

This permits us to make several interesting comparisons:

Force Strength Ratio (Israeli/Syrian)	1.16 (in favor of Israel)
Combat Power Ratio (without CEV)	0.55 (or 1.82 in favor of Syria)
Combat Power Ratio (with 2.5 Israeli CEV)	1.38 (in favor of Israel)

On the basis of this essentially static comparison, the Force Strength Ratio tells us there should be a standoff between the Israelis and Syrians in Lebanon. (The data is not sufficiently precise for us to evaluate the slight calculated Israeli preponderance). The Combat Power Ratio—without the CEV—is hardly more useful, since it tells us that the Syrians will decisively repulse the Israeli offensive. A meaningful comparison of the opposing forces can be made only when combat power comparison includes consideration of the CEV. But this too does not indicate an Israeli superiority as overwhelming as was actually demonstrated on the battlefield between the evening of June 8 and the morning of June 11.

Let us continue the analysis by dividing the three days of serious fighting into two phases of about 36 hours each, and looking at each of these separately.

Figure 2
Estimated Opposing Initial Syrian and Israeli Force Strengths
Late June 8, 1982, Bekaa Valley Battle, Phase I

	Israeli	Syrian
Troops	35,000	22,000
Tanks	800	300
Aircraft Available for Close Support	275	225*
Non-organic Air Defense Missile Launchers (SAMs)		120**

* Reduced to 195 by mid-afternoon, June 9
** Reduced to about 12 (8 launcher units) by mid-afternoon, June 9

Figure 3
Estimated Opposing Initial Syrian and Israeli Force Strengths
Early June 10, 1982, Bekaa Valley Battle, Phase II

	Israeli	Syrian
Troops	34,000	28,000
Tanks	750	400
Aircraft Available for Close Support	250	130
Non-Organic Air Defense Missile Launchers (SAMs)	–	12

A manpower equivalent comparison of the opposing forces late on June 8 is complicated by the fact that early in the afternoon on June 9 the IDF took out most of the Syrian SAMs. Thus, it may be estimated that over the first 36-hour period not more than 10% of the Syrian SAM strength was effective. It is also estimated that less than half of available aircraft were operational. Those estimates are reflected in the following comparison:

	Israeli manpower equivalents	Syrian manpower equivalents
Troops	35,000 × 1 = 35,000	22,000 × 1 = 22,000
Tanks	800 × 100 = 80,000	300 × 100 = 30,000
Aircraft (or sorties)	275 × 250 = 68,750	100 × 200 = 20,000
Air Defense Missiles	none	12 × 200 = 2,400
Force Strength (total)	183,750	74,400
Terrain	—	× 1.5
Posture	—	× 1.4
Combat Power (without CEV)	183,750	156,240

This time the comparisons are as follows:

Force Strength Ratio (Israeli/Syrian)	2.47
Combat Power Ratio (without CEV)	1.18
Combat Power Ratio (with 2.5 Israeli CEV)	2.94

This combat power ratio of 2.94 takes into consideration the previous historical combat power superiority of Israeli troops over Syrians (about 2.5 CEV), and suggests that a one-sided Israeli success was again to be expected. That is the way it was.

The Israelis advanced an average of about 10 kilometers that day, through the extemely rugged terrain on both sides of the Bekaa Valley. Applying the advance rate factors for posture (0.7) and terrain (0.6) shown previously, this means that the Israelis could have expected to advance about 24 kilometers on flat terrain against the Syrian combat power opposition actually encountered ($10/(.6 × .7) = 23.8$). In figure 4 (a QJM advance rate table) we can see that the standard, unmodified advance of a mixed armored and mechanized force with a combat power superiority of 2.94 is about 17 kilometers on flat terrain. Thus, the Israelis advanced farther than this figure would indicate, suggesting that the CEV was somewhat more than 2.5, about 3.5. (The calculation is: $(2.5 × 24)/17 = 3.53$.)

Figure 4
Standard (Unmodified) Advance Rates (Sr) on Flat Terrain
(in km/day)

Resistance Description	P/P*	Armd Div	Mczd Div	Inf Div	Horse Cav Force
Intense[1]	1.00-1.09	4.0	4.00	4.00	3.00
Near Intense	1.10-1.19	4.5	4.25	4.25	3.25
Strong, Intense	1.20-1.29	5.0	4.50	4.50	3.50
Near Strong/Intense	1.30-1.39	5.5	4.75	4.75	3.75

Strong	1.40-1.49	6.0	5.00	5.00	4.00
Near Strong	1.50-1.59	7.5	6.25	5.75	5.00
Moderate Strong	1.60-1.74	9.0	7.50	6.50	6.00
Near Moderate Strong	1.75-1.89	10.5	8.75	7.25	7.00
Moderate	1.90-2.09	12.0	10.00	8.00	8.00
Near Moderate	2.10-2.39	14.0	11.50	9.00	10.00
Slight Moderate	2.40-2.69	16.0	13.00	10.00	12.00
Near Slight Moderate	2.70-3.09	18.0	14.50	11.00	13.50
Slight	3.10-3.59	20.0	16.00	12.00	15.00
Near Slight	3.60-4.49	25.0	25.00	14.00	20.00
Negligible Slight	4.50-5.49	35.0	35.00	16.00	25.00
Near Negligible	550-6.49	45.0	45.00	20.00	31.00
Negligible[2]	6.50 plus	60.0	60.00	24.00	40.00

* Combat Power Ratio
1 If the P/P is less than 1.0, use advance rate of 1.0 km/day.
2 For armored and mechanized infantry divisions, these rates can be sustained for 10 days only; for next 20 days standard rates for armored and mechanized infantry forces cannot exceed half these rates.

Now for the data at the beginning of the battle phase from dawn of June 10 to noon of June 11. It will be remembered that the results of this day's fighting led the Syrians to accept a ceasefire. The figures below reflect Syrian reinforcements, and force attrition on both sides due to estimated combat and non-combat causes.

	Israeli manpower equivalents	Syrian manpower equivalents
Troops	34,000 × 1 = 34,000	28,000 × 1 = 28,000
Tanks	750 × 100 = 75,000	400 × 100 = 40,000
Aircraft (or sorties)	250 × 250 = 62,500	50 × 200 = 10,000
Air Defense	none	none
Force Strength	171,500	78,000
Terrain	—	× 1.5
Posture	—	× 1.4
Morale (Syrian morale had been badly shaken on the 9th)		× 0.9
Combat Power (without CEV)	171,500	147,420

This permits us to make the following comparisons:

Force Strength Ratio (Israeli/Syrian)	2.20
Combat Power Ratio (without CEV)	1.16
Combat Power Ratio (with CEV)	2.90

Again, an overwhelming Israeli success was to be expected, when the Israeli CEV is taken into consideration.

On June 10 the Israelis again advanced an average of more than ten kilometers. Taking into consideration the difficult terrain and the previously prepared Syrian defensive positions, such an advance should not have been expected without a substantial Israeli CEV superiority. Using Figure 4, and the procedure used to calculate the CEV on June 8-9, we calculate a CEV of 3.6. ($(2.5 \times 24)/16.5 = 3.6$) The Israeli CEV would have been calculated even higher had we not taken into consideration the lowered Syrian morale.

Thus, on the basis of the Israeli advance rate we can calculate an Israeli/Syrian CEV in the Bekaa Valley battle as in the range of 3.5 to 3.6. It must be recognized, of course, that this calculation is based upon gross, estimated, aggregated data.

Another way of estimating CEVs is to compare the casualty inflicting capability of the two opponents.

There is no way of assessing the daily casualties for either the Israelis or the Syrians. However, we can compare the overall casualty rates of the Israelis with the estimated losses for the Syrians. From Figure 5 one can see that the total Israeli casualties against the Syrians were about 1,082; the total Syrian casualties are estimated to have been about 4,150.

Figure 5
Estimated Israeli and Syrian Losses
Bekaa Valley Battle, June 8-11, 1982

	Israeli	Syrian
Personnel Casualties		
Killed	195	800
Wounded	872	3,200
Missing & POWs	15	150
Total	1,082	4,150
Tanks	30*	400
Aircraft (including helicopters)	0	90
Air Defense Missile Launchers (SAMs)	0	120
% Casualties/Day	1.05	5.53
Casualties inflicted by 100/day	4.01	1.41
Casualty inflicting capability/100/day	4.01	0.69

* Minor damage was inflicted on perhaps 100 more Israeli tanks.

The Israeli figures are close to accurate; the Syrian figures are estimates only. On the basis of these figures the Israeli daily casualty rate (average strength about 34,500) was about 1.05% per day; the estimated Syrian casualty rate (average strength about 25,000) was about 5.53% per day. The casualty *inflicting* rate for 34,500 Israelis was 4.01 Syrian casualties per day per 100 Israeli soldiers. The casualty *inflicting* rate for the 25,000 Syrians was 1.41 Israeli casualties inflicted per day per 100 Syrian soldiers. However, we must remember that the Syrian capability on the defense was multiplied by a factor of 1.4 for posture, and 1.5 for terrain. Thus, without those advantages (as shown in Figure 4) the normalized casualty-inflicting *capability* of the Syrians was about 0.69 Israelis per 100 Syrians per day.

The ratio of Israeli casualty-inflicting capability to that of the Syrians, therefore, was 4.01/0.69, or 5.81. From previous analyses of World War I, World War II and earlier Arab-Israeli wars data, we know that the ratio of opposing casualty–inflicting capabilities is approximately the square of the CEV. Applying this "New Square Law" to the estimated casualty data from the Bekaa Valley battle, the square root of 5.81 should be the equivalent of the CEV value for the Israelis. This value is 2.41.

The record is very clear that the average relative combat effectiveness superiority factor (CEV) of Israelis with respect to Syrians was about 2.5 in the 1967 and 1973 wars. With less assurance, because of less confidence in more aggregated data, we have demonstrated—in two independent sets of calculations—that the Israeli CEV with respect to the Syrians in 1982 was between about 2.4 and about 3.4. Thus we can conclude that the gap in combat capability between Syria and Israel (and *not* the gap in military technology) is certainly not closing, and may even be still widening.

FOOTNOTES:
1. T.N. Dupuy, *Elusive Victory, The Arab-Israeli Wars, 1947-1974* (New York, Harper & Row, 1978), Appendices A and B.
2. The Quantified Judgment Model (QJM) is a mathematical simulation of historical combat. It is a relatively simple, aggregated model of land and air battle which was derived from factual historical combat data. While the QJM cannot, of course, predict with absolute accuracy the course of future battles, it can—to the extent that the principles and trends of historical combat can be extrapolated into the future—provide useful insights to military planners concerned with major aspects of future warfare. For a detailed description of the QJM see *Numbers, Predictions and War* (New York, Bobbs-Merrill, 1977).

Appendix B
Support of the War in Lebanon by the Israelis *

Source: Jerusalem Post, July 2, 1982

Question: In view of what is known to you, do you think the operation in Lebanon was justified?

Answer:

Yes, definitely	77.6 per cent	
Yes, reservedly	15.7 per cent	
TOTAL YES		93.3 per cent
No, definitely	2.8 per cent	
No, reservedly	1.8 per cent	
TOTAL NO		4.6 per cent
Undecided		2.1 per cent

Question: In your opinion, was the extent of the operation too big, too small, or on desirable scale?

Answer:

Too Big	32.6 per cent
Desirable Scale	55.8 per cent
Too Small	6.4 per cent
Undecided	5.2 per cent

* Based on the Public Opinion Polls conducted by the Modi'in Ezrahi Research Institute in Israel, for the Jerusalem Post. A sample of 1,236 Israeli adults were polled during the third week of the war, between June 21 and June 30, 1982.

Glossary

A-4 Skyhawk	Carrier Based Strike Aircraft (USA)
A-6E Intruder	Carrier Based Strike Aircraft (USA)
A-7 Corsair II	Carrier Based Strike Aircraft (USA)
AK-47 Kalashnikov	Assault Rifle (USSR)
APC	Armored Personnel Carrier
BMP	Infantry Combat Vehicle (USSR)
BRDM-2	Armored Wheeled Reconnaissance Carrier (USSR) (Air Portable)
BTR-60	Amphibious Armored Personnel Carrier (USSR)
BTR-152	Armored Wheeled Reconnaissance Carrier (USSR)
ECM	Electronic Counter-Measures
F-4 Phantom	Tactical Fighter (USA)
F-14 Tomcat	Tactical Fighter (USA)
F-15 Eagle	Tactical Fighter (USA)
F-16 Falcon	Tactical Fighter (USA)
Gabriel	Sea to Sea Missile (Israel)
Gazelle	Anti-Tank Attack Helicopter (France)
Grad	Surface to Surface Missile (USSR)
HETZ	Armor Piercing Ammunition
Kfir	Combat Aircraft; Tactical Fighter (Israel)
Merkava	Main Battle Tank .105 mm gun. 56 tons. (Israel)
Mirage	Combat Aircraft; Tactical Fighter (France)
MiG-23 Flogger	Combat Aircraft; Fighter Interceptor (USSR)
MiG-25 Foxbat	Combat Aircraft; Fighter Interceptor (USSR)
Reshef	Missile Fast-Patrol Boat (MFPB) of the Reshef Class (Israel)
SAM	Surface to Air Missile
SA-2 Guideline	Surface to Air Missile (USSR)
SA-3 Goa	Surface to Air Missile (USSR)
SA-6 Gainful	Surface to Air Missile (USSR)
SA-7 Grail	Surface to Air Hand Carried Missile (USSR)
SA-8 Gecko	Surface to Air Missile (USSR)
SA-9 Gaskin	Surface to Air Missile (USSR)
Sagger	Anti-Tank Missile (USSR)
SU Sukhoi	Strike Aircraft (USSR)
SCUD	Surface to Surface Medium Range Missile (USSR)
T-34	Medium Battle Tank 85mm gun; 32 tons (USSR)

T-54	Main Battle Tank 100 mm gun; 36 tons (USSR)
T-55	Main Battle Tank 100 mm gun; 36 tons (USSR)
T-62	Main Battle Tank 115 mm gun; 37.5 tons (USSR)
T-72	Main Battle Tank 125 mm gun; 41 tons. (USSR)
TOW	Tube Launcher, Optically-tracked, Wire-guided, Anti-Tank Weapon (Missile)
Tu	Tupolev Medium Range Bomber (USSR)
Ze'ev (Wolf)	Ground Launched Rocket equipped with homing device (Israel)
ZSU-23-4 Shilka	Quad Self-Propelled 23 mm Anti-Aircraft Gun (USSR)

SELECTED BIBLIOGRAPHY

Books

Barakat, Halim, and Peter Dodd. *Refugees: Uprootedness and Exile.* Beirut: Institute for Palestinian Studies, 1958.

Barker, A.J. *Arab-Israeli Wars.* New York: Hippocrene Books, 1980.

Bethmann, Eric W. *Decisive Years in Palestine 1918-1948.* Washington, D.C.: American Friends of the Middle East, 1959.

Brzezinski, Zbigniew. *Power and Principle: Memoirs of the National Security Adviser, 1977-1981.* New York: Farrar, Strauss and Giroux, 1983.

Carter, Jimmy. *Keeping Faith. Memoirs of a President,* New York: Bantam Books, 1982.

Clausewitz, Carl von. *On War.* Princeton, New Jersey: Princeton University Press, 1976.

Dawisha, Adeed I. *Syria and the Lebanese Crisis.* New York: St. Martin's Press, 1980.

Deeb, Marius. *The Lebanese Civil War.* New York: Praeger, 1980.

Dupuy, Trevor N. *Elusive Victory: The Arab-Israeli Wars 1947-1974.* Fairfax, Virginia: HERO Books, 1984.

Eshel, David. *The Lebanon War, 1982.* Jerusalem—Tel Aviv: Steimatzky, 1982.

Fahmi, Ismail. *Negotiations For Peace in the Middle East: The Arab View.* Baltimore, Maryland: Johns Hopkins University Press, 1983.

Gabriel, Richard A. *Operation Peace for Galilee. The Israeli-PLO War in Lebanon.* New York: Hill and Wang, 1984.

Gilsenan, Michael. *Recognizing Islam: Religion and Society in the Modern Arab World.* New York: Pantheon, 1983.

Gordon, David C. *The Republic of Lebanon: Nation in Jeopardy.* Boulder, Colorado: Westview Press, 1983.

_____ . *Lebanon: The Fragmented Nation.* Stanford, California: Hoover Institution, 1980.

Hadawi, Sami. *Bitter Harvest; Palestine 1914-1979.* Delmar, New York: Caravan Books, 1979.

_____ . *Crime and No Punishment.* Beirut: Palestine Research Center, 1972.

Harkabi, Y. Ehoshafat. *Palestinians and Israel.* Jerusalem: Keter Publishing, 1974.

Hirst, David. *The Gun and the Olive Branch.* London: Faber and Faber, 1977.

Heller, Mark A. *A Palestinian State: The Implications for Israel.* Cambridge, Mass.: Harvard University Press, 1983.

Heller, Mark *et al. The Middle East Military Balance 1983.* Tel Aviv: The Jaffe Center for Strategic Studies, 1983.

Herzog, Chaim. *The Arab-Israeli Wars.* New York: Random House, 1982.

International Institute for Strategic Studies (IISS). *The Military Balance 1983-1984.* London: IISS, 1983.

Jansen, Michael. *The Battle of Beirut: Why Israel Invaded Lebanon.* London: Zed Press, 1982.

Khalidi, Walid. *Conflict and Violence in Lebanon: Confrontation in the Middle East.* Cambridge, Mass.: Harvard University Press, 1979.

Luttwak, Edward, and Dan Horowitz. *The Israeli Army.* London: Penguin Books, Ltd, 1975.

Meibar, Basheer. *Political Culture, Foreign Policy, and Conflict: The Palestine Area Conflict System.* Westport, Conn.: Greenwood Press, 1972.

Neff, Donald. *Warriors for Jerusalem.* New York: Linden Press/Simon and Schuster, 1984.

Nabib, Selim. *Beirut: Frontline Story.* London: Pluto Press, 1983.

Peck, Juliana S. *The Reagan Administration and the Palestinian Question: The First Thousand Days.* Washington, D.C.: Institute for Palestine Studies, 1984.

Pranger, Robert J., and Dale R. Tahtinen. *Nuclear Threat in the Middle East.* Washington, D.C.: American Enterprise Institute for Public Policy Research, 1979.

Randal, Jonathan C. *Going all the Way: Christian Warlords, Israeli Adventurers, and the War in Lebanon.* New York: Viking Press, 1983.

Rubenberg, Cheryl A. *The Palestinian Liberation Organization: Its Institutional Infrastructure.* Belmont, Mass: Institute of Arab Studies, 1983.

Salem, Elie. *Prospects For a New Lebanon,* Washington, D.C.: American Enterprise Institute, 1982.

Schiff, Ze'ev, and Ehud Ya'ari. *Israel's Lebanon War.* New York: Simon and Schuster, 1984.

Sinai, Anne, and Robert I. Sinai. *Israel and the Arabs: Prelude to the Jewish State.* New York: Facts on File, Inc., 1972.

Ulanoff, Stanley M., and David Eshel. *The Fighting Israeli Air Force.* New York: Arco Publishing, Inc. 1985.

Vance, Cyrus. *Hard Choices: Four Critical Years in America's Foreign Policy.* New York: Simon and Schuster, 1983.

Articles and Papers:

Alexander, Edward. "Israel in the Dock." *Encounter*, September/October 1982.

Aviran, Reuven. "Operation Peace for Galilee: A Crossroad in Syrian Involvement in the Lebanese Crisis." *Ma'arachot*, September, 1982.

Barach, Boaz. "The Arab Deterrent Force; A Legal Appraisal." *IDF Journal*, No. 2, December, 1982.

Ben-Dor, Gabriel. *"The PLO and the Palestinians."* The Jaffe Center for Strategic Studies Tel Aviv University. Memorandum No.8, February, 1983.

Bloom, James J. "From the Litani River to Beirut: A Brief Strategic Assessment of Israel's Operations in Lebanon, 1978-1982." *Middle East Insight*, No. 2, 1982.

_____ . "The-Six-Days-Plus-Ten-Weeks War: Aspects of Israel's Summer Campaign in Lebanon." *Middle East Insight*, No. 5, January/February, 1983.

Brown, Dean L. "Middle East Problem." Paper No. 23. Middle East Institute, Washington, D.C., 1982.

Caplan, Neil, and Ian Black. "Israel and Lebanon: Origin of Relationship." *The Jerusalem Quarterly*, No. 27, Spring, 1983.

Carus, Seth W. "The Bekaa Valley Campaign." *The Washington Quarterly*, December, 1982.

Cordesman, Anthony H. "The Sixth Arab-Israeli Conflict." *Armed Forces Journal*, August, 1982.

Cragg, Kenneth. "By the Fig and the Olive: Perspective Round Jerusalem." *American-Arab Affairs*, No. 4, Spring, 1983.

Danaher, Kevin. "Israel's Use of Cluster Bombs in Lebanon." *Journal of Palestinian Studies*, No. 12, Summer/Fall, 1982.

Dupuy, T.N. "A Proposed Step Toward Middle East Peace." *Strategic Review*, Fall, 1981.

Farghal, Mahmoud H. "Islamic Ideology: Essence and Dimensions." *American-Arab Affairs*, No.4, Spring, 1983.

Furlong, R.D.M. "Israel Lashes Out." *International Defense Review*, No. 8, August, 1982.

Gichon, Mordechai. "Peace for Galilee: The Campaign." *IDF Journal*, No. 2, December, 1982.

Golan, Galia. "The Soviet Union and the PLO." *Adelphi Paper*, No. 131, 1976.

Guindy, Fadwa el. "The Killing of Sadat and After; A Current Assessment of Egypt's Islamic Movement." *Middle East Insight*, No. 5, January/ February, 1983.

Hamid, Rashid. "What is the PLO." *Journal of Palestine Studies* No. 4, 1975.

Israel Ministry of Defense. "National Security Issues." Jerusalem: 1982.

Kahan, Itzhak, *et al.* "The Commission of Inquiry into Events at the Refugee Camps in Beirut." Final Report, February 1983. (Authorized English Translation). Tel Aviv: Kabat, Ltd., 1983.

Laipson, Ellen B., and Clyder R. Mark. "Israeli-Palestinian Confrontation." Congressional Research Service, Washington, D.C. 1983.

Mallison, Sally V., and Thomas W. Mallison. "Israel in Lebanon, 1982: Aggression or Self-Defense?" *American-Arab Affairs*, No. 5, Summer, 1983.

Ma'oz, Moshe. "Israel and Arabs After the Lebanese War." *Jerusalem Quarterly*, No. 28, Summer, 1983.

Mas, Beni. "Peace for Galilee: Main Combat Operations." *Ma'arachot*, September, 1982.

Mead, James M. "The Lebanese Experience." *Marine Corps Gazette*, No. 2, February, 1983.

Norton, August R. "The Political Mood in Lebanon." *Middle East Insight*, No. 5, January/February 1983.

Norton, August R. "Israel and South Lebanon." *American-Arab Affairs*, No. 4, Spring 1983.

Pa'il, Meir. "The West Bank and Gaza: A Strategic Analysis for Peace." *Outlook* Paper, No. 3, 1981.

Peterson, Erik R. "Interview with Hatem Husseini, Member of the Palestine National Council." *American-Arab Affairs*, No. 5, Summer, 1983.

Rahall, Nick J. "Lebanon and U.S. Foreign Policy toward the Middle East." *American-Arab Affairs*, No. 2, Fall, 1982.

Roberts, Cynthia A. "Soviet Arms Transfer Policy and the Decision to Upgrade Syrian Air Force." *Survival*, July-August, 1983.

Robinson, Clarence A. Jr. "Surveillance Integration Pivotal in Israeli Success." *Aviation Week and Space Technology*, July 5, 1982.

Salem, Saeb. "One Lebanon, Not Two: The End of Carnage." *Middle East Insight*, No. 5, January/February, 1983.

Sayigh, Yezid. "Palestinian Military Performance in the 1982 War." *Journal of Palestine Studies*, No. 4, Summer, 1983.

Schueftan, Dan. "The PLO after Lebanon: Origin of Relationship." *The Jerusalem Quarterly*, No. 27, Spring, 1983.

Tlass, Mustafa. Partial Response by the Syrian Ministry of Defense to the Questionnaire on the Lebanese War, submitted by the authors to the Syrian Minister of Defense. Damascus, 1983.

Tucker, Robert W. "Lebanon: The Case for War." *Current News*, Special Edition, December, 1982.

Wright, Clifford A. "The Israeli War Machine in Lebanon." *Journal of Palestine Studies*, No. 2, Spring, 1983.

Yariv, Aaharon. "Reflections on a Solution of the Palestinian Problem." *Jerusalem Quarterly*, No. 23, Spring, 1982.

_____ . "The War in Lebanon: The Effects on Israel's Strategic Situation." The Jaffe Center for Strategic Studies, Tel Aviv University, Memorandum No. 8, February, 1983.

Zinger, Yoel. "Peace for Galilee: The Prisoners." *IDF Journal*, No. 2, December, 1982.

Documents:

Israeli-Lebanese Agreement Signed May 19, 1983. Official English Text. U.S. Government Release, 1983.

Palestinian National Covenant. Palestinian Research Center, 1969.

Palestinian Terrorist Training in the Soviet Union. Report to Arafat. English Translation. Document Captured by the Israeli Forces in Lebanon in 1982.

Protocol of Talks between the PLO and the Soviet Delegation in Moscow, November 13, 1979. English Translation. Document Captured by the Israeli Forces in Lebanon in 1982.

United Nations Resolution of Partition 181, November 29, 1947. U.N. Press Release, 1947.

United Nations Record of General Assembly Plenary Session, May 14, 1948. U.N. Press Release, 1948.

United Nations Security Council Resolution 242, November 22, 1967. U.N. Press Release, 1967.

United Nations Security Council Resolution 425, May 19, 1978. U.N. Press Release, 1978.

United Nations Security Council Resolution 508, June 5, 1982. U.N. Press Release, 1982.

United Nations Security Council Resolution 509, June 6, 1982. U.N. Press Release, 1982.

United Nations Security Council Resolution 521, September 19, 1982. U.N. Press Release, 1982.

White Paper on Peace Initiatives Undertaken by President Anwar Al-Sadat. Official Egyptian Publication. 1978.

INDEX